TRADITION AND TRANSFORMATION IN EASTERN NIGERIA

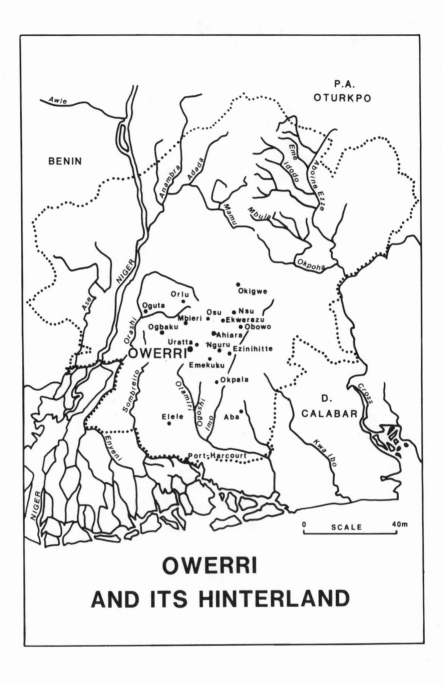

OWERRI

AND ITS HINTERLAND

Tradition and Transformation in Eastern Nigeria

A Sociopolitical History of Owerri and Its Hinterland, 1902–1947

Felix K. Ekechi

THE KENT STATE UNIVERSITY PRESS
Kent, Ohio, and London, England

Library of Congress Catalog Card Number 88-30111
ISBN 0-87338-368-0 (cloth)
ISBN 0-87338-383-4 (paper)
Manufactured in the United States of America

Library of Congress Cataloging-in-Publication Data

Ekechi, Felix K., 1934–
    Tradition and transformation in Eastern Nigeria : a sociopolitical
history of Owerri and its hinterland, 1902–1947 / Felix K. Ekechi.
        p.   cm.
    Bibliography: p.
    Includes index.
    ISBN 0-87338-368-0 (alk. paper).   ISBN 0-87338-383-4 (pbk. : alk.
paper)
    1. Owerri (Nigeria : Division)—Politics and government.
    2. Owerri (Nigeria : Division)—Social conditions.   I. Title.
DT515.9.O87E39   1989
966.9′4—dc19   88-30111
                                                                          CIP

British Library Cataloging-in-Publication data are available.

Dedicated to

Kemakolam, Chidi, Okechukwu, and Chinyere

CONTENTS

PREFACE

This work is an attempt to explore the dynamics of social and political change in the former Owerri Division of Nigeria since the establishment of British rule in the early part of this century. It was hoped that the study, conceived in 1967, would form a part of the Eastern Nigeria local history scheme, which was then sponsored by the History Department of the University of Nigeria, Nsukka under the late Professor J. C. Anene. Unfortunately, the outbreak of the Nigerian Civil War (1967–70) interfered with the scheme and consequently prolonged the completion of this study. Since 1973, however, I had been intermittently collecting materials on the subject in both Nigeria and Europe. Several trips were made to Nigeria to consult the National Archives at Enugu and Ibadan, as well as to collect oral traditions from the different sections of the old Owerri Division and beyond.

This present work is indeed a part of a larger work, still in progress, on the history of the Igbo-speaking people. It should also be stressed that this study is by no means a comprehensive history of Owerri and its hinterland. Primary attention has been given to the patterns of sociopolitical change, and consequently very little is said of the economic aspect of Owerri history. I hope that this omission will be corrected in a future work. Moreover, this itself is full of many gaps, largely caused by the paucity of source materials. Despite these weaknesses, however, it is hoped that this book will make a modest contribution to the study of Owerri local history. Should it stir others to do more investigative work and thus enlarge or even correct many of the issues raised here, much of my objective would have been realized indeed. Furthermore, I hope that this study will generate interest in the study of the history of other towns in Imo State.

Until recently scholars have not paid any serious attention to the social and political developments in the Owerri area since the advent of British rule in Nigeria. The most recent study is that of Dr. Cletus E. Emezi, whose doctoral research dealt with the patterns of political change in Owerri (1978). It remains unpublished, but I hope he will publish it eventually to provide further source material for the study of Owerri history.

The emergence of Owerri in modern Nigerian political history dates from 1902 when it was made a district headquarters. In 1917 it was designated a third-class township—even though it remained a township only in name until recently. From 1902 until 1947, however, Owerri became one of the major political nerve centers of British administration in Nigeria. Not only was it a district headquarters, it also served as the divisional and provincial capital. When in 1947 the provincial capital was moved to Umuahia (for reasons yet unknown), Owerri's political preeminence vis-à-vis other townships in the province began to wane. In fact, the political decline had started before 1947. The political reorganization of the 1930s, following the Women's Revolt of 1929, had significantly accelerated the political demise of Owerri. For prior to the dismemberment of the Owerri Native Court in 1935, most towns in the old Owerri Division, especially those in the Oratta and Isu areas, attended court sessions at Owerri. With the creation of new group courts in several areas, the apparently existing client-state relationship came to an abrupt end. The only remaining political unifying factor was the district officer, still stationed at Owerri. Thus, the many towns and villages which had formerly been under the jurisdiction of the Owerri Native Court were now virtually independent. Indeed, for all practical purposes, Owerri had sunk into relative political insignificance following the relocation of the provincial capital to Umuahia in 1947.

Since 1976, however, Owerri has bounced back into political prominence, having been selected as the capital of Imo State, which was created in 1976. Today, as never before, Owerri is steadily growing into a major metropolis. As a state capital, its population has more than doubled, and infrastructural developments have been proceeding at an incredible pace. There is no doubt that Owerri is now among the leading educational and cultural centers in the state as well as in Nigeria as a whole.

Portions of this book (especially chapters 1–3) have already appeared in the *Nigerian Statesman* (September 1979). I am grateful to Mr. H. K. Offonry, then Managing Director of Imo Newspapers Limited, and his staff for the encouragement to enlarge the original study for publication as a book monograph. I would like to express my deep debt of gratitude to Kent State University for its financial support and for granting me time to undertake the research in both Nigeria and Europe. Special thanks must be given to Professor Eugene Wenninger, Director of Research and Sponsored Programs at Kent State University, for his continued interest and cooperation in my research endeavors. Acknowledgment is also given hereby to the American Philosophical Society for its financial assistance during my

1979 and 1983 fieldwork in Nigeria. I must express my deep debt of gratitude to my brother William D. Ekechi and his wife Philomena for their many kindnesses during my periodic visits to Nigeria. Without their assistance, especially in making their car available to me, the fieldwork for this study would not have been possible to carry out. For transportation was the greatest handicap I experienced during my research trips.

Many other people and institutions have provided valuable assistance, and I am sincerely grateful to all who have helped me in one way or another. However, special acknowledgment must be made of the services of the officials at the Nigerian and British archives. The officials at the Nigerian Archives at Ibadan, the Public Record Office, London, and the Rhodes House Library, Oxford, were extremely helpful. The Chief Archivist at Enugu and his staff deserve particular mention for bending over backwards to accommodate my frantic demands for records. I thank them heartfully for tolerating the many inconveniences and for providing the needed materials. In fact, their enthusiasm in respect to my research project provided me with greater stimulus for action. Also, I would like to thank the archivists of the missionary societies in England (Church Missionary Society), France (Holy Ghost Fathers), and Rome (Society of African Missions) for their assistance in locating documents.

Furthermore, I am sincerely grateful to the many men and women who provided information during my fieldwork in Owerri. Fuller acknowledgment is given in the endnotes. But I wish to express my very sincere thanks to the Owerri Council of Elders (Qha Owere Nchi Ise) for their enthusiastic cooperation and support during my 1979 fieldwork. I am equally grateful to Eze Ugochukwu of Nkwerre, the Venerable Archdeacon F. E. Chukwuezi of St. Paul's Church, Nkwerre, and the members of the Ekwe Society of Nkwerre for the information they provided. Above all, I must thank the Right Reverend Bishop B. C. Nwankiti, Anglican Bishop of Owerri Diocese, for his assistance in locating source materials and providing answers to many of my nagging problems. My thanks also go to Mrs. Marge Evans and Mrs. Marilyn Zehner for typing the manuscript.

Finally, my greatest debt of gratitude goes to my wife Regina without whom this work would have been impossible. Her patience and endurance during the many periods I had to be away from her and our four lovely children enabled me to complete the research and the writing. In moments of great trial and crisis, she always managed to put on a happy face and thus spurred me on. "Continue with your research," she wrote me on one occasion in Nigeria; "come back when your money runs out. We are well, although there are occasional crises in the house." Need I say, in fact, that without her cooperation this research project would hardly have become a reality. To you, my dear wife, I am grateful.

1. OWERRI AND THE ESTABLISHMENT OF BRITISH RULE

OWERRI BEFORE THE BRITISH ADMINISTRATION

Owerri Town is made up of five villages: namely Umuọrọrọnjọ, Ama-wom, Umuoyeche, Umuọdu, and Umuoyima. These villages, except Umuoyima, trace their descent from a common ancestor, Ekwema Arugo. Umuoyima village is said to have migrated from Umukoto Nekede (a neighboring town), hence the intermarriage between Umuoyima and the other four villages, a practice that is forbidden (*nsọ*) among the agnatic villages. But according to an elder from Umuoyima, Oyima was one of the sons of Ekwema, but was forced to flee to Nekede because of an alleged homicide. When he later quarrelled with his host village over the claim of *mgbada* (deer) game, which was killed by one of his sons, his "brothers" reportedly invited him to return home instead of surrendering the game to Nekede claimants.[1] This seems to be a distortion of the tradition of Oyima's relationship with the other Owerri villages. In fact, its main purpose is probably to legitimize Oyima's position as an integral part of Owere Nchi Ise, that is, as a legitimate member of the five villages of Owerri.

The traditional history of Owere (Anglicized Owerri), like that of many other Igbo towns, is essentially the story of migrations and settlements. According to tradition Owerri was founded by a legendary hero called Ekwema Arugo, whose original home was Uratta, about four miles from Owerri Town. Tradition holds that Ekwema left his ancestral home of Uratta as a result of a quarrel between himself and his "brother" Ndumoha. According to the most pervasive version of the tradition, Ndumoha was the older brother of Ekwema. Because he was financially unable to provide the materials for the funeral ceremony (i.e., "second burial"), of their father, it devolved on the younger Ekwema, "a wealthy man" (*Ogaranya*), to procure the materials, which included a cow. Upon the conclusion of the funeral ceremonies, Ndumoha demanded the heart (some say head) of the cow by right of seniority; but Ekwema allegedly refused and thus compelled Ndumoha to summon the council of elders (*Nde Ǫha*) for an arbitration. The elders reportedly sided with Ndumoha, citing an Igbo adage to buttress their decision: *Aka ji aku kwaa nna ya; ǫwuu nwa ǫpara gburu ya* ("Any son who is in a better financial position to provide materials for the father's funeral, should do so, insofar as it is not the first son who killed his father"). Ekwema, however, defied the Ǫha by refusing to surrender the coveted part of the animal and thereby aroused Ndumoha's hatred of him. It was therefore Ekwema's alleged breach of *Omenala* (customary practice) that earned him the nickname "Owere," "the taker," from which Owerri was derived.

Agonized by Ekwema's violation of *Omenala,* Ndumoha then took practical steps to get rid of him. As tradition says, he purchased a gun (*Oro*) with which to wage war against Ekwema. This gun, we are further told, was purchased from Ngwa traders, a subgroup of the Igbo, who probably acquired it from the Aro. In time, civil war broke out between the two brothers. "Ekwema, being unable to stand the unslaught [*sic*], collected his people and well wishers and ran towards his Canan."[2] More specifically, Ekwema fled with his pregnant wife and his son, Ikenegbu. They travelled via Egbu, a neighboring town of Uratta, from whence Ekwema obtained fire, and finally settled at the foot of a hill, now commonly known as Ugwu Ekwema (Ekwema's Hill).

The following is a slightly different version of the tradition. In contrast to the foregoing account, which was collected from individual informants at Owerri and Uratta in 1975, the testimony reproduced below represents, for all practical purposes, the "official" version of Owerri history. This is so because it reflects the collective testimony of the Owerri Council of Elders (Ǫha Owere Nchi Ise). Here is the tradition as it was read to me by the secretary, in English (1979):

> Ndumoha and Ekwem [*sic*] were of the same parents. When Arugo died his son Ekwem buried him. Being a wealthy man, whose funeral should consist of goats and cows, Ndumoha could not afford to do it; and so, Ekwem bought [a] cow and celebrated the funeral of his father. When the cow was slaughtered, Ndumoha asked for the heart of the cow, but Ekwem refused and claimed that, as he bought the cow and celebrated the funeral of his father, he was entitled to the heart. This brought a serious quarrel between both of them.
>
> The matter was later decided by the townspeople and [the] elders, who awarded Ekwem the heart for reasons that he bought the cow. The decision of the elders infuriated Ndumoha, and he nursed a great hatred against Ekwem, planning to kill him.
>
> As time goes on, there was a hunting spree in which Ekwem's young men killed a big bush pig and brought it home. Ndumoha ordered that the pig should be slaughtered at his *Ǫbu Ozuzu* [ancestral tree]. Ekwem refused, and slaughtered it

at his *obi* [entrance hut]; [he] shared the meat among the townspeople, and gave Ndumoha some share, which he refused.³

Having refused, other townsmen refused [their shares] as well, and brought back their shares, which Ekwem gathered and took away. The talk in the town was: "Has he taken the meat? *Owerela?*" They answered, "Owerela! . . . "Owerela!" which gave him the name "Owere." Ndumoha became infuriated. He gathered his men and seriously planned to kill Ekwem. The news came to Ekwem and he, too, gathered his own people and fled by night.

He passed through Egbu, where he branched to his son-in-law's house. His son-in-law asked him in but he refused and asked for fire. His daughter became apprehensive of danger and became restless. In the morning . . . she and her husband followed the sound of [her father's] drum to a hill in the forest, where they found her father and the people in the forest. They were roasting yams.⁴

Whatever the reason(s) for Ekwema's migration, and more will be said on this later, it is clear that some lineage conflict triggered the flight. In any event, Ekwema is said to have prospered at his new hillside settlement. For, while there, his wife gave birth to another son, Azuzi, whom he nicknamed "Abaole," meaning that he was born in exile. Later he and his family discovered a clear and glittering stream (*Ogbuamuma*), now known as Otamiri River. It was apparently the discovery of this river that forced him to settle at the hillside. To have crossed the river would have permanently severed his relationship with Uratta. Buoyed by his possessions (blessings?), particularly the seemingly limitless stretch of unoccupied land, Ekwema is said to have exclaimed in evident ecstasy, *"Ewerelam ihem choga, anabajem ole!"*("I have now obtained my heart's desire [what I want]; where else shall I go!") In other words, being now in control of a vast unoccupied land, Ekwema and his family decided to stay permanently at Ugwu Ekwema, which is now the site of the Owerri Civic Hall (between Egbu and Owerri).⁵

Ekwema and his family commemorated their sojourn at Ugwu Ekwema a year later. This entailed, among other things, the roasting of yams and corn. Thereafter, this commemoration became an annual festival, known today as *Oru Owere* and aptly described as "the most important traditional annual festival of the people of Owerri Nchi-Ise."⁶ In essence, Oru Owere is "Owerri People's National Day," marking the founding of Owerri by Ekwema Arugo. Oru Owere also symbolizes the cultural separation of Owerri from Uratta in that Uratta people celebrate *Ǫnwa Oru* (harvest festival). Ǫnwa Oru, unlike Oru Owere, is celebrated during the dry season (*Ǫkǫ-chi*), or the harvest season. Oru Owere, on the other hand, is celebrated in the rainy season (*Udu mmiri*), or the farming season.

It would appear that Oru Owere, which is today celebrated with great "pomp and festivity," is a recent event. According to Geoffrey E. Emenako, "The children of Ekwema Arugo did not consider it appropriate or necessary to continue to celebrate Ǫnwa-Oru, when they had freed themselves from allegiance to Uratta." But then "two or three generations later, certain prodigies and calamities were rife and took a big toll of the population." Consultation of the oracle, however, revealed that failure to celebrate Ekwema Arugo's sojourn at Owerri had been responsible for the calamities. To appease the spirit of the great ancestor, Oru Owere thus evolved. This annual festival takes place on Orie Owere market day, in the sixth month of the local calendar year (July). During the Oru Owere season, which lasts for forty days, peace and harmony reign. To quote Emenako,

> The season is marked with peace and harmony, whereby no man or woman must fight or quarrel, no debts must be collected, and freedom of movement is guaranteed, even to our slaves in the olden days. In the days of old there would be ceasefire between neighbouring towns and villages at war with any Owerri Town or any Owerri Compound throughout the season of the festivals. Armed hostility could resume at the end of the festival season.[7]

Like Oru Owere, the colonization of what is now the five Owerri villages apparently came after Ekwema's death. According to a local historian, "Like Joseph of the Old Testament, Ekwema had nothing but a glimpse of Canaan; he never entered into the site now known as Owerre [Owerri]. Death overtook him at Ugwu Ekwema, where he was laid to rest till this day."[8] It was his descendants, therefore, who presumably occupied various portions of the "limitless" farmland; hence Owerri may appropriately be described as "the land of the taker." Subsequently, too, Ekwema's descendants established the central Orie Owere Market and planted the phallic Ǫbu Ozuzu, a communal tree which now serves as the symbol of unity among the five villages.

The Ekwema Arugo saga raises a number of interesting questions. First and foremost, is Ekwema a historical figure? And is the animal motif in the narrative to be accepted as a historical fact? Or is it simply an example of the "complex stereotype" which, as Jan Vansina has pointed out, is found in most African traditional narratives? We should point out at this juncture that contrary to the commonly held belief in Owerri, Arugo was not, in fact, Ekwema's father, but his mother! Thus the narratives which suggest that the funeral ceremony was for their father Arugo are inaccurate. Arugo, it has also been suggested, was actually one of Ndumoha's father's wives who, as it now appears, had Ekwema by a previous marriage.[9] Accordingly, Ekwema would be the stepson of Ndumoha's father and therefore, Ndumoha's stepbrother. However, in the elastic African extended-family relationship, there is no term for "stepbrother" in the Igbo language. Consequently Ndumoha and Ekwema may be regarded as brothers. Furthermore, Ndumoha's father was Orii, the second son of Atta, the father of

Uratta (i.e., the children of Atta).[10] Ndumoha in fact was the first son of Orii. Was the funeral ceremony then for Orii? This is very unlikely. It is perhaps more likely that the conflict between Ndumoha and Ekwema had arisen over the burial of Ekwema's mother, Arugo, rather than his father. More will be said on the probable source of the conflict later.

Ekwema may have been a historical figure nonetheless, despite his somewhat shadowy past. In my opinion, the animal story, which embellishes the tradition, appears to have been invented for possible social and political ends. In this case, it may have been a clever structural device to explain a social relationship between Owerri and Uratta, a characteristic feature of most African traditions of origin. "Oral tradition," affirmed John D. Fage, "is often in reality an explanation, in quasi-historical terms, of existing or of currently relevant past social or socio-political relationships." Thus the Ekwema narrative appears to fulfill a social function: to establish a social or historical "charter" of Owerri, suggesting that Owerri and Uratta, now distinct social and political entities, were originally shared by one and the same people. Thus as Vansina reminds us, we must "be aware" that traditions have practical functions. He writes,

> A tradition is affected by the purposes and functions which it fulfils. An informant may alter the content of a testimony in order to make it correspond better with his own private purposes; social influences may force a tradition to follow a certain direction because in this its social function is more adequately fulfilled. . . . The private purposes of the informant lead to falsification, the social function to error.[11]

Owerri, of course, still acknowledges Uratta as its ancestral homeland, hence the popular saying that *"Owere wu Owere wu Uratta."* In other words, any "true son" of Owerri traces his ancestry to Uratta. Nevertheless, Owerri maintained political and cultural ties with its other neighbors—Ihitte, Awaka, Egbu, and Naze. These were formerly grouped politically under one court and are still known culturally as Umu Ala Enyi (literally, the children of the settlers in the land of elephants). Ala Enyi (the land of elephants) thus suggests a region where elephant hunting may have been an important aspect of the economy. In Owerri folklore it is said that an elephant was once shot at Egbu but fell at Owerri (at Ekwema's Hill) and thus made Owerri the righful owner. In popular Owerri parlance, *"Egbu egbuola [enyi], Owere ewere."*[12]

Since the 1977 local government reorganization, Owerri Town has been linked politically with Uratta. Both towns form what is now the Owerri Uraban community. In other words, Uratta and Owerri share a common electoral constituency, an obvious recognition of their primordial relationship.

Of course, oral traditions are not necessarily accepted at their face value; the historian must endeavor to explain or interpret what they mean. In Vansina's words, "More interpretation is needed from the historian than when he or she deals with full written records."[13] In this context the animal story might have been intended not only to explain the evolution of Owerri but also the dispersal of Uratta people. For we learn that in the remote past, Owerri, Egbu, Awaka, and Ihitte, now separate towns, were at one time part of Uratta. On the other hand, the reported conflict between Ekwema and Ndumoha may have stemmed from a land dispute which ultimately forced Ekwema to flee in search of his own "Canaan."

Land disputes, often described in historical literature as arising from "land hunger," generally forced members of a lineage to migrate or to split. A cursory look at Igbo traditional history in general reveals that land hunger in fact played a crucial role in the dispersal of the Igbo in precolonial times.[14] In the Ekwema case, land dispute seems very likely to have been a decisive factor in splitting the lineage, as reflected in Ekwema's exclamation: *"Ewerelam ihem choga, anabajem ole."* In other words, Ekwema had finally attained his heart's desire; he was now satisfied and thus in no mood to return to his original homeland. The reason for the above is probably this: in Igbo culture, an adopted son (*nwa ekuru luta di*) has no claim to the stepfather's inheritance, especially land. The scenario of this land question may have been as follows: Ekwema may have been unsuccessful in his bid for a portion of his "father's" land. Dispute over land then gave rise to the alleged "civil war" between him and Ndumoha. But, being the master of all he surveyed at the new settlement, that is, abundance of land, Ekwema had no apparent reason to continue his journey any farther. Besides, said one informant, "beyond Uratta land was plentiful. And no one owned the land" there. If our postulation here is accepted, it therefore appears that the colorful animal story represents what Vansina has described as a "complex stereotype," meaning a skillfully embroidered tradition to explain "a disagreeable past event without upsetting existing cultural values." In other words, the alleged Ekwema-Ndumoha dispute over the rightful owner of the heart of the cow might really have been an attempt to legitimize Ekwema Arugo's forced migration, or perhaps expulsion, from Uratta. It must be remembered that people's recall of traditions, as Elizabeth Tonkin has observed, may at times "be purposeful, dependent on the interest of the teller," and that "oral tradition is utterly dependent on social understanding. What are the key concerns for a community, its ideological as well as its political and economic dispositions, and how are they encoded?"[15]

Yet, there is another problem with the animal story. By all accounts, Ndumoha was reputed to be a wealthy man, an Ogaranya. He was, in the words of an informant, "big, wealthy, powerful, high-tempered, and feared."[16] If he was an Ogaranya, why could he not afford the funeral ceremony of his "father"? In this connection, the impulse for Ekwema Arugo's migration must be sought elsewhere, and, as I have suggested, the land hypothesis may offer a possible solution to the problem.

More research on this is needed, of course, before we can speak with greater confidence on its being the probable cause of the Ndumoha-Ekwema imbroglio. But time is running out, as most of the knowledgeable custodians (elders) of the traditions are fast disappearing from the scene. For instance, when I returned to Owerri for further fieldwork in 1983, only one out of the ten elders I interviewed in 1975 was still alive! Even then, he had become quite incapacitated to be of any further assistance. This example, among many, illustrates the urgency for collecting the rich African traditions before they all vanish or become so badly "tainted" with literary sources that the historian faces the increasing possibility of extensive feedback in the traditions.

Finally, let us look at the chronological implications of the tradition. Is it possible, for instance, to determine when Ekwema Arugo's migration took place? In essence, when exactly was Owerri founded? As students of oral tradition are well aware, it may be nearly impossible to assign exact dates to most traditional histories.[17] Yet, in the Ekwema case the mention of firearms (Oro) offers the possibility of some kind of relative dating of the event. For one thing, firearms may have come to Igboland by way of the Europeans during the Atlantic slave trade. Even though it is not immediately clear when they were first introduced to the Igbo, it is known nonetheless that either the Portuguese or the Dutch must have sold guns to Aro traders on the Cross River basin, from whom they probably reached Ngwa traders. The Aro traders of Arochukwu were, of course, the distributors of firearms in much of southeastern Nigeria and beyond. A former British official has speculated that the Aro probably acquired firearms by the eighteenth century,[18] but this has been disputed by his contemporaries. According to P. A. Talbot, the Portuguese or the Dutch introduced guns in the Cross River area perhaps by as early as the seventeenth century or even earlier. With the use of guns "obtained from the white traders," wrote Talbot, Aro mercenaries, "the Abam, Abiriba, Awhawfia [Ohaffia] and Edda, conquered all the people who resisted their influence or killed their agents" and thereby established their commercial dominance.[19]

If the Oro evidence in the tradition can be historically confirmed, then the Ekwema Arugo saga must have taken place in the era of the Europeans. Thus the evolution of Owerri must have occurred in the period of the slave trade, that is, between the fifteenth and the eighteenth centuries when firearms proliferated in the Bights of Benin and Biafra. However, the Oro element in the tradition may or may not in fact be significant. What seems important to keep in mind in this particular instance is the timelessness of oral traditions. Timelessness, in our case, can be demonstrated by ignoring time[20] and paying attention to the "once upon a time" motif in African oral tradition. It is against this background that the views of indigenous Africanist historians should be appreciated. A "historian should not," wrote A. E. Afigbo in his rejection of Western historical emphasis on chronology,

> put an unfair question to his source, no matter what that source may be. . . . For instance, since the conception and arrangement of time in a non-literate African society are different from the conception and arrangement of time in literate Western society, it is a violation of this principle to put to the oral tradition of a non-literate African community questions about duration and chronology which presupposes answers that make sense only against the Gregorian calendral scale.

To this C. C. Ifemesia adds, "Why should we allow Western scholars to impose their own concepts of history and time on us? We should write the history of our people in the manner in which our people understood their history and time."[21] Rejection of this "imposition" of historical time is certainly in accord with the ongoing process of decolonizing African studies. In the words of critical African writers, the role of the African intellectual is among other things "to help release African culture [and history] from the death-grip of the West." And they added, "At this point in history it is Africa's mission to intensify its decolonization and pursue it into liberation."[22]

OWERRI AND ITS NEIGHBORS

Although Owerri has become politically important in the twentieth century by reason of its being an administrative and judicial nerve center of the British administration, there is no evidence of its having assumed any dominant position vis-à-vis its other neighbors prior to the establishment of British colonial rule. Its political preeminence during the period of study rests therefore on the advent of the British government. By 1935 some twenty-five to thirty different towns were brought into the vortex of Owerri political and judicial authority. It is true, of course, that its market, Orie Owere, attracted traders from far and near. Its strategic location in the yam and palm oil belt also made it an important distributing center. During the era of the slave trade, the market served as an important slave mart. Aro slave dealers and the agents of the Chukwu oracle are said to have frequented the market. Like the famous markets of Uzoakoli, Ogobende, Orie Amaraku, and others, Owerri market was an important slave mart. "Slaves were sold like fowls, goats, dogs and other animals. There were special sections of the market where slaves were sold. And slave dealers came and bought as they wished."[23]

Traditional sources indicate that Owerri constituted a very important staging center for the Aro slave trade. The Aro traders from Arochukwu, who dominated much of the commercial life of southeastern Nigeria, frequented Orie Owere Market. It was from here, informants insist, that Arochukwu slavers made forays into Oguta and other nearby places. In the process, there developed an understanding between the Aro and the Owerri people whereby the Aro would receive cooperation from their Owerri hosts in the slaving operation. In return, the Aro refrained from enslaving any Owerri man, that is, any person of the Oratta group[24] who made a pilgrimage to Arochukwu. Should an Oratta man "be eaten" (enslaved) while consulting the oracle (Chukwu), then an Aro man was bound to be enslaved as well. This reciprocity treaty gave rise to the popular saying in Owerri that *"Chukwu anaghi eri onye Oratta,"* meaning that an Oratta man was immune to enslavement while consulting Chukwu.

This traditional account is substantially supported by documentary evidence. For example, a European woman missionary at Egbu, who visited Arochukwu between 1907 and 1909, reported that Arochukwu informants told her that in precolonial days there was friendly cooperation between them and Owerri people in matters of trade and religion. "They told us," she wrote, "the Arochukwu people and the Owerris were in league, and help was given them as they passed through with their slaves, that district being on the main route" for the purchase and sale of slaves. On the other hand, she went on, even though "many thousands" who went to consult the oracle at Arochukwu "never returned," the people from "the country round Ebu" always returned. They were "never killed or sold as slaves" because of the mutual understanding between them and the Aro.[25]

In precolonial days the Aro were great traders. They used the influence of the Chukwu oracle to promote their trade. In central Igboland the oracle was generally known as *Chukwu oke abiama,* known to the Europeans as the "Long Juju" of Arochukwu. Its fame spread to practically all of Eastern Nigeria and beyond. There was hardly any part of Igboland where the Aro could not penetrate. Many of the Aro traders were, of course, bona fide agents of the oracle. As they settled in the communities, they collected information on the social, political, and economic situations of the areas and relayed such intelligence back to the priests of the oracle at Arochukwu. Moreover, they conducted clients to the oracle or brought back oracular pronouncements, charms, and medicine to the local people. For these services the Aro demanded payment in money or in kind, thus making the operation evidently profitable. However, the destruction of the shrine of the oracle in 1902 has led to the decline of Aro influence. But there are people of Aro stock in many places today who still exert varying degrees of political influence. In the Owerri area they are to be found in Umuoyeche village in Owerri Town, Umuakali Naze, Orji Uratta, Obudi Agwa, Oguta, and other places.

The physical destruction of the shrines of oracles in Igboland during the era of colonial conquests did not necessarily imply that the local people no longer consulted oracles. As a matter of fact, new locations were often established and pilgrimages to the oracles continued as usual. The Igwekala or Igwe of Umunoha, for example, is said to have been destroyed in 1902. But consultation of the oracle continued, though in attenuated form, until the 1960s. In the opinion of the local people, Igwe is indestructible. Hence during the 1940s and 1950s Umunoha agents of Igwekala played similar roles as the Aro. Posing as traders, these agents travelled from village to village hawking *Mmiri agwa,* a quininelike liquid supposed to cure stomach ailments. In the process of their travels, the agents studied local conditions and relayed them to Igwe priests. And like the Aro traders, they too conducted clients to the oracle. One of these "traders" was a frequent visitor to my father, and it was he who advised him to consult Igwe around 1946. Repeated attempts by the Nigerian government "to end the racketeering business" of Igwekala had little effect.[26] As one shrine was captured and destroyed, another emerged somewhere else within a short time. This explains why, to some people, Igwe is not only mysterious but indestructible. Indeed, despite the so-called final assault on Igwe camp in 1963 by the East Regional Government of Nigeria, the hold of Igwe on Umunoha people remains firm. One major problem about the Igwe operation, as this writer learned by experience at Umunoha in 1975, is that the people most familiar with it adamantly refuse to talk about it. Thus it remains a mystery to outsiders.

The Establishment of British Administration

Oral and literary evidence seems to suggest that Owerri did not enter into the British scheme of things until the period of the Arochukwu expedition of 1901-2. Nor is there any evidence that Europeans visited the town earlier, even though, as some have suggested, the Royal Niger Company, which operated at Oguta since 1884, knew about Njemanze Ihenacho Okorie, the most prominent man in Owerri at the time.[27] It was in fact during the preparation for the Arochukwu expedition that Owerri was selected as one of the military bases of operation. There is no record, however, that the survey group was in Owerri for that matter. The choice seems to have been based on the so-called central base theory of colonial occupation. According to this theory, towns which appeared centrally located and from where easy access could be gained into neighboring towns were considered vitally important as military bases. Also, towns believed to have harbored anti-European sentiments were selected not only as military bases but as administrative centers. Since there were no known cases of anti-British feeling here prior to 1902, it would appear that the first rather than the second theory explains the choice of Owerri as a military base and eventually as an administrative headquarters.

Prior to the Arochukwu expedition, Eastern Nigeria was carefully surveyed and mapped out for military purposes. It was during this time that Owerri was designated a "strategic military station."[28] Owerri thus became one of the four major military centers for the Arochukwu operation, the others being Oguta, Akwete, and Bende. When the expedition started in November 1901, two of the four military columns, those from Oguta and Akwete, were ordered to converge at Owerri. The military contingent from Oguta (column 1) arrived on December 5 followed by the Akwete column (number 3) on December 9. From Owerri the two columns proceeded to Bende en route to Arochukwu.

Colonial soldiers from Oguta are said to have followed the traditional trade routes between Owerri and Oguta and were guided by Aro slave dealers who were familiar with the trade routes. Here is an example of the African factor in the saga of European conquest. There are, unfortunately, very scanty literary accounts relating to the military operations in Owerri Town, although oral sources provide ample details. When the data for this section of the study was collected in 1975, there were informants who remembered the encounter with the British very vividly. Some indicated that they were young men at the time.

After experiencing stiff opposition at Oguta and elsewhere, the soldiers finally reached Umuguma. From here a message was sent through one Agogha Ekeze, the headman of Umuguma, to Njemanze Ihenacho Okorie of Owerri, warning him that the British were coming to his town. Njemanze (alias Odogwo) was at the time a wealthy and influential man (an Ogaranya), having acquired great wealth from slave trading and through inheritance. Another prominent man in the town was Igwigbe Okoroji Abazu. Unaware of who the soldiers were and suspicious of their intentions, Njemanze, Igwigbe, and the elders decided to refuse the soldiers free entry. But the soldiers were determined to enter Owerri anyway. So the commander of the expeditionary force allegedly sent back word to Njemanze informing him rather peremptorily that whether he and his people agreed or not, the soldiers were coming: *"Ekwe abia abia! Ekweghi abia abia."*[29] After encountering spirited opposition at Umuguma and other neighboring towns, the soldiers ultimately entered Owerri in full force. They are reported to have been too numerous and strange.

Upon entering Owerri the soldiers are said to have gone wild—looting farms and seizing animals. Fear coupled with anger forced Njemanze to advise his people to refrain from all forms of contact with the intruders. They were not to be provided with food nor water nor even fire. Occasional clashes between the local people and soldiers are said to have occurred at the market square where the soldiers camped. The soldiers are said to have seized foodstuff from market women without payment. Farms and yam barns (*ọba*), especially those belonging to Njemanze, were looted. Animals were also seized. Naturally such unfriendly behavior infuriated as well as frightened the local inhabitants. One informant likened this experience of British presence to that of the Nigerian occupation of Owerri (1968) during the Nigeria-Biafra war: "When they [British soldiers] came, we lost almost all we had. Now [1975], too, we have nothing. Everything we have has vanished, including our yams!"[30] It is alleged that the Aro traders even suggested that the soldiers should be attacked and their belongings seized. No such action was attempted, however, for fear of government reprisals. *"Ujọ okwere onye vuọ Beke!"* Literally, no one dared to assault the white man because of fear.

According to British official report, the attitude of the Owerri people toward the government during this period (1901) is said to have been "distinctly friendly." Consequently, while armed resistance, as noted earlier, was reported at Oguta, Umuguma, and other places, no such military opposition emerges from the documents in respect to Owerri Town. One wonders what must have been responsible for this rather atypical passivity. Oral evidence collected at Owerri throws some light on the matter. It would appear from this source that Owerri people were utterly frightened by the destructive manner of British penetration. "They came in hordes, shooting and seizing animals. They burned farms and houses." In addition, it seems that only a few Owerri people possessed guns for armed resistance. One Ohagwa Nduma is said to have offered a symbolic resistance by firing at the soldiers at the market square. According to our source, Ohagwa was keeping watch at the market when the soldiers arrived. Believing they were hostile busybodies, he fired at them. When the soldiers returned fire one Onyewuchi Ejiogu from Umuodu village is said to have been fatally wounded. This created a general panic. According to informants, "Cannon thundered, smoke filled the horizon, and fear and panic seized every man and woman." To many, "this strange event" presaged the end of the world! As the sound of gunfire reverberated, consternation grew, leading ultimately to desertion from the villages so as to escape "the disastrous war of the whiteman."[31] This episode is immortalized in local folklore as *igba ǫsǫ ǫgu Beke,* the flight from the whiteman's war.

Desertion of towns and villages thus became a phenomenon of the conquest period. Indeed, in Igboland as a whole, whenever people expected trouble from the colonial army, they generally deserted their villages. In the words of a British officer, as soon as people in a village got wind of the approach of the soldiers, they quickly took "all their goods and chattels, including their wives and children, [and] retreat[ed] into the bush." In the Owerri case, most people are said to have fled to the neighboring towns of Egbu and Uratta. Njemanze, for example, is said to have fled to his relative Anumudu of Orji Uratta, while another prominent man, Osigwe Mere, fled to Umuoba Uratta.[32]

It should be noted that from this time on soldiers symbolized colonial presence, destruction, terror, and brutality. Their arrival in any town or village invariably caused considerable uneasiness, fear, and, as mentioned, desertion. It was this perception of the soldiers as destroyers that helped create an atmosphere of social distance between the military and the civilian population. It also fostered an enduring hostility not only toward the imperial forces but also toward political officers as well. In large measure, to be sure, the traditional fear of the Abam, Ada, and Ohaffia warriors was now replaced by fear of the British—and much more so. Whereas the reputed Abam headhunters might have but a few heads as a mark of prowess,[33] the "visit" of colonial forces heralded new forms of social disaster: "They burnt down whole villages, wantonly destroyed farms and other property, seized goats and cattle, took hostages, and demanded heavy ransom." It is against this background that the significance of the statement made by the Owerri Divisional Union to the Jones Commission in 1956 should be understood: "When the Europeans came to this division they did not come as friends."[34]

By 1901 Owerri had only been terrorized, not effectively colonized. Effective colonization took place after Owerri had been declared district headquarters. At the conclusion of the Arochukwu expedition (March 24, 1902), a detachment of the military regiment under Major Henry L. Gallwey returned to Owerri in April. This military contingent, numbering about two hundred, formed the nucleus of the military garrison at Owerri. In addition, there were some fourteen police constables stationed here. Although this military garrison was expected to be temporary, it nevertheless remained solidly entrenched up to the First World War due largely to continued colonial resistance. Backed by this military presence, Gallwey negotiated with Njemanze and Igwigbe (another prominent man) for the cession of lands to the government. Unfortunately we have no official record of this transaction; our reconstruction here is based on oral sources.

Njemanze is said to have shown Gallwey some pieces of land which the government could use, but was alarmed and outraged by Gallwey's land-grabbing proclivities. Not only did Gallwey refuse the sites allocated to him, he is reported to have demanded more land than the concessionaries were willing to allow. Angry protests to Gallwey's land policy stemmed from the fact that he had taken the best arable lands instead of accepting the "bad bush" (*ǫhia ǫjǫǫ*) that had been allocated to him. Secondly, by claiming lands beyond those owned by Njemanze and Igwigbe, Gallway was in essence asking both men to alienate lands on which they had no traditional authority. Under normal circumstances Gallwey's choice of land would have been rejected. But the presence of the soldiers probably forced Njemanze and Igwigbe to acquiesce.[35]

Shortly after the negotiations, the consul-general, Sir Ralph Moor, visited Owerri (May 1902) and proclaimed it a district headquarters. Harold Morday Douglas, formerly at Akwete, was appointed the district commissioner (DC). On May 11, 1902, Moor held a conference with the headmen from Owerri and neighboring towns, ostensibly to explain government policy to them. According to Moor the meeting was attended by traditional headmen from twenty-three different towns within a twelve-mile radius of Owerri. This may be an exaggeration; it is much more likely that headmen from the immediate neighborhood attended. These may have included leaders from Uratta, Egbu, Emekuku, Naze, Nekede, Irete, Avu, Ogbaku, and elsewhere. Whatever the case, the meeting yielded results. At its conclusion Moor inaugurated the Native Council and appointed some of the traditional leaders as members. It was not until a year later that a Sierra Leonean, Isaiah Yellow, was appointed clerk of the council. And in May 1903 the Owerri Native Court was established.

The early members of the court were basically men of wealth and power (Ogaranya). Unfortunately, the official list of the warrant chiefs had been lost, but by 1912 those referred to as "chiefs" in Owerri Town included Njemanze (Amawom), Nwagbaroacha Anumudu (Umuǫrǫrǫnjǫ), Uche-wuako Obi (Umuoyeche), Emeto Chiekezi (Umuodu), and Ukegbu (Umuoyima). Presumably these were also among the original court appointees. Evidently those who were granted warrants in the early days of British rule were not necessarily scoundrels or riffraff or opportunistic and ambitious men. Rather, they seem to have been men who had traditional legitimacy of authority. However, their position and role under the new administration differed fundamentally from what they were in pregovernment days. In the olden days, for example, the rich received authority *from the people* in recognition of services rendered, and they invariably lost it if they acted in an oppressive manner. In other words, the check-and-balance mechanism inherent in the Igbo political system prevented autocracy and dictatorship. During the colonial era, on the other hand, rich men, to quote C. K. Meek, "assumed (or were forced by Government to assume) *uncontrolled* authority in their own towns."[36]

The native courts seriously subverted and undercut indigenous political organization. And their locations, as Robert L. Tignor has observed, "forced previously autonomous communities into new political units," thus creating political restlessness. We shall return to this later. To the British, of course, the native courts represented new departures in colonial administration. They were now vital instruments of sociopolitical change. Here is Sir Ralph's view of the role of the native courts in Southern Nigeria:

> These courts are not only the basis of the judicial system, but, also, of the Administrative and Executive systems of the Protectorate. It is on these courts that the Government mainly relies for the dispensing of justice among the natives, for the establishment of peace and good order in the territories, for the carrying out of all Administrative and Executive work among the natives themselves, for the furtherance of Trade, Education, Agriculture, etc., throughout the territories.

The creation of the Owerri Native Court and the appointment of warrant chiefs heralded the era of judicial and political transformation. For example, by investing the chiefs with paramount "authority over their boys," a practice which had no place in Igbo traditional political system, Moor and others invariably sowed the seeds of political corruption and social disintegration. Indeed, in traditional Igbo society, authority was diffused and never did any one man hold the position of a ruler of a town. In other words, no one person was regarded as possessing paramount authority over other people. Instead, authority was exercised by various groups including headmen, elders, priests, titled men, secret societies, and age grades. Because of the democratic nature of the society, decisions were based on consensus rather than on majority rule. This reflects the equality principle in Igbo democratic organization. This "natural communism," as one British administrator quaintly described the indigenous system of government, was then "suspended by an autocracy, and the autocrats were anything but benevolent."[37] In essence, Moor's action as well as those of his followers constituted a serious political scandal that shook Igbo political organization to its very foundation. More will be said on this later.

Moor was not oblivious to the revolutionary character of his political reorganization. Nor was he so naive as not to realize that the chiefs he had appointed would hardly be obeyed if left alone to enforce their authority, hence his insistence that the government should back the chiefs up with necessary military power. Otherwise, he stressed, they would never be obeyed by their people. In any case, Moor viewed his exploits at Owerri with evident satisfaction. Given the "unsettled" nature of the new district, he pointed out, the establishment of a military garrison and the presence of the district commissioner would ensure "thorough government control in the district . . . in a short time." Moreover, considering the fact that the district was rich in palm produce and the local people skillful traders, Moor felt satisfied that the reorganization he had carried out in the district would invariably contribute to the promotion of trade. And in the tradition of the time, he assured his superiors that what had been accomplished would lead to the civilization of the Africans. Naturally, the Colonial Office was pleased with "the new order of things" effected in Southern Nigeria, and Moor was heartily congratulated for "the time and effort" he had given to advance the British Empire and to promote trade and civilization in Eastern Nigeria.[38]

As might be expected, the British knew very little about the new district. Neither Moor nor Douglas knew exactly the boundary limitations of the new district nor of course did they have any conception of the population therein. The 1902 boundary definitions simply said that the Owerri District was "bounded on the South by the Northern Boundary of Degema District, on the West by Eastern Boundary of Agberi District, on the North by the Northern Boundary of the Protectorate and on the East by the Western Boundaries of Opobo and Bende Districts." This, to say the least, is vague. If there were maps to indicate these boundaries, they have not survived. After further military expansion, new boundary arrangements were drawn in 1905 which remained extremely vague, confusing, and imprecise even to the experts. As a result, there were occasional boundary disputes between officials in Owerri, Okigwe, Bende, Degema, and other districts. "The only sound way of disposing them" (the disputes), it was suggested, "is to accept the *de facto* boundary and insist on its observance." Investigations in England and Nigeria have as yet failed to provide any clear-cut delimitation of the old Owerri District. Nor have I seen any maps on the matter. With the expansion of administrative authority, however, officials were then more concerned with divisional boundaries than district delimitations. Even then, by 1938 the boundary of Owerri Division had not yet been precisely defined. "The Division is bounded on the North by the Okigwe Division, on the East by the Bende and Aba Divisions, on the South-West by the

Ahoada Division and on the North-West by the Orlu District, Okigwe Division. The Imo River forms the Eastern boundary; the other boundaries are not marked by geographical features and have not been surveyed."[39] By the end of 1947, Owerri Division covered about 1,085 square miles with an estimated population of six hundred thousand.[40]

2. THE CONSOLIDATION OF BRITISH ADMINISTRATION

AGGRESSION AND RESISTANCE

The history of the establishment of British authority in the Owerri Division, as elsewhere in Nigeria, is basically the story of conquests and fusions. Indeed, beyond the immediate environs of the headquarters, government authority was virtually nonexistent. None of the towns and villages outside of Owerri Town acknowledged the imperial pretensions of the government. Umunoha and its neighbors, for example, continued to conduct their business unmindful of the government at Owerri. Hence the "pacification" process continued until after the First World War. This involved a series of military expeditions, known more popularly as "patrols" or "operations," designed to bring different towns and villages under the pale of the colonial government. "In the Uri Operations" of 1902, wrote A. Haywood and F. A. S. Clarke, "the object was to punish this tribe for raiding and stopping trade" and also to destroy the Igwe oracle, which was terrorizing the district. "For these purposes a force of about 350 Rifles was assembled at Oguta under Colonel Montanaro on 3rd April. . . . On 25th–26th an entrenched camp was found at Omonoha [sic]. This was captured after 4½ hours' engagement. From 27th [April] to 15th May various towns which had collaborated in the disorders were punished and the Igwe Juju was destroyed."[1]

The expansion of government authority in the early years devolved on the DC, Harold Morday Douglas (1902–6) and his immediate successors. Born in 1874, Douglas joined the British overseas service in 1894. He came to Southern Nigeria in 1897 from Las Palmas, Canary Islands, where he had acted as British consular agent and acting vice-consul (1894–97). On December 7, 1897 he was appointed acting district commissioner (ADC) at Calabar. From here he was transferred to Akwete in 1900.[2] After the Arochukwu expedition he was relocated to Owerri in 1902. By the time of his retirement on July 20, 1920, Douglas had occupied several positions in

Nigeria, the highest rank he attained being that of a second class Resident. He died in Northern Rhodesia (Zambia) on May 24, 1926.

During the Arochukwu expedition Douglas acted as a political officer and was decorated with a medal and a shoulder clasp for meritorious service. The commander of the Aro Field Force reported of Douglas, "Mr. H. M. Douglas was very useful to me at the time of the Obegu raid and acted with energy on several occasions during the operations."[3]

For the people of Owerri and the division as a whole, the appointment of Douglas as the district commissioner heralded an era of storm and stress. For the first time in their lives people in the division began to experience the real impact of European colonialism—loss of political sovereignty, personal dignity, and freedom. They were then subjected to personal abuse, insults, humiliation, and exploitation. To them, in fact, Douglas symbolized all that was bad in European imperialism. His personal eccentricities are still vividly remembered. The overall picture of him which emerges from both oral and literary evidence is of a man who was affected with the arrogance of power and who often exploded under the slightest provocation. According to sources, he was obstinate and tempestuous. His authoritarian personality, imperial obstrusiveness, and almost pathological addiction to brutality made him very unpopular throughout Southern Nigeria. Not only was he an overbearing and intolerant bureaucrat, but he is also said to have shown neither respect for age nor regard for those in positions of authority. Owerri informants were almost unanimous in alleging that he often slapped chiefs publicly. As an illustration of his high temper, for instance, Douglas is said to have thrown a pot of gum (*eso*) on the face of one Nwagbaraocha Anumudu from Umuọrọrọnjọ village for allegedly not bringing a full pot of gum from his people as ordered by the DC. Njemanze is also said to have been disciplined. Again, it was alleged that Douglas often flogged elders for coming late to meetings! Because he was *Beke ọjọọ* ("a bad Englishman"), he was feared, and the local people tried to stay clear of his sight as much as possible. "Black Douglas," as he was pejoratively called, was "a hard man" in the eyes of Africans as well as among his European contemporaries. The Africans found him to be irritatingly imperious and cruel.[4] European contemporaries also deplored his overbearing attitude toward Africans. His reputation for intolerance and high-handedness drew this pungent criticism from the Anglican bishop on the Niger:

Adopt a kindlier and more generous attitude towards a subject people. . . . From what I heard from the people as I passed through your district . . . your system of administration appears to be nigh unbearable. The people complained bitterly of your harsh treatment of them, while those who accompanied me

(through your district) do not cease to speak in the strongest terms of your overbearing manner towards them. They say they have never received such treatment
at the hands of a British officer.[5]

In official circles, too, Douglas faced harsh criticism. In 1914, for example, Douglas was sharply reprimanded by the governor for the maltreat-
ment of his African subordinates. The Nigerian *Times* also joined in the
condemnation when Douglas had physically assaulted an interpreter (Mr.
Braid) and his houseboys, John and Peter. In explaining his behavior toward the interpreter, Douglas told the governor that Braid had "talked
back" to him in an "insolent" and disdainful manner when he was re-
proached for what he had done (which was not explained). Braid is said to
have retorted, "I do what you tell me." At that point, said Douglas, "[I was]
so furious at his insolence that I sprang up and struck him twice with my
fist, knocking him down." Braid suffered some facial abrasions and was
treated at the hospital.[6] He later reported the incident to the governor.

The press fiercely criticized Douglas for his "intolerance and ill-
treatment of subordinates." He was also assailed for his insensitivity and
unbridled arrogance. In a letter to the governor on January 17, 1915
Douglas alleged that the "vicious" attack on him by the press was simply "a
deliberate effort" on their part "to get me into as much trouble as possible."
He also claimed that Braid's telegram was definitely "instigated" by the
press and other enemies. Indeed, said Douglas, "the whole matter appears
to me to savour of malicious persecution on the part of the writers of the
papers." The governor, however, disagreed and branded his action as ir-
rational and indefensible. Douglas was therefore firmly told that his conduct had been viewed as a gross violation of official code of conduct and
that this "intemperate action" would certainly "militate" against his future
promotion.[7]

As already indicated, the establishment of British colonial presence at
Owerri did not imply that the people had accepted British colonial rule. On
the contrary, we find that Douglas's attempts to assert his authority were
fiercely resisted everywhere. The defiant mood of the people was reflected in
the several messages that were sent to Douglas and his soldiers to "come
and fight; we are ready." Given this atmosphere of hostility toward the
administration, it is not surprising that people would refuse to make roads
as ordered by Douglas. The degree of resistance to government political
pretensions may be appreciated from this report about the people of Ahiara in the present Mbaise local government. "The Ahiaras on the Owerri-
Bende road," Douglas reported in 1903, "have refused to submit [to the
government] and are now sending messages to ask when the Government
intends visiting them. . . . I have made many efforts to get the people to

come in [to Owerri to settle palaver], both through friendly chiefs and by visiting as near [to] their towns as is safe, but they refuse to have anything to do with the Government."[8] In other places the situation was practically the same.

Defiance of British authority was almost universal throughout the division. In some cases hostility toward the administration was expressed by the destruction of government property, beating up of colonial agents, especially court messengers, or even murder of European and African officials. In other cases, resistance was expressed by refusing to make roads or carry loads for colonial officers. These will be treated later. In any case, such challenges to government authority were met with prompt government military action. Take the case of the murder of one Chief Nwogu Umaru of Ngor in Janury 1905. In that year the chief, said to have been "friendly with the government," was killed by dissidents from Norie who seemed frustrated by the onerous demands of the government through the chief. A court messenger sent to investigate the matter was assulted and chased out of the town. When C. T. O'Connell, the acting district officer, attempted to enter the town with a small corps of soldiers, he too was driven out. Suspecting (rightly) that government intervention was imminent, the people of Ngor and Norie formed a military alliance and bound themselves to an oath "to resist the government" by whatever means necessary. Under the command of Lieutenant Half-penny, a military patrol was dispatched on April 21, 1905 to the Ngor-Norie area to punish the towns concerned and to "pacify" the entire region. The scale of resistance alarmed Half-penny. In the encounter, four of his soldiers were killed and fifty-three wounded. Half-penny was therefore forced to ask for reinforcements. On April 22 he launched a surprise night attack and succeeded in penetrating into Norie. War raged until early May. In the end, Ngor, Norie, Isuobiangwu (Obiangwu), Umuohiagu, and other surrounding towns were reported to have been "thoroughly subjugated and brought under the rule of the Government." In the opinion of Captain P. K. Carre, "the prompt and severe punishment inflicted on the Ngors must prove a useful factor in raising the government's prestige in the Owerri District, and be of assistance in bringing any disaffected tribes to their senses."[9]

Several other towns in the division were similarly treated. Truculent towns were particularly earmarked for subjugation and incorporation. Thus several wars of conquest were undertaken from 1903 onwards. In fact 1905 seems to have been a critical year for the administration. Demands for carriers and laborers for road construction significantly accentuated local anticolonial sentiment. In his report on the attitude of the people in the Owerri District for 1905, Douglas noted among other things that "with the exception of a few towns all the country [*sic*] . . . is decidedly hostile to the Government." In the Mbaise clan and especially in Ahiara, anti-British feeling was markedly intense. The defiant mood of the people of Ahiara was patently clear from the closure of all their roads to government agents and even to neighboring towns (especially Nguru), said to be friendly to the administration. To Douglas, this challenge to government authority was intolerable. But lack of sufficient military force to teach Ahiara a "sharp lesson" precluded an earlier invasion.[10] However, it was the murder of one Dr. Stewart, a medical officer attached to the Southern Nigeria Expeditionary Force, at Onicha (Ezinihitte) in Mbaise in November 1905 that provided the occasion for the military invasion of Ahiara and the other towns in the area.

THE AHIARA EXPEDITION

The historic episode of the Ahiara expedition of 1905–16 has been treated by this writer in some detail elsewhere.[11] It will suffice to examine the major aspects of the crisis here. Dr. Stewart was believed (wrongly) to have been killed and eaten by the people of Ahiara. The tragic incident seems indeed to have been triggered by sad memories of British brutality and overrule. Local recollections of British atrocity in this area prior to the murder of Dr. Stewart clearly suggest that British brutality and other forms of oppression rankled. It is said, for example, that during the Arochukwu expedition, Ahiara young men were seized by the expeditionary force and compelled to carry loads for the soldiers. Individuals who resisted are said to have been harshly treated, some reportedly bludgeoned to death. Several towns and villages were also ordered to provide food and water for the soldiers. To induce the people to comply with government demands, some prominent elders are said to have been seized as hostages and sent to Owerri, a distance of some twelve miles. The practice of seizing prominent people as hostages to induce local compliance to government authority was, of course, widespread in Nigeria during the colonial period. According to informants, some of the old men died from sheer exhaustion en route to Owerri. On the whole, the hostages either died or were incarcerated. In fact, when Governor Walter Egerton visited Owerri in April 1905, he regretfully observed that the Owerri lockup had too many people,[12] some of whom might have been the Mbaise victims.

Obviously, this high-handed behavior of the soldiers rankled the Africans and thus created an atmosphere of bitterness and hostility toward the government. Moreover, the alleged disappearance of highly respected and cherished elders not only inflamed the spirit of revenge but made the people more determined than ever to resist British imperial pretensions. A military patrol sent to Ahiara in March 1905 as a means of crushing Ahiara's "persistent insubordination" further exacerbated tensions. Therefore, when Dr. Stewart was captured in November 1905, having lost his way en route to Umuahia (some sources say Calabar), Opara Nwaeberike of Ahiara, whose father is said to have been among those interred at Owerri, insisted that Dr. Stewart's life should not be spared.[13] Seen from this perspective it would appear that the murder was at least in part a clear example of retaliatory violence. Indeed, whatever else may be said of this tragic incident, one fact is patently clear: the swiftness with which demonstrations spread upon the capture of Dr. Stewart is an indication of the social depth of grievances against the British administration. The London *Times'* contention that Dr. Stewart was killed primarily for cannibalistic reasons has no foundation whatsoever. But the *Times* was right when it remarked that the people firmly believed (though wrongly) "they had killed a great enemy"[14]— Douglas.

The episode of Dr. Stewart is certainly one of the most celebrated events in Anglo-Igbo relations during the early decades of the twentieth century. Accounts of the circumstances that led to the death of Dr. Stewart are somewhat confusing and at some points clearly contradictory. The account that follows is therefore a simplified version. British official account insists that Dr. Stewart was accompanying an expeditionary force as a medical officer. He is said to have left Owerri on November 15, 1905 en route to Bende, but he lost his way and was then captured and killed by the people of Ahiara. Before he was killed, we are told, he was first paraded publicly and forced to march from market to market. He was finally brought to a market square where he was "stripped and tied up," beaten to death, and his body "cut up and shared among the towns."[15] There is the legend that Dr. Stewart's bicycle was hung on the tree at the market square to prevent it from running away!

There is yet another version, this one from a European contemporary whose reconstruction of events should be treated with great caution. Here is the account given by A. Haywood, who participated in many of the military campaigns.

This Medical Officer was a new-comer in Nigeria, and as such unaccustomed to the hazards of travelling by himself in the bush. It appears that he was travelling on his bicycle alone along a bush-path when he lost his way. Being exhausted by nightfall he came across a native hut, where he lay down to rest. The occupant, said to be an old woman, alerted the tribe to his presence. He was probably killed while still asleep. His body was cut up into small pieces and distributed by way of fetish, with the idea that those eating a portion would be protected from harm by any white man and be released from his domination.[16]

Oral evidence collected in 1973 reveals that contrary to popular opinion Dr. Stewart was killed at Afor Ukwu Onicha in Ezinihitte and not at Ahiara. The attribution of guilt to Ahiara may have derived from: (1) its intransigent attitude toward the British government; (2) false rumors emanating from its Nguru neighbors that Dr. Stewart was murdered by Ahiara people (it should be pointed out here that Ahiara and Nguru were archenemies at the time; Nguru young men even volunteered to fight on the side of the British against their inveterate enemy); (3) the emotional public demonstration at Ahiara following the killing of the medical doctor which may indeed have been construed as evidence of guilt. It is said that the people of Ahiara, who apparently regarded the death of Dr. Stewart as a form of retaliation against British overrule, paraded at the various sections of their town. As the crowd paraded with obvious excitement they are said to have sung: "We have killed the white man who killed our fathers and elders." Perhaps they thought they had killed Douglas, the bugbear of the people.[17]

British response to the killing of Dr. Stewart was predictably immediate and harsh. Since Ahiara was believed to have been responsible for the "intolerable" murder, it was to be severely punished. In an urgent telegram to the district officer at Owerri, Divisional Commissioner W. Fosbery instructed that "full reparation for this outrage" should be exacted on Ahiara people. Accordingly, a massive military expedition was launched against Ahiara and other towns. The military operation began on December 7, 1905 and lasted until April 15, 1906. Although the major concentration here is on the famous Ahiara expedition, it is well to remember that the operation was simply part of the wide-ranging 1905 punitive expedition which overwhelmed most areas of former Eastern Nigeria. Actually, many Igbo towns, including those in the Owerri Division, had by late 1905 demonstrated their uncompromising attitude toward the British government by closing their roads to all British officials and agents. The British government, of course, was equally determined to exert its full authority in the whole territory. It therefore declared in no uncertain terms that all roads "must be opened and tribes through whose territory the road passes made to understand once and for all that they must carry out the requirements of the Government."[18] And because both sides remained decisively uncompromising, serious confrontation was inevitable.

The resistance, according to British accounts, was "serious" and formidable. As soon as Major Trenchard crossed into Ahiara from Udo, Ahiara people began firing at the enemy from their trenches. As Trenchard conceded, "The most continued and obstinate resistance was met with trenches and stockades being found everywhere." It appeared indeed that British aggression might be stopped. For days the war raged and, according to Trenchard, the colonial army was almost overwhelmed. As he put it, the noise made by the guns of the enemy was "utterly deafening." And in a letter to the British Colonial Office, the acting high commissioner reported, "The opposition to the punitive force is serious and I anticipate that some time must elapse before the Ahiara country is adequately punished."[19]

The British did not of course anticipate the degree of resistance thus encountered. Trenchard therefore had to call for reinforcements from Onitsha and Aba. Thereafter he made a desperate attempt to silence Ahiara guns. At two o'clock in the morning of December 13 a surprise attack was directed at Ahiara strongholds. This was followed by unwanton burning and destruction of houses and farms. Local property was also looted. It was this war of attrition that ultimately forced Ahiara people to desert their homes and seek refuge among their neighbors to the north. British soldiers pursued them into Obizi, Eziudo, and Onicha. Again, all the towns affected deserted their homes and fled to Obowo. On December 14, 1905 a decisive battle was fought at one o'clock in the afternoon. This was the battle of Alaike ("Aliki"). Here, as informants described it, "force was met with force." In Igbo parlance, it was here that *ike na ibe ya jiri zuru.* The colonial army actually faced a formidable force from Ahiara, Obizi, Eziudo, Onicha, and Obowo. The fierceness of the battle might be appreciated from Major Trenchard's report in which he stated: "There is not a single town here that has not fired at us." He boasted, however, that he was able to deal "severe blows" on the enemy in spite of heavy odds. Government casualties were reported as nine killed and two "dangerously" and "severely" injured. Trenchard also claimed to have recovered the skull of Dr. Stewart,[20] but this report of 1932 by the district officer at Owerri casts serious doubt on the accuracy of the claim: "Vigorous attempts were revived last year without success to discover more [about the Ahiara incident] and recover Dr. Stewart's head. Further efforts are not likely to achieve any better results, and failure might do harm." Thus the impression is that Dr. Stewart's head was never recovered because it was carefully hidden from the British. It is in fact speculated that Dr. Stewart's skull is now a local heirloom.[21]

At the conclusion of the operations, the whole of present-day Mbaise local government area was effectively brought under Owerri jurisdictional authority. The entire area was disarmed because, as the government argued, the continued possession of firearms "would be a constant source of danger to the future peace of the country." Those who were reluctant to surrender their guns for fear of being left defenseless were cajoled to turn them in with the assurance that there was "no [further] need for the retention of such arms as the Government will provide the protection of the people concerned."[22] In all, about 17,966 guns were confiscated, a clear reflection of the large quantity of arms in the possession of colonial resistors.

Shortly after the "pacification," the DC visited Ahiara and its neighbors and appointed headmen whom he entrusted with the responsibility of reporting any serious breaches of the peace. According to official records, "these Headmen turned out their people to make roads, thus making the area more accessible and possible to control, while also encouraging trade." One wonders very seriously whether these headmen were the accepted traditional rulers. For as both the written and oral sources indicate, many of the traditional rulers had been seized as hostages and incarcerated at the government prisons at Owerri and Onitsha. According to Governor Egerton, many of these elders died at the Onitsha prison. Many others who had been arrested in connection with the death of Dr. Stewart, were reported as having died in prison as a result of inadequate care and from dysentery. In some places, to be sure, those who were chosen as headmen had no traditional basis of authority as the cases of Chief Onyekwere of Udo and Chief Okpokoro of Onicha would suggest. Both are said to have been political upstarts, men who rose to power because of their close association with the soldiers during the Ahiara expedition.[23]

As another way of keeping the whole clan under strict surveillance, a native court was established at Obohia in 1907. Because of political problems and pressures from Chief Nwaturuocha of Nguru, the court was transferred from Obohia to Nguru in 1909. In 1929 the Nguru court was destroyed as a result of the women's revolt of that year. Thereafter, sessional courts were opened at Obohia, Itu, Ife, and Inyiogugu in response to the "home rule" movement of the 1930s.

It is well to remember that none of the measures indicated above served singly or collectively to eliminate completely local animosity toward the British administration. The people in the area as well as elsewhere in the division seemed determined never to compromise with European colonialism. Thus, political agitation continued well into the 1950s. In some places, some warrant chiefs even sided with their people in resisting onerous government orders. Chief Chilaka of Umunama and Chief Abii of Eziudo were examples of chiefs who united with their people in resisting imperial exploitation. In several other places the local people vented their vengeance at the court clerks, court messengers, police constables, and even chiefs. All over the division there were reports of "acts of violence" being perpetrated against these agents of British imperialism.[24]

Court messengers, derisively called *"Kotima [Courtima] otula ntu,"* were indeed "jacks of all trades" during the colonial era. They performed all sorts of jobs ranging from the noble to the ignoble. For example, they "guarded the properties of the courts, maintained order during court sittings, guarded criminals under arrest, carried messages between the district officer and court clerks." They also looked after government rest houses. In addition, they acted as work overseers and served summonses. Wherever the district officer or the court clerk or even the chiefs wanted a job done, the court messenger would be there. Mostly corrupt, they were nonetheless courageous in the performance of their duties. As the district officer (DO), Captain Ambrose, said of them, "The feat of the *Courtimas* was often little short of marvelous. They could lug a prisoner out from a place that I would not have cared to put my nose into without an escort."[25] In spite of the fact that they were poorly paid, their occupation appeared popular among some classes of people, perhaps because of the extra money or presents (yams) that were given to them during the delivery of summonses.

However, the court messengers appeared to be the greatest victims of public frustration against colonial rule. In report after report they are said to have been beaten up by angry villagers as they attempted to serve summonses or to arrest criminals. In 1910 L. L. Tew, the district commissioner (DC) at Owerri, reported that court messengers were physically assaulted by many of the Mbaise towns and villages. Onicha, Ogbe, Otulu, Ihitteafoukwu, Umuokirika, and others were specifically identified as places where court messengers were generally beaten up or molested. Evidently, villagers viewed court messengers as agents of British oppression and so the "ruffling up" of the court messengers was an expression of defiance of the government's authority.

ORACLES AND COLONIAL RESISTANCE

In the Owerri-Oguta sector there were similar reports of acts of violence against court messengers and warrant chiefs. In such places as Ogbaku, Izombe, Ejemekwuru, Nkwesi, and Uli, among others, where government and Niger Company encroachments were considered by the people as an attack on their independence, there were attempts to reassert local independence. This included the assertion of local rights to collect tolls on traders who passed through the area. In pregovernment days, traders ordinarily paid tolls to local potentates or headmen as they passed through their territories. In return they were guaranteed security by the local rulers. The government and the company of course adopted the ideology of free trade which deprived the local rulers of their independence as well as their source of income. So, in an attempt to restore their traditional rights, headmen in the above-mentioned places closed their roads to traders and insisted on payment of the traditional tolls. Warrant chiefs who sought to enforce government orders on free trade found themselves in the throes of mass revolt. When court messengers were sent to arrest the rebels, they too were attacked.

Naturally, the Niger Company agents, who considered the so-called lawless situation inimical to trade, demanded government intervention. Tew, the district commissioner, assured the company of government determination to enforce law and order which would promote trade. "In my opinion," he said, "no permanent result could be obtained except by frequent use of Military Patrols. I am now more convinced than ever of the necessity of such measures." Accordingly, punitive military patrols were launched in the affected areas. As might be expected, the effects were quite unsettling as entire villages were obliterated, farms burnt, and local properties plundered or seized. In some cases, casualties were high. In the Nguru patrol of 1916–17, for example, between thirty and forty people were killed in the town of Onicha alone.[26]

Many of these colonial resistance movements in various parts of the Owerri Division and beyond, especially from 1909 to 1911, were in fact inspired by oracles. Thus, as we shall soon see, religious ideology was an important factor in anticolonial protests. For example, as the British colonial administration sought to extend its colonial influence, various towns and villages consulted powerful oracles, believing that these oracles would enable them "to drive out the white man from the country" and thereafter cleanse the society of "the pestilence" of the imperialists.[27] In essence, supernatural intervention through the agency of local oracles became central to the maintenance of political independence and the restoration of the traditional way of life.

Before examining the pattern of this anticolonial protest, it might be useful to discuss briefly the importance and role of oracles in traditional Igbo society. Oracles occupied a very important place "in the total theological framework of . . . African religious systems."[28] In other words, oracles functioned as religious institutions and hence were a potent force in African social and religious life. Like their other African counterparts, the Igbo generally consulted oracles in times of trouble or for the solution to situational problems. When individuals or social groups were beset by misfortunes, for instance, they generally consulted oracles either to discover the identity of the mystic agents of their troubles or to ward off the enemy, whether evil spirits or even individuals. Childless couples often consulted oracles in order to have children. In times of war also social groups or towns consulted oracles, generally for the purpose of overcoming the enemy. In many instances the priests of the oracles or specialist doctors (*dibia*) prepared special war medicines (*ọgwu agha*) purporting to instill in the warriors a sense of invincibility.[29] Besides, the consultation of the oracle promoted intergroup solidarity as the people concerned bound themselves together through the swearing of the sacred oath to fight against the forces of imperialism.[30] With respect to the colonial wars, the sacred oaths tended to embolden the people to defy the authority of the white man and his imperial agents. To quote Frank Hives, a former British colonial official involved in colonial conquests, "No orders given by the Government were to be obeyed, and messengers sent by the Government, such as police and Court messengers, were to be beaten and driven out" from the towns and villages.[31] Thus, oracles galvanized the local people toward revolutionary action. More will be said on this later.

Above all, oracles functioned as judicial institutions. The Igbo, for example, consulted oracles, especially powerful oracles such as Chukwu, Igwekala, Amadioha Ozuzu, Agbala, or Ogbunorie, to name a few, for the purpose of settling disputes. "Perhaps the most powerful of all legal instruments in Iboland," wrote C. K. Meek, a well-informed colonial anthropologist, "were certain well-known oracles which functioned as the highest courts of appeal." Indeed, when disputes which proved too difficult for the extended-family or the village assembly arose, pilgrimages were made to the oracles in order to establish guilt or innocence of the individual or group concerned. The Arochukwu oracle was particularly the most famous and authoritative judicial institution in Igboland. From the foregoing, it is clear that oracles influenced Igbo religious, political, social, and judicial life. Hence the Igbo, as Meek correctly observed, "regard the destruction of the oracles [by the British] as an abominable outrage."[32]

Returning to the wave of resistance to British imperial authority, it is interesting to note that the Ogbunorie oracle, located at Ezumoha in the then Okigwe Division, provided the inspiration for the widespread uprising during the period from 1909 to 1911. Of the Ogbunorie oracle, the DC at Owerri reported,

> There is reported to be a big juju called Obonorie [Ogbunorie] which, as far as I can gather, is at Nsu. . . . This juju is becoming a serious danger to this district, as people from nearly all parts [of the district] are visiting it and professing that it enables them to disregard the white man, and their chiefs, and the courts. I have known about it for some time, but it is only lately that there have been open manifestations of it, even in the most friendly towns.

He went on to describe the pattern of this widespread resistance against

imperial authority. "At Oguta I learnt that [my] carriers had been refused
water by certain compounds of Obaku [Ogbaku] and that at Ejemekwuru a
police whom I sent with a message to the head chief had been driven out of
the compound." Elsewhere too, especially in the Okigwe Division, we learn
that the influence of Ogbunorie was widespread and that the local inhabitants were extremely hostile to the government. In the words of the local
DC, "Practically the influence of the Obonorie Juju . . . has affected the
whole of Omoduro [Umuduru] N.C. jurisdiction." Hostility to the government, he added, was manifested in the people's threat "to attack Omoduro Station itself." In some towns, he went on, the people have driven
away their chiefs.[33] The DC at Okigwe, as well as his counterpart at Owerri,
admitted that they were quite helpless to deal militarily either with the
recalcitrant towns and villages or with the oracle itself—hence the elaborate preparations that were later made to deal with the Ogbunorie oracle
and to suppress the widespread rebellion in the two divisions.

At this juncture it is important to point out also that the Ogbunorie
oracle was widely reputed as a powerful oracle. Its fame seems to have
derived from the fact that it "killed" a woman said to have sworn falsely by
it, hence its perception as the *Ome ire,* or the spirit of action.[34] It was also
known as the god of truth and justice in that "Ogbunorie does not kill the
innocent." In Igbo parlance, *"Ogbunorie anaghi egbu n'ugha."*[35] More specifically, the local people seemed to have had great confidence in the power
and impartiality of the oracle, especially when they swore oaths, using its
sacred water (*mmiri Ihiafor*) as the object of oath.

Furthermore, the local people generally believed that because Ogbunorie was a powerful spirit, it would certainly "kill anyone" sent by the British
to wage war against them or to enforce the obnoxious laws. Thus confidence in the omnipotence of the oracle seemed to have propelled the various towns and villages to offer a stiff resistance against British imperial
pretensions. Indeed, when soldiers were sent to crush the rebellions inspired by Ogbunorie, the encounter proved far more bewildering than originally anticipated. In the words of the military officer engaged in the pacification, "The enemy were found waiting in large numbers. War drums were
being beaten and the enemy wore a menacing aspect." Everywhere, he conceded, "we were fired upon." The reference here was to Obowo where, in
the words of S. K. Given (ADC), there was absolutely "no sign of submission" to government authority nor any evidence that the people were even
in the mood to parley with the administration. Instead, "they are preparing
for [more] active resistance." A punitive military action thus followed.

On the 22nd [September] I left Owerri with Captain C. G. Ashton, Dr. J. S.
Smith, and one section of No. 5 Company with a Maxim, visited several com-

pounds of Obako [Ogbaku], and camped at Ejemekwuru, leaving police at Obako to guard a friendly chief's compound and patrol the road between there and Owerri. Compounds of Obako visited were found deserted and only a few people were seen in the distance. . . . On the 23rd we visited all compounds S[outh] of Oguta road and came upon several bush camps in which slight opposition was encountered from individuals. On the 24th we moved back to Obako through the bush visiting all the compounds of Ejemekwuru and Obako. These were all deserted. There was a little "sniping" occasionally. On the 25th we worked back towards Owerri on both sides of the main road through Orogwe, part of which had been affected by the Obonorie Juju, and Ndegu [Ndegwu] and camped at Irete. On the 26th we visited all compounds of Irete and Ndegu S. of the main road, [and] found several bush camps from which some shots were fired. . . . On the 27th we moved to Ubomiri North of the Oguta road and tried to induce all the people to come in, but without success. All compounds but one were deserted, the people being reported to have run to Orodo, Umaka, Awo, and Mbieri, towns lying to the North and East. On the 29th we visited Ifakola, which was deserted, and Omonoha [Umunoha], where evry [*sic*] thing was satisfactory, and returned to Ejemekwuru, where we stayed till the 2nd October but without being able to get the people to come in [to parley]. On October 2nd the escort returned to Owerri.

In all, only about ten "enemy soldiers" were reported killed, while the colonial troops apparently sustained no casualties. But in addition to the "considerable damage" inflicted on the different towns and villages, which included the wanton destruction of houses and farms, the local people were forced to make roads "in the interest of trade and other kindred objects [objectives]." Gloating on his seemingly spectacular achievement, the DC remarked, "There is no doubt that . . . the volume of trade finding its way to the factories should be more than doubled. With the special view of the furtherance of trade, the roads have invariably been made direct from market to market."[36]

Because the pacification was ineffective in either stemming the tide of anticolonial protests or in "rid[ding] the country thoroughly and finally of [the] baneful influence" of Ogbunorie, a well-coordinated military action was then launched in December 1910. This war, regarded as the war to end all wars, is treated here as the Ogbunorie war.[37] In the words of Given, "The Obonorie Juju is deep seated . . . [and] is . . . much more widely spread than was previously imagined. The country seems tainted with it, and undoubtedly until it is stamped out there will be no peaceful termination of the business." He acknowledged, of course, that "it is extremely difficult with a small number of troops to deal with adequately"—hence the full mobilization of the soldiers in the Owerri, Okigwe, and Onitsha divisions to deal "adequately" with the Ogbunorie oracle. Under the command of Major G. T. Mair, the "final" solution to the Ogbunorie menace began. From December 19, 1910 until mid-February 1911, war raged. Ezumoha, "the headquarters" of Ogbunorie, was "bombarded for weeks," and in the words of Ezumoha elders, "the destruction was too much." One informant in his seventies added that the soldiers in fact "burnt down all the houses around; they [also] killed my uncle Abogu."38

At the conclusion of the war, several towns were "thoroughly subjugated" and made to accept British colonial rule. The objective of the punitive expedition also was achieved. Said Captain Ambrose, "We accomplished the work of destruction [of Ogbunorie] by cutting down and burning all the trees around the water, and adding the skull altar to the bonfire." In addition, two sacred crocodiles which resided in the lake surrounding the Ogbunorie shrine were killed and retrieved with extraordinary anxiety. The reason for this was the "rumour" that these crocodiles had golden anklets on their legs. "This . . . piece of information," affirmed Captain Ambrose, "caused a little stir and excitement among the officers, each of us speculating as to who would be the lucky one to get the anklets and become rich for life."39

Interestingly enough, it was Captain Ambrose who, perhaps anxious to "become rich for life," shot and retrieved the two crocodiles from the Ogbunorie lake. Following is the account of his exploits.

Choosing a narrow path out of the market place, I went along with my men. We had not gone half a mile, and were descending a rather steep hill in the very dense bush, when I saw my point, Ali Keffi and Gana Bida, two choice rascals, suddenly come to the *Ready;* they were gazing fixedly at something down below us, to the right of the path. Running forward with my carbine ready, I looked in the same direction, and through a clearing in the bush saw a sheet of water about fifty yards below me. It was surrounded by bush, and the small stream ran into it out of a cave. In the middle of the little lake, lying on the surface of the water, was a crocodile about seven feet long, and another the same size was basking on a ledge of rock at the mouth of the cave. I shot this one first . . . and then took the other, which was quite undisturbed by the first shot and had not stirred.

But the anticipation of becoming rich for life proved chimerical; for the crocodiles "wore no golden anklets, nor even brass ones!" Groaned the captain, "How the legend got about that they had golden anklets, I do not know; anyhow, it was a sad disappointment to us to find that the story was untrue."40

The operations, as we have already noted, resulted in the extension of British colonial rule. Hence, through military force, the British government consolidated its political authority. What followed was massive exploitation and oppression.

3. THE ERA OF COLONIAL EXPLOITATION

ROAD BUILDING

Colonial exploitation and other forms of social oppression accompanied British military conquest. To ensure effective administration and quick movement of troops, the British compelled the towns and villages to build roads. These linked them with one another as well as with the headquarters. In the process, forced labor became the chief instrument for the development of the colonial estate.

By the Roads and Rivers Proclamation of 1903 district commissioners had the power to compel ablebodied men and women through their chiefs to provide free labor. Failure to comply with the chiefs' orders resulted in the imposition of fines or imprisonment or both. Even chiefs who failed to provide men and women for road work were at times flogged, fined, or removed. A classic case is that of Chief Obi of Emekuku whose warrant was suspended in January 1910 for six months. According to DC D. E. Price, Chief Obi was instructed to mobilize laborers for work on the Owerri-Udo-Bende road. But contrary to the chief's assurances that the work had been done, the DC discovered later that this was not the case. "On the 18th instant," remarked Price, "I passed along that [road]" and discovered that, with the exception of one small area near a school, "nothing had been done" at all. As a result, Chief Obi's warrant was revoked as a warning to him and to others "that warrant holders should be an example to others" in regard to honesty. In a letter to the provincial commissioner requesting the endorsement of his action, the DC wrote, "I beg to attach Chief Obi's warrant with the request that the H.P.C. will be good enough to endorse it as suspended for a period of six months or less at the discretion of the DC."[1] The suspension was endorsed, but on August 26, 1910 Chief Obi was reinstated and thereafter complied faithfully with government behest.

On the whole, Owerri chiefs actively cooperated with the administration in the recruitment of labor. Examples are Chiefs Nkwazema of Nekede,

Obi of Emekuku, Nwansi of Akabo, and Nwaturuocha of Nguru, to name but a few. In many instances these chiefs diverted the laborers to their own farms and so became invariably full partners in colonial exploitation. There were even chiefs who used the compulsory labor policy to settle old scores or to enhance their personal prestige and authority. Certain villages or compounds, for example, were subjected to onerous and arbitrary labor demands, such as providing laborers or carriers when in fact it was not their turn to do so. The abuse of power was so rampant among the chiefs that one district officer seemed utterly disgusted with them. "The Owerri chiefs have a most unenviable reputation for skill in extortion and injustice."[2] Some chiefs of course were ultimately either removed or imprisoned because of their unscrupulous and extortionate behavior or for misgovernment. Among such chiefs were Chief Onyejiako of Ogbaku, Chief Nwaturuocha of Nguru, Chief Duru Ubochi of Awa, and many others.

Forced labor, as we shall see, was indeed the hallmark of the colonial system. In the context of colonial idealogy, a good system of transportation was the sine qua non for economic development. Without it, "progress" was impossible, as Joyce Cary once remarked. "The first need in Africa has always been communications. Trade, order, peace . . . all start from the free and safe harbour, the open river, and the cleared road. Africa had never had them and could not progress without them." Many colonial officials in Nigeria wrote in a similar vein, pointing out, of course, the administrative and "civilizing" effects of good roads. "It is impossible to overrate the importance of good roads in this country as a civilizing factor in opening up remote districts apart from the benefit derived by administrative officers in being able to travel more expeditiously through their districts."[3] In other words, the new roads facilitated quick movement of troops as well as economic exploitation. Thus, for colonial apologists the new system of transportation signified progress and modernization. Critics of imperialism, however, are not as sanguine as its advocates.

In purely conceptual terms, the principal objection to the prevailing notion of modernization is that it unsoundly rests on a strictly a priori assumption that for all societies there is only one direction of significant change, culminating in the essentials of modern Western society. This conceptual attachment to a unilinear model of change has on reflection seemed to critics to be partly rooted in a naive faith in general social evolution or the inevitability of "progress" and partly in implicit cultural and ideological bias which arbitrarily (even if unconsciously) places the societies that one is most familiar with or admiring of at the top of a descending scale of human virtue. A closely related objection is that the concept entails a dichotomization of significant social qualities which are not necessarily mutually exclusive and thence the attribution of each of the two sets of qualities thus derived to imaginary classes of societies, called "modern" and "traditional" respectively. The essence of the empirically based objections is that the work of many scholars dealing with a wide range of cultural and geographical contexts suggests that the image of any apparently "premodern" society implicit in this approach is often false or significantly distorted; and/or that the acquisition of ostensibly "modern" qualities is possible under a considerable diversity of cultural conditions.[4]

In the Owerri Division, the architect of road construction was H. M. Douglas. By the time he left Owerri for Onitsha on November 8, 1906, he had in fact built over two hundred miles of roads, most of them radiating from Owerri. Throughout the division Douglas is still remembered as *"Beke ogbu ama,"* the great European road builder. To this day, the main thoroughfare in the Owerri Township bears his name—Douglas Road. On the other hand, he is equally remembered as a hard man who would not brook any African opposition. Chief Njemanze, for example, is said to have initially opposed Douglas's road building policy on the grounds that it was onerous and exploitative. His refusal to provide men for roadwork as ordered by Douglas led to his being declared persona non grata at Owerri. Consequently, he was for a time deported to Degema.[5] By the time he returned, he had mellowed significantly, and like most of the other chiefs he recruited laborers and carriers with reckless abandon. In the process, he and Chief Nkwazema gained prestige and wealth as well as notoriety from their labor recruitment activities.

Resistance to road work was widespread. Other than direct taxation, no other colonial exaction provoked as much resentment and resistance as forced labor. It should be emphasized here that impressment into road work was clearly an infringement of individual freedom and liberty. Also, road construction was resented because it was burdensome, precarious, and largely unremunerative. Moreover, those involved in road construction were often separated from their families and their occupations for long periods of time—hence the strong resentment and resistance. In several cases, chiefs were strongly warned "not to come again with messages from the whiteman" demanding road work. Chiefs and court messengers sent to enforce the order were also physically threatened on occasion. To enforce their authority, however, chiefs often invited soldiers or police to come and punish their people. Fearful of the consequences, many people, of course, complied with the chief's behest while others deserted the villages on learning of the "visit" of the soldiers. "In those days," said an informant at Owerri in 1975, "we were constrained to flee to the bush rather than serve as road workers or carriers. For days we slept in the bush in order to avoid capture. My son, it was an unforgettable experience [*ọbughi ihe eji ọnu akọ*]."[6]

The resentment of compulsory labor and the violence that greeted the enforcement of the policy confounded the British administration. To the officials it seemed unreasonable that the Africans should resist the compulsory labor policy since they paid no direct taxes. In pregovernment days, it was argued, "natives" made roads "for their chiefs." It was hard for the administration to understand, therefore, why the Africans should not do the same for the British government. Besides, reasoned Governor Egerton, the Africans stood to gain from the infrastructural developments. In his words, roads "are a necessary material factor" in the civilization of the African peoples.[7]

Whatever the arguments, colonial road building was a hated task. In report after report, the district officers pointed to the high incidence of armed resistance. Said the officials: "The people refuse to make roads"; "the order to make roads was resisted"; "they say they have nothing to do with the Government." When communities defied government orders, district commissioners often sent military patrols to punish the people involved. It was partly the refusal to make roads that led to the invasion of Obinze and Mbutu Okohia, among others, in 1903. After "severely punishing" these towns the military officer reported, "Obinze, near Nekede on the Isiokpo road, was visited [March 31] and several compounds [were] destroyed. These people have consistently refused to obey orders given to them by their District Commissioner." Mbutu, which offered dogged resistance, was equally "taught a sharp lesson."[8] In the end these towns were compelled to construct roads, erect government rest houses, and provide carriers when needed.

There can be little doubt that the widespread resistance to forced labor irked the government officials. Towns which defied the government had to be humbled. Hence the town of Eziama, near Okpala, was ruthlessly dealt with in 1904. Resistance was fierce, but the crucial battle of Nkwala led to government victory. This is how Douglas explained the Eziama debacle: "Ever since the Government came across the Imo [River] the Eziamas have refused to come to meetings or to obey summonses or to allow their people to do so, and refused to make roads. They were repeatedly warned, and finally in March 1904 all the compounds of Eziama were destroyed by No. 2 Column; the Chiefs afterwards came in and agreed to do everything the Government laid down; they were told at once to make their roads."[9]

Before the punitive expedition, police constable William Jumbo had been sent to Eziama to supervise the construction of roads. According to him, Eziama chiefs were summoned to a meeting and told to make roads, but "they repeatedly refused to work, always making excuses." He further testified: "I stayed there [for] two months and could get nothing done."

Two months after the military operation Douglas revisited Eziama and found that of all the villages only Umuokoro compound had done a bit of work. Infuriated by the people's audacious challenge to government authority, Douglas seized several of the chiefs as hostages, believing that by doing so he would ultimately induce the people to engage in road building. In his own words, "I left Constable Wabara behind to see if the removal of the Chiefs would have any effect in inducing them to make their roads." It does not appear that the DC's tactics had any positive effect. For as Wabara testified during the prosecution of Eziama chiefs, he had great difficulty inducing Eziama people to do any work at all. As a result of this stubborn resistance, several of the Eziama leaders were sentenced by Douglas to six months of hard labor each. "But," remarked Douglas, who was both prosecutor and judge, "if at the end of three months the District Commissioner is satisfied that all their roads are made and in good order, the other three months will be rescinded."[10]

By his active road building, Douglas had undoubtedly initiated a farreaching communications revolution in the division. European contemporaries, especially the Christian missionaries, found the roads extremely useful because they tended to provide better security and faster means of communication. This explains the reason for the high praise they lavished on Douglas as they visited his district. Governor Egerton, himself a strong advocate of road building, also seemed particularly impressed with the nature of the roads during his visit in 1905. Compared with other districts, Owerri appeared to him to be far in advance of all other regions in Southern Nigeria. Said Egerton, "Mr. Douglas has done wonderfully good work in his District. There is no district in the Protectorate that can even compare with Douglas' for the roadwork that has been done." Not only did he shower high praises on this taskmaster, but he pledged his moral and financial support as well. Douglas was, for example, assured of favorable consideration of his road building requests and was encouraged to complete work on the road linking Oguta and the Imo River via Owerri and, if possible, to continue it as far as the Cross River. Douglas was also assured of support for the construction of bridges over the Otamiri River at Owerri and Imo River at Okpala. Impressed generally with the state of the roads, especially with respect to their width, Egerton recommended: "Until the Engineer appointed for road construction is able to visit Douglas' District, it is unnecessary to call upon him to have drains cut, or to have further work done on his roads." Of the roads Egerton noted: "These roads are nearly forty feet wide. . . . The surface is wonderfully good considering that no side drains have been dug nor has any portion of the forty-foot-way been properly formed for wheel traffic. . . . The width of the roadway is sufficient to allow for the erection of the telegraph line without interfering with the traffic and without the Telegraph Construction Party having additional clearing to do."[11]

Governor Egerton's praise was not confined to Douglas alone. He equally appreciated the enormous contributions which the local communities and their chiefs had made. For this reason he heartily congratulated the warrant chiefs for their cooperative effort in the burgeoning communications revolution. In places like Ulakwo, where significant road work had been undertaken, Egerton not only thanked the chiefs but promised them a handsome "dash" of £25 upon the construction of an embankment on the Otamiri River. At Owerri Town too he expressed deep gratitude to the local people and their chiefs for their support of the government and implored them to continue "the excellent work" they were doing in the area of road building. As for the neighboring towns which still resisted government intrusion, the governor called upon the chiefs to lend a helping hand in ensuring the success of the government's pacification program. Said Egerton, "I asked them if they have any relatives or friends in the few towns adjacent to the Aba road that are still unfriendly to the Government [and] to advise them to surrender their war guns and give up the evil practices of slave dealing, making war on their neighbours and preventing travellers from passing through their country [*sic*]." The chiefs reportedly "promised to do so."[12]

While on the whole the chiefs cooperated with the administration in its road building scheme, they occasionally raised objection to the "extreme demands" of the district officers. Because these officials often demanded a large number of laborers and carriers rather suddenly, they said, it was often difficult to recruit the requisite number of people at such a short notice. The chiefs therefore pleaded with the governor that at least four days' notice should be given them for the provision of carriers and laborers rather than the hitherto "quick" demands. Egerton considered their views to be fair and "reasonable" and assured them that district commissioners would oblige accordingly, "except when very urgent work was in hand or when carriers were wanted suddenly."[13]

Although the new roads had certain advantages over the old pathways, they had several handicaps. Because they were not of metallic construction, they were generally waterlogged during the rainy season, and so many of them remained impassable. Unfortunately, many of the same roads remained waterlogged and impassable during the rainy season even in 1979. Another serious defect of these roads was their lack of shade trees. In pre-government times, the traditional footpaths with their rows of shade trees provided ample shelter to the pedestrians. The new roads, on the other hand, exposed travellers to the blazing heat of the sun, especially during the dry season, because of their barrenness. Indeed, European contemporaries pointed to the ordeal of travelling along these "wide unshaded roads."[14] For those on bare feet it was utterly uncomfortable to travel on the new roads in the dry season. However, attempts were made to remedy the major handicaps, especially the barrenness, by planting *ugba (ugbakala)* trees along the roadsides. The planting of these trees is generally associated with Douglas—hence the reference to "Ugba Douglas."

In addition to providing essential shade or shelter for pedestrians, the ugba trees also proved to be of economic value. The seeds, known commercially as *apachelo-nuts* or oil bean seeds, were used locally as new sources of food and trade. Because of their commercial value the colonial administration encouraged the planting of ugba trees "on a large scale" all over Southern Nigeria.[15] In the Owerri area, women from Mbieri, in the Mbaitoli Local Government Area, became specialists in the preparation of oil bean seeds. To this day, ugba constitutes an important article of trade in the local markets. Prepared by itself or with meat or kola nuts (*ọji*), ugba is a most cherished delicacy in most areas of Southern Nigeria and particularly in Owerri.

THE CARRIER SYSTEM

Forced labor was not limited to road building. In fact, as in the case of road work, ablebodied men were forced to carry loads for government officials or to carry building materials for road or railway construction. Government officials and even missionaries were often carried in hammocks (*ndọgọlọ*) during their travels. Carriers were not only exposed to the dangers of life and limb but were hardly adequately remunerated, hence the stiff resistance to the carrier system. Besides, the loads were generally heavy and the carriers made to carry them for long distances. A man now in his late nineties who claimed to have been a victim of the forced labor policy recounted his experiences in this manner:

The loads were heavy. And we travelled for many, many miles without food or rest. On many occasions we, the carriers, decided to stop and rest or to find something to eat. Often, however, this brought almost instant harassment from the soldiers, or the DC, or the overseer. My son [Nwam], remember we travelled through unfamiliar places and many of us were deeply concerned about our safety. So, apart from the bad treatment from the officers, fear of losing our lives weighed heavily on our minds. This is why we often dropped the loads, escaped into the bush and returned home. But if you were caught, that was the end of your life.[16]

While admitting that there were irregularities in the carrier system, the colonial officials argued, however, that since porterage was the pillar of the Nigerian economy, the government could not help but compel men to carry loads. Said the colonial secretary, "Where there are no other means of transportation, the natives must be utilized for the purpose of transport." The governor agreed. "It must never be overlooked that the Government cannot go on without it, trade cannot go on without it, the people cannot even be fed without it. It is the basis of the whole life of the country." Others attempted to rationalize the system by invoking its "wonderful civilizing influence." By carrying loads for Europeans or carrying them in hammocks, it was claimed, the African would develop "good feelings" towards the whiteman through close contact with him. Indeed, said one official, the social value of the carrier system might be seen in "the dissipation of the inborn fear which the untutored West African has of the whiteman."[17]

Since the carrier system was seen as a necessary evil, it is clear that Africans who refused to carry loads for the government would be punished for it. Consider the case of Azaraegbelu in Emekuku. During the 1903-4 dry season operations, Douglas had asked the local headmen to provide carriers for military purposes. The order was resisted on the ground that the government had no legal authority over the people. Consequently, it was agreed that a punitive military operation should be sent "to thoroughly subdue these very stubborn people." Accordingly, Azaraegbelu villages were heavily bombarded, and many of their houses razed. Because of the stiff resistance encountered, an army of occupation was left in the area for several weeks, and as might be expected, they spread devastation and desolation.[18]

This military occupation and the ravage that accompanied it is known popularly as *iri ọlulu*. This appears to have been a consistent British policy in Southern Nigeria. According to Governor Egerton, "Where a town refuses to submit to Government [orders or] control or supervision, it is our policy . . . to occupy it . . . until the chiefs and the people have been made thoroughly to understand that Government laws must be obeyed."[19] In the case of Azaraegbelu, it does not appear that the policy was effective. For despite the severe punishment inflicted on the people, the headmen continued to refuse to provide carriers. According to Douglas, carriers were ultimately provided by friendly chiefs from other parts of Emekuku. And so the exploitation continued.

RAILWAY SCHEMES AND DEVELOPMENT

Proposals to revolutionalize the transportation system in Owerri included the construction of a railway. While road transportation provided a measure of economic development, administrators felt that the construction of a railway would accelerate the commercial activity in this area. Hence, in 1904 a monorail was projected to be constructed between Owerri and Isiokpo. This railway was considered vital for the full exploitation of the commercial opportunities in the Isiokpo-Owerri region. Thus, in his frantic appeal to the Colonial Office, the acting high commissioner, Leslie Probyn, called attention to the commercial benefits to be derived from the construction of a forty-mile railway from Owerri to Isiokpo, the latter being an important palm oil market. Traders from the Owerri Division, he said, generally brought palm produce (mainly palm oil) to Isiokpo by road and took back only dried fish. To Probyn this was simply an inefficient pattern of trade which should be improved by the construction of a monorail. "It is important," he urged, "that this work should be put in hand at once; [for] at present produce cannot be brought out in quantity neither can trade goods be introduced."[20]

Probyn's scheme called for the building of the railroad along the existing Owerri-Isiopko trade route at an estimated cost of £18,000. Recognizing, of course, that this amount of money might elicit negative reaction from the highly economy-conscious Colonial Office, he took pains to explain details of the proposal to the authorities. First, he assured them that labor costs would be minimal since free labor would be provided by local communities. Direct labor costs, he said, would simply consist of the salary of a European foreman experienced in bridge construction and "grants-in-aid to native tribes who have to do exceptional work." All in all, labor costs were estimated at about £3,000. The remaining £15,000 would be for the cost of rails, freight, sleepers, and rolling stock. In addition, he pointed out that the railway would facilitate the shipment of government building materials to Owerri.[21]

The reaction of the Colonial Office to the scheme was markedly unenthusiastic. Whereas Probyn had urged that work on the project should start "at once," London authorities, on the other hand, felt that the proposal should "lie on the table for the future." As one senior official noted, "I do not see that the matter is urgent." The Colonial Office did recognize the added benefits to be derived from the proposed improvement on the transportation system, but financial considerations prompted the officials to delay the railway scheme. In their minds, the special financial needs of

Northern Nigeria seemed of greater consequence than the proposed Owerri-Isiokpo railway. Given "the responsibility of the Southern Protectorate to contribute towards the Northern Nigerian administration," argued the Colonial Office, it seemed rather inadvisable "at the present time" to engage in a scheme that involved so large an expenditure. Consequently, Governor Egerton, upon his return from leave, was notified that Probyn's pet scheme could not be entertained.[22]

Even though the scheme had been scuttled at the Colonial Office, the issue was not actually dead. In fact, local officials were asked to determine the feasibility of the project for possible future action. It was for this reason that Probyn's proposal was submitted to the divisional commissioner, W. Fosbery, for evaluation. His elaborate report to the governor on this issue is particularly interesting in view of the fact that his argument against the project was not primarily based on financial consideration, even though he was not unaware of the huge outlay involved. Rather, his opposition was directed at what he perceived as the relative unimportance of Owerri in the commercial life of the division. After a "careful consideration of the proposal," he wrote, it was not possible to recommend the construction of the proposed railway largely because of the probability of a shift in the pattern of trade in the Owerri and Niger Delta areas. "I am of opinion," he said, "that the clearing of Imo River and its tributaries, the Ota[miri] River with its branches, will so alter the circumstances under which trade has been carried on at Isiokpo and other markets on the New Calabar river in the past, as to render the construction of the projected rail inadvisable." In essence, Fosbery felt that fuller use should be made of the cleared waterways before the railway project could be considered: "I think it would be premature to lay a rail in any part of the Degema or Owerri Districts until the water-ways have been made use of as far as practicable and that money would be expended to more advantage if, employed in clearing water-ways already mentioned, [during the] next dry season."[23]

But it was Fosbery's view that Owerri was not a vital commercial center, and this persuaded him to recommend that the proposed railway should not be undertaken. In support of his stand, Fosbery offered these points: (1) that the bulk of the produce at Isiokpo, New Calabar (Kalabari), and Okrika markets "has been brought from the Ngwa country on the left bank of the Imo River and from the Uratta country between the Imo River and Owerri"; (2) that the people living between Isiokpo and Elele did not produce oil to any great extent, "having in days gone-by lived on tolls collected on produce passing [through] their towns"; (3) that there appeared to have been "a considerable falling off" of trade at the Okrika and Kalabari markets due to the fact that palm produce from the Ngwa region had been intercepted by the recently opened markets on the Imo River. As a result of the latter, he said, Okrika traders had quickly "transferred their canoes to the Imo River." Finally, Fosbery argued that the opening of the Otamiri and Sombiero rivers would invariably alter the pattern of trade in the Niger Delta and its hinterland.[24]

Probyn had emphasized that a monorail between Isiokpo and Owerri would facilitate the transporting of government stores to Owerri. Fosbery, however, countered that in fact the amount of such stores would be substantially small and that it was even "highly probable" that the military garrison at Owerri would be removed. He furthermore contended that it was very likely that Owerri itself would soon no longer be the administrative headquarters of the division. Finally, he argued that since the Isuama people in the Owerri Division "have been in the habit of hiring themselves out as carriers to the oil producers in the Uratta country, and have transported produce to the markets on the New Calabar River and to Okrika," it seemed rather inadvisable to destroy this important porterage system. In his view then the railway project was not necessary.[25]

It should be pointed out that Owerri, as noted earlier, remained the administrative headquarters until 1947. Nor was the military garrison removed until after the First World War. In any case, the governor found Fosbery's objections persuasive and so informed the Colonial Office that "it would be inadvisable to construct the projected railway." Egerton did not share Probyn's enthusiasm in the enterprise and instead was of the opinion that priority should be given to road building. Thereafter, he insisted, it might be possible "to lay down monorails at the sides of the principal roads." He observed again that railways "should only be laid where there is no water transport available." In fact, Egerton was much more disposed to having a monorail built in the Kwa-Ibo or Cross River area rather than in the Owerri sector because, as he said, the former region was "extraordinarily populated and . . . very rich in oil palms" but has had its trade undeveloped because of "the absence of transport facilities." For this reason he strongly recommended the building of good roads in the area and the construction of a railway line linking Itu, Ikot-Ekpene, and Calabar.[26]

Although Egerton had disapproved of the Owerri-Isiokpo railway, this did not mean that railway projects were no longer considered. In 1909, for example, he proposed the construction of a railway line between Afikpo and Abakiliki as a means of stimulating the already increasing volume of trade in this sector. As in the Owerri-Isiokpo case, however, the Colonial Office demurred, again for financial reasons. However, if the governor wanted to implement his scheme, the Colonial Office indicated, then the Southern Nigerian administration should bear all the expenses as no subsidy would be forthcoming from London. It would appear that, other than financial considerations, opposition to railway projects in Eastern Nigeria at this early stage was due to the lack of international commercial rivalry. In Northern Nigeria, it was fear of French interest in the Hausa trade that influenced the authorization of funds for the building of the Lagos-Kano railway. In fact, colonial officials, especially Lord Frederick Lugard, saw the building of railways in Nigeria partly in terms of a direct response to international rivalries. On this Lugard wrote, "The extraordinary efforts made by France in the matter of railway extension in West Africa would appear to force upon the British possession of Nigeria some corresponding effort as a measure of defense, even though it might have been considered premature from the point of view of development only. It is, therefore, chiefly from the former standpoint that the urgency of railway construction should, in my view, be considered."[27]

In spite of the lack of support from London, Egerton continued to press for funds for the construction of railway lines in the eastern provinces. In 1910 he strongly urged that funds should be provided "to undertake the much needed and certainly profitable Itu-Owerri railway at no distant date." He justified the project on grounds that trade on the Owerri-Itu axis was flourishing and needed an efficient and faster system of communication. Trade in the region, he emphasized, was "far more important than most of the Crown Colonies." No specific action to the Owerri-Itu scheme seems to have been taken. Nor was any serious consideration given to the projected Itu, Ikot-Ekpene, Owerri, and Oguta railway line. One senior official at the Colonial Office simply minuted that Egerton's report for 1910 clearly showed "a satisfactory record of progress" in the eastern provinces. Thus, plans for linking strategic places in Eastern Nigeria with a single railway line were treated with benign neglect. In 1906 Lord Elgin, the British colonial secretary, said, "In dealing with railway communication in [Nigeria], I think it is generally agreed that eventually there will have to be two main lines, one in the eastern part of the territory and one in the western. We need not discuss the one in the eastern part at present, as the country is not ready for it."[28] But the discovery of coal at Ngwo (Udi) in 1909 provided a compelling impulse for the building of the Eastern Railway, which started in 1913 from Port Harcourt and reached Udi in 1926. It bypassed Owerri, however.

After the First World War the initiative for infrastructural developments appears to have shifted from the colonial administration to local communities and the chiefs. Indeed, by the 1920s and 1930s it had become clear to the people of Owerri that "social progress" in Owerri was markedly slow due primarily to official neglect. Even some colonial administrators echoed similar sentiments.[29] Believing therefore that improvement in the transportation system was fundamentally vital for economic and social development, the Owerri Town Planning Committee petitioned the administration for the construction of a direct road from Owerri to Aba, a major commercial center. Part of the 1925 committee recommendation states: "In view of the ever increasing amount of motor traffic between Aba through Owerri to Port Harcourt, Onitsha and Oguta, the Committee strongly advises the reconstruction of a direct road (discussed for some years) from the crossroads beyond the River Worio [Nworie] to meet the Aba road outside Owerri Town. This scheme will involve the making of about a mile of Motor Road and the erecting of a permanent bridge. The total cost is estimated at £1000."[30]

No official action was taken on this proposal until some years later. However, when Governor Sir Hugh Clifford visited Owerri in 1925, the chiefs renewed the railway issue. The governor was made to understand that the establishment of a railway line at Owerri was absolutely essential if Owerri was not to remain backward vis-à-vis other townships. Hence the chiefs requested that Owerri, Onitsha, and Aba should be linked by a railway. The reply was negative. Said the governor, "There are other places in Nigeria where the Railway is required and the Government will have to consider the most important of these places first. At present there is a Railway at Aba, but that does not necessarily mean that there will immediately be a Railway at Owerri. But if one is found necessary and advisable it will be considered in turn with others."[31]

In 1926 when the administration began to consider the extension of railway lines from Port Harcourt, it was proposed that Owerri should be one of the centers linked by rail with Port Harcourt. Oguta was also proposed but later rejected. Feasibility studies were carried out but little came of it. Owerri chiefs once again renewed the campaign for the construction of a railway at Owerri in 1934. In that year, a petition was submitted to Governor Donald Cameron. It stated,

We the representatives of Owerri District have the honour most respectfully to submit this letter before you for your kind consideration and favourable approval.

We beg to state that we are surprising [*sic*] for not having Railway Engine in the town of Owerri which can run to Aba, Onitsha, Oron and all . . . other places. We are cognizant of the fact that it would have enabled the fund of the Railway to rise as most of us will rejoice to participate in rendering our assistance by passages to the different countries [*sic*] and the booking of our luggages. We place the matter before you to enable us to get Railway Engine in our country [*sic*].[32]

Again, as in 1925, the response was both negative and disappointing. For despite the assurances of local support and the economic potential of the projected railway extension, the governor informed the petitioners that their request could not be entertained.[33] For all practical purposes this was the last to be heard of the railway question. Today there are some who contend that the absence of a railway in Owerri is a material factor in the general underdevelopment of the area. Had a railway been built as was proposed, some argue, there would have been marked social and economic development in the Owerri area similar to Aba and other major townships. In this respect, the stunted economic development of Owerri is blamed on the colonial administration's official neglect.

Ironically, there is also the view that the failure to construct a railway at Owerri stemmed directly from the strong objection of the chiefs and elders. These are said to have entertained the fear that the building of a railway would inevitably pervert traditional morals. Women and young girls would take advantage of the opportunities provided by the railway to engage in prostitution; marriages would be ruined. According to one source, "They feared they were going to lose their wives."[34] Clearly, this view is in direct contrast to all the literary evidence we have so far cited. It has, for example, been amply demonstrated that it was the chiefs and others who requested the extension of a railway to Owerri. Their primary interest was the economic development of Owerri. Moral questions hardly entered into their considerations. Certainly the failure to construct a railway must be blamed on the colonial government's policy rather than on the alleged opposition of the chiefs.

DOUGLAS AND THE NIGERIAN ADMINISTRATION

As we have seen in this chapter and the preceding one, H. M. Douglas was unquestionably instrumental in the political and infrastructural transformation of Owerri. By the time he left Owerri, he had laid a firm foundation for effective British rule in the whole division. Yet despite the favorable evaluations by his superiors as an "energetic political officer" and an untiring road builder, Douglas was not really the favorite of the Nigerian colonial authorities. There were several reasons for this, including his eccentric personality, his stubborn and outspoken tendencies, as well as his pugnacious inclinations. To some of his superiors Douglas was a "nasty" man who often behaved in a manner "unbecoming of an officer." Nevertheless, it was Douglas's vituperative attacks on the Nigerian colonial administration and "those at the head of affairs" in Nigeria and at the Colonial Office in London,[35] that ultimately brought his downfall and forced retirement from Nigerian service by 1920.

This study of the conflict between Douglas and the administration is interesting in many ways. First, it helps to destroy the myth that European colonial officers almost uniformly conformed to the colonial ethos of refraining from criticizing the government openly while still in service. As Sir Grattan Bushe, formerly of the British Colonial Office, put it, "serious criticism" of government policies by colonial officials "is a thing which is not done" at all.[36] But by "seriously" criticizing the Nigerian colonial government, Douglas invariably deviated from the typical colonial norm. In short, he was a rebel. Secondly, his telling criticism of the "system" and diatribes against the top men at the head of affairs suggest that all was not well in the Nigerian colonial service. More specifically, an analysis of Douglas's criticisms, as well as evidence from other sources, clearly reveal that the European colonial administrators, especially those in the junior cadre, had a relatively rough time. Thus the story of the fall of Douglas is inextricably linked with the British colonial administration in Nigeria. In this case, it illuminates our understanding of British colonial administration and administrators.

The distance between Douglas and the Nigerian colonial authorities had crystallized between 1914 and 1918; it was at this period that Douglas had virtually become persona non grata in Nigeria largely because of his open criticism of the administration and the top bureaucrats. Not only did he openly denounce what he called the "iniquitous system" of administration in Nigeria, but he lambasted the British Colonial Office for its alleged breach of contract with colonial officials. Thus for all practical purposes Douglas had become, perhaps unwittingly, a thorn in the flesh of the administration and hence adjudged "unfit to hold his position of responsibility." For convenience, we shall treat Douglas's imbroglio with the authorities under two separate but related topics—namely, (1) his umbrage with the Nigerian administration and the authorities, viewed by him as a "legitimate expression of opinion"; and, (2) confrontation with the Colonial Office.[37]

As the sources reveal, Douglas seemed deeply distressed by the state of affairs in Nigeria from about 1914 if not earlier. One source of his annoyance, as we learn from him, derived from the apparently slow pace of promotion in the service. For years Douglas had remained senior district officer; but in 1914 he was finally promoted to the rank of resident (second class). It was during this period (1914–19), when he served as the resident of Warri Province, that Douglas seemingly let "cowardice . . . be dead," to borrow from Dante's *Divine Comedy*. In other words, his patience with the colonial administration had reached a breaking point, and henceforth he became a "prickly" officer.[38]

His exasperation with "the state of affairs," which he cynically referred to as "the system," arose from his perception that chances for promotion in the service had become bleak under the administration of the governor-general, Sir Frederick Lugard. It must be remembered that Nigeria became administratively one country in 1914. In that year, Lugard (later Lord) amalgamated the Northern and Southern provinces and thus introduced a uniform colonial administration in Nigeria. Hitherto, the two provinces were administered separately. Unfortunately, the amalgamation era (1914–18) coincided with the period of the First World War. Hence, their combined impact fostered a great deal of uneasiness, as this study will unravel. In fact the "Lugardian era" ushered in a period of administrative turmoil, social discontent, and political confusion.[39]

For Douglas and certainly for most of those in the public service—European and African—the Lugardian era was a period of storm and stress, a time of general discontent arising, according to Douglas, from the benign neglect of "those at the head of affairs" in Nigeria. For Douglas, what seemed even more discouraging was the lack of any prospect of things ever getting better, a situation he blamed on Lugard's "parsimony in dealing with personnel," as well as his alleged social dissonance with administrative officers. Accordingly, Douglas wrote to the lieutenant-governor expressing outrage at the low salaries of colonial officials, particularly those of the junior ranks. As he put it, given that "Nigeria is one of the richest colonies in the [British] Empire," it seemed ironic that the administration should pay low salaries to those officials. Douglas also expressed dismay at what he perceived as a terrible deterioration of the conditions of service in Nigeria, adding, "I consider the position and prospects of political officers unsatisfactory, and I suppose there was not a more dissatisfied lot of men to be found in the Empire than in Nigeria." In characteristic fashion he explicitly blamed Lugard for the manifold problems: "It is indeed to be regretted that Sir Frederick Lugard has been so [pre]occupied with the affairs of amalgamation that he could not come more in touch with his officers. Had he been able to it would probably have saved a deal of heart-burning and general loss of esprit de corps which is bound to occur where unredressed grievances exist, and cannot but undermine both individual and general efficiency."[40]

If Douglas expected corrective action, his impertinence probably made this unlikely. As he acknowledged, the lieutenant-governor treated the letter with contempt, noting simply in his response, "Do you really think so?" This curt response tended to reinforce Douglas's impression that the top officials in the Nigerian administration were manifestly "insensitive and unresponsive" to the grievances of junior officers.[41]

Yet there were other factors that galvanized Douglas to action, such as the war bonus question. Just before the end of the First World War, the British government is said to have granted workers in the public service a war bonus, perhaps to ease the economic impact of the war on government officials. Its distribution among administrative officials, however, provoked considerable agitation. According to Douglas, a special committee known as the War Bonus Committee was set up to make recommendations as to its distribution. To ensure an equitable distribution, the committee "unanimously" adopted the resolution to pay "a minimum flat rate of £120 per annum" to all officers. But the Nigerian authorities allegedly ignored the recommendation and paid officers according to their own private formula. In doing so, Douglas contended, they invariably treated categories of officers quite preferentially. Hence Douglas protested, acting, he put it, as the "spokesman" of the disgruntled officers. Following is the text of his telegram to the colonial secretary in Nigeria (Southern Provinces): "Re War Bonus. . . . My view is present scheme creates undesirable and invidious distinctions and appears to have been framed to satisfy second class officers who are in a position to enforce their demands and the remainder worked on a basis of how little could be offered to higher grade officers in order to keep them quiet."[42]

Instead of treating the telegram as representing the collective opinion of disgruntled officers, the Nigerian authorities regarded it as a purely "private matter." Hence Douglas was charged for its transmission to England. As usual, Douglas was outraged at the surcharge, as well as the negative attitude of the officials toward the grievances he expressed. "Government's action concerning my telegram," he complained to the colonial secretary, "has shown clearly that there is no intention of any notice being taken of the view [*sic*] and complaints of officials in spite of His Excellency Sir Frederick Lugard's minute concerning 'natural spokesmen' and his expressed readiness to listen to officers who consider they have grievances."[43] Believing that it was useless to seek any redress for grievances from the Nigerian authorities, Douglas therefore took the decisive step of confronting the Colonial Office. This, as it turned out, was his fateful leap into the abyss.

In his letters of December 28, 1918 and January 13, 1919 Douglas expressed his frustration and dissatisfaction with the Nigerian administration and its top officials. In enumerating the sources of discontent or, as he put it, "the points which cause irritation and annoyance," Douglas alerted the colonial secretary that the curtailment of administrative allowances was particularly irritating, given that the cost of living had risen sharply due to the war. In addition, he bemoaned the "decreased prospects" for promotion in the service and the apparent inequity in the Nigerian administrative system. These irregularities, he contended, not only fostered a sense of despair among the junior officers, but also engendered a crisis of confidence in the public service. Douglas was equally critical about the prevailing policy on promotions, arguing that it was neither humane nor fair. "There are cases where officers have received no promotion for over 12½ years and have been on their maximum salary for over 8½ years." Should officers not be deemed "worthy of promotion," he suggested, they should "be notified" as a matter of policy, adding that, "owing to slow promotion [in the service] personal allowances should be automatic after five years on maximum salary."[44]

Douglas, of course, was directly affected by the promotions policy. By 1918 he was among those who had received no promotion for some years and, as it appears, had been on maximum salary "for over 8½ years." This perhaps explains his criticism of the policy and concern over "the decreased prospects of political officers in general and the position of second grade Residents in particular." With special reference to the slashing of the salary of residents, Douglas protested that "the highest salary they could now look forward to [is] £1,000 per annum whereas formerly it was £1,200 per annum with a corresponding pension." In addition, he objected to the practice of paying substantive residents the same salary as "relieving Residents." According to Douglas, "Residents in charge of Provinces drew exactly the same pay and allowances as relieving Residents. Yet the onus of the good running of the province and the writing of the Annual report fell on the Resident in charge, the relieving Resident merely carrying on." Even though the Nigerian authorities considered his complaints not "justified by the facts," Douglas stood firm. "My facts," he informed the Colonial Office, "appear to me to be perfectly clear, and justified. I have not been enlightened as to what the [Nigerian] Secretary of State's facts are."[45]

On the question of promotions, it must be noted that advancement in the colonial service was admittedly slow[46] and was often based on examinations —including language examinations and character. As for Douglas, his language incompetence and his unsavory character seem to have adversely affected his promotion. After all, he was explicitly warned in 1915 that his violent proclivities could "militate" against his promotion. With regard to the language question, Douglas's performance in the language examinations was rather unsatisfactory, even though he rationalized it by arguing that his frequent transfers from one area to another did not allow him the necessary time to sufficiently master any one language. Yet, excellence in examinations did not necessarily ensure promotion. Major U. F. H. Ruxton, formerly lieutenant-governor of Southern Nigeria, confirmed that "good manners and right conduct tell for promotion *more than elsewhere,*" and added, "It is the Machine that counts and not the individual."[47]

On the question of allowances, Douglas charged that Lugard's tight mon- ✻
ey policy was directly responsible for the curtailment of administrative allowances, and he voiced his irritation and annoyance at "the reduction to
half of travelling allowances." Such a reduction seemed particularly callous
when officials were more than ever engaged in "extended tours and over-
work" due to sharply reduced staff. He also decried the inadequate provision of houses—"the abolishment of bush allowance [simply] because a
mud and thatched house has a cement floor"—and he expressed annoyance
at the imposition of conservancy fees, which he described as "a very sore
point." Of equal annoyance, he informed the secretary of state, was the
government's refusal to pay for officers' wives when they travelled to or
from Nigeria, as well as the policy of compelling officers to pay for the
"return passage" of their servants when on transfer and travelling by government vessel. Noting also that allowances in the Gold Coast (Ghana)
were considerably higher than in Nigeria, Douglas accused the Nigerian
authorities of apparent disinterestedness in the welfare of administrative
officers. Furthermore, he criticized the inadequate allowances paid to officers "in bush stations" for transporting their personal belongings, as well
as for the meager allowances paid for carriers when an officer was on
transfer. All in all, Douglas said the Nigerian administration was not only
lacking in human consideration, but seemed unwilling to bring relief to
administrative officials.[48]

Douglas's criticisms appear extraordinary and unprecedented to be sure.
But they must be seen in their colonial context. Colonial officials were paid
all sorts of allowances for various reasons, including, for instance, "bush
allowance" for living in what was considered uncomfortable conditions,
travelling allowances "for journeying with cook and servant from one ram-
shacle rest-house to another," as well as a host of other fringe benefits. The
primary justification for these allowances, according to I. F. Nicolson, was
that "they cost less than the payment of higher salaries, or the capital expenditure to make permanent improvement."[49] Besides, administrative
allowances "made comfort a means of solvency for some officers." In other
words, the allowance scheme tended to make the colonial service a little
more attractive. Hence, when allowances were either curtailed or eliminated, officials naturally murmured.[50] For Douglas, tinkering with the allowance question indicated the administration's lack of concern for the
welfare of the junior officers. It is instructive to note that a disgruntled
officer testified in 1919, after Lugard's retirement, that the government's
stringent financial policies "definitely" put his family "on the high road to
beggary."[51]

The First World War, as already noted, aggravated Nigerian problems,
too. Not only did it shatter the economy and consequently cause economic stagnation in the country, it also unleashed widespread social dis-

content and political unrest. In fact, the sharp rise in the price of consumer goods, especially imported commodities, accentuated local difficulties. To the African and European administrative class alike, the war, which coincided with the era of Lugard's governor-generalship, thus intensified economic distress and administrative discontent. In Nicolson's words, "The public service—British and African—had been brought to the brink of despair by a long process of worsening conditions, and had little confidence that their situation would be improved."[52] It was these "worsening conditions" indeed that propelled Douglas's criticisms and complaints.

To make matters worse, Douglas circulated his critical letter of December 1918 to as many junior officers as possible, perhaps to shore up their support. In justifying his action, Douglas argued that since his previous telegram was treated as "a personal matter . . . I therefore consider I am entitled to circulate my opinion, which I believe to be that of the great majority of officials in Nigeria." In other words, he believed that the views expressed in his letter of December 28, 1918 represented the collective voice of "the great majority of officials,"[53] especially the junior ones.

Commenting further on the war bonus question, Douglas let it be known that the administration's unilateral action on the matter was directly responsible for the formation of the European officers' labor union or, as he called it, "the combine." The term "combine" referred to the formation of the European Civil Servants Association (CSA) in 1917, dubbed the "Bolshie Society," obviously in reference to the Bolshevik Revolution in Russia.[54] The association, composed of senior officials in British West Africa, acted as a pressure group to secure benefits for its members. To Douglas, this unionization of senior officials was inevitable, given the Colonial Office stinginess. Said Douglas, "It has been patent to me for many years that such action would come sooner or later as . . . individuals had a poor prospect of any serious notice being taken of their grievances or views." Besides, he insisted, "the tone of the Secretary of State's reply to the War Bonus Committee is enough to rouse men, who have hitherto been content to remain passive, to action that will have, I believe, far reaching effects."[55]

The unforeseen consequence of the formation of the Civil Service Association, as Douglas viewed it, was the introduction of "undesirable and invidious distinctions" in the service. In other words, the CSA had sharpened class consciousness, for there were now two classes of men, the "haves" and the "have-nots." In his perceptive analysis of the impact of the CSA on the non-unionized junior officers, Douglas observed, "When a body of men who have combined and are in a position to enforce their demands, makes a threat, the Government submits but does not apparently deal with the matter from the view of what is fair and reasonable, but from the point of how little will the [junior] men accept." In his by now familiar confrontational style, Douglas accused the Nigerian colonial authorities of failing to treat fairly junior officers "who have no 'Union.' " Instead, said Douglas, these officers "are offered a sop which apparently it is hoped will keep them quiet." Yet as already noted, Douglas actually approved of the formation of the CSA.

How can it but be expected [that] men will combine when after doing extended tours and extra work owing to depleted staff with vacancies to promotion unfilled, with the price of everything practically double, they see on every hand bonuses being granted and wages raised up to 50% [for top officials] and when a few joined and put forward the suggestion that perhaps they, too might receive something, they are told they are not considering the public interest.[56]

Still directing his invectives at the top bureaucrats, Douglas charged that these men were exploiters, "literally . . . taking money out of the officials' pockets" under the guise of financial exigency. By systematically slashing allowances, by not filling vacant posts (thereby compelling officers to do "extra work"), by ingenuously depriving officers of their "short period of home life" in England, again because of unfilled vacancies, the government, said Douglas, invariably "saved hundreds of pounds" at the expense of officers who "impaired their health both by the extra work and long hours." And, he asked, why was it that the men at the head of affairs tended to rob Peter in order to pay Paul, as it were? Here is his answer to the rhetorical question: "A feeling, I am sure exists, that it redounds to the credit if not at times to the pecuniary advantage of [these] higher officials if they can cut down the allowances of junior officers or in any other way save a few pounds to the Government or increase the revenue by making trivial pecuniary demands of the officials."[57]

Equally remarkable was the alleged conspiracy of silence over the "system of sweating," or the exploitation, of officers that prevailed in Nigeria. Again, Douglas asked why administrative officers remained silent over these irregularities in Nigeria. As before, he attributed it to selfish motives: "Junior officers are afraid to speak for fear of injuring their prospects and seniors too for that matter even though they may have got as high as they can reasonably expect to get and some (I hope very few) may possibly be thinking of an I.S.O. or C.M.G. as the price of their silence."[58]

Having lashed at the men at the head of affairs in Nigeria, Douglas then directed his criticisms at the Colonial Office. Agitated, as the tone of his letters revealed, by what he regarded as unfair denials of leave pay to the families of deceased officers, Douglas charged that the attitude of the Colonial Office smacked of rank ingratitude. Said Douglas, "After perhaps doing two years in the country the official is told that if he dies his wife and

family will not even get the money for the full pay leave he has earned."
What is even worse, he continued, is that "up to recently the victim . . . was charged for his coffin," a clear indication that the Colonial
Office had no regard for officers in the colonial service. Had it not been that
the press exposed this "iniquitous system," he went on, no serious attention
might have been given to it at all. "Perhaps when a few more grievances are
ventilated further justice will be done," he concluded.[59]

Indeed, to Douglas, the nonpayment of death benefits and the nonprovision of coffins for deceased officers represented a "soulless action" on the
part of the Colonial Office. "It is hardly believable that a Government or
Corporation could deprive a man's dependents of say anything from a few
pounds to five hundred or more pounds of hard and justly earned leave pay
because he had the misfortune to die before he could enjoy it, and add to the
injury by charging him for his coffin." Again, he asked: Why does this
happen? "The only reason I can suggest," replied Douglas, "is that it [the
government] is speculating" that:

> (a) On the possibility that the victim's widow knows nothing about any pay or
> allowances that may be due to her husband.
> (b) That if she does, the chances are she will not put forward a claim either
> because it is a too distressing matter to be discussed or from fear of being consid-
> ered mercenary and trying to make capital out of her bereavement.
> (c) That if she does put in a claim, a reply signed by some clerk purporting to
> emanate from the Secretary of State will effectually silence her.[60]

Yet this was not all. As far as Douglas was concerned, the Colonial Office seemed not to believe in the sanctity of contracts, as its action seemed to
suggest:

> But surely the Government having contracted in the first instance to pay a man
> so much salary (that no one will dispute naturally ceases at death) and so much
> full pay leave for every month served is morally if not legally bound to fulfil its
> obligations whether the man dies or not. To say that because a man dies before he
> has been able to enjoy the leave earned, Government has no further liability in the
> matter, is, I am of opinion . . . unjust. In addition to this if the victim dies in
> West Africa the Government saves the cost of his passage home and his full pay
> for the voyage, which more than counterbalances his funeral expenses.[61]

Surely few colonial administrators if any ventured to openly criticize
the government as Douglas did. Even Sir Hugh Clifford, regarded as a radical governor, was prudent enough to know the limits of official criticism of
policy. In 1920, for example, when he levelled biting criticisms on the Lugardian system of administration, he quickly recognized that his radical

ideas had no sympathy at the Colonial Office. Said one senior official, "If we can direct Sir Hugh Clifford's great energy from destroying all that is best in Nigeria to pushing on a policy of improving communications and harbours and building houses for officers his term of office will be a useful if one-sided one." The colonial secretary rubbed it in: "I think we should tell Clifford politely but firmly that we did not send him to Nigeria to upset everything which his predecessor has done."[62] Predictably, official reaction to Douglas's unprecedented criticisms was uniformly harsh. Indeed, as discussed later, the authorities viewed his "act of disloyalty" as reason enough for his dismissal.

Upon reading Douglas's letters (before forwarding them to the Colonial Office), the acting lieutenant-governor, Colonel H. C. Moorhouse, expressed shock at the "intemperate" tone of the letters. As he put it, not only did they "overstep the widest limits of criticism," but they "have the misfortune . . . to be in extremely bad taste." Thus in his covering letter Moorhouse expressed outrage at Douglas's "outspoken criticism" of the government.

> In my opinion the letter is a model of bad taste apart from the fact that I do not believe its contents would be endorsed by the large majority of officials. I myself gave an interview some time ago to the Chairman of the Civil Service War Bonus Committee and I have recently met a deputation of the Railway Committee on the same subject. Their attitude and remarks were in marked contrast to that of Mr. Douglas and I can only regret that one of my officers, especially of the standing of Mr. Douglas, should have put forward such a letter.

Moorhouse disputed Douglas's claim that "there was not a more dissatisfied lot of men to be found in the Empire than in Nigeria," adding that some of the sources of annoyance which Douglas indicated had already been discussed with him. "I have never known Mr. Douglas so modest as to discontinue the discussion of a subject because he considered his hearer to be unsympathetic."[63]

Commenting further on Douglas's letter item by item, Moorhouse firmly rejected the aspersions cast on the motives for the cutbacks in allowances and the nonpayment of death benefits. With respect to the alleged "scandal" in the press about the nonprovision of coffins for deceased officials, the deputy governor insisted that Douglas's allegation "is incorrect," arguing that the matter was not actually "ventilated in the press" but "arose from the consideration of . . . a British Non-Commissioned Officer who had recently died." Whatever the case, Moorhouse considered Douglas's charge that the Colonial Office was "soulless" in its treatment of officers to be absolutely "insulting."[64]

On the question of allowances, especially leave pay, Moorhouse expressed the view that "leave is a privilege and not a right" and that Douglas seemed to have ignored this fact. Yet he agreed that officials were entitled to accumulated leave pay and, if they were deceased, their relatives should receive the leave pay. However, while endorsing Douglas's views on this issue, Moorhouse absolved his government from blame. "As a matter of fact this Government has [earlier] recommended that such leave pay should be automatically paid to the relatives of a deceased officer but Your Lord's predecessor was unable to agree to the proposal." Regarding Douglas's contention that allowances were higher in the Gold Coast than in Nigeria, Moorhouse doubted its accuracy, but insisted that the scale in Nigeria was probably "as high as in the Gold Coast." Whatever the case, he seemed persuaded that travelling allowances "should be paid in full except when detention allowance becomes payable, i.e., after 7 days at any one place." Also, commenting on Douglas's complaint about housing, Moorhouse conceded that "there are very few furnished rest houses and the difficulty met with in calculating whether a rest house should be considered as one for which detention allowances can be drawn is not inconsiderable. This I know from my own experience."[65]

Turning to the question of inadequate payment of allowances for carriers, Moorhouse rejected any increases on grounds that this matter had previously been "thoroughly examined at the time the General Orders were framed," adding, "I am not aware of any widespread dissatisfaction on the subject." As for the policy on "bush allowances," he justified government's stand on the matter.

Bush allowance is only abolished in cases where a bush house has a cement floor and is furnished. I have myself lived for many years in bush houses and I have seen many such here. When they have a cement floor and are furnished they are quite as comfortable and indeed cooler than a permanent house and I do not think any junior officer who has lived in such a house would willingly give it up in order to live in a permanent house of the kind erected in Lagos and elsewhere for an officer of that class. I cannot therefore regard the present regulation on the subject as unfair.

But on the imposition of conservancy fees, Moorhouse endorsed Douglas's sentiments. "There is no doubt," he conceded, that "this is felt to be a grievance and personally I consider that the difficulty of collecting it does not compensate for the irritation that it engenders. With this the Acting Lieutenant Governor [of the] Southern Provinces entirely concurs." He also agreed that the return passage for servants of officers on transfer should be free, especially "when travelling by Government craft."[66]

Finally, Moorhouse dismissed Douglas's contention that the government should pay for the passage of an officer's wife. "Such a proposal, in my opinion, shows that Mr. Douglas has not fully considered it." He added, "It is only in Africa that officers do not have to pay their own passage and in no Colony in the Empire is a wife's passage paid so far as I am aware except as in Colonial Regulation 121." Fully convinced that Douglas's letter of December 1918 far exceeded "any possible limit of justifiable criticism," Moorhouse then recommended appropriate sanction(s) for his evident disloyalty.

> Had Mr. Douglas been long resident in a lonely bush station I could have found many excuses for this letter, as such a life is apt to lead an officer to take a distorted view of matters in general. This is not however the case as he has only recently returned from leave and is stationed at Warri, where there are many Europeans. I have therefore nothing to plead in extenuation of this letter, which in my opinion shows that he fails to realise the loyalty which the Resident of a Province should give to the Government and that on the contrary he has by writing such a letter and showing it to his junior officers done all that lies in his power to create disloyalty in the Service both to this Government and to your Lordship's office.[67]

The acting governor, A. G. Boyle, was equally furious upon reading Douglas's letters. "Mr. Douglas should be relieved as soon as possible," he advised. "His pension papers should be put up when he can be relieved."[68] The Colonial Office staff seemed even more outraged—hence the sharp denunciation of Douglas's "scandalous" statements, his "nastiness," and "downright effrontery." Not surprisingly, they recommended that Douglas should immediately be relieved of his job so as "to make way for younger men who are better fitted for the post." In the view of one senior official, Douglas should not be invited merely to resign, for "he might refuse to do so, and then it would be too late to take action." Rather, he should be warned that if he refused to retire voluntarily, he would be tried and then dismissed. Continued the official, "Govt. cannot afford to tolerate such attacks from a senior European officer if it hopes to maintain discipline among the subordinate staff." The general feeling at the Colonial Office was that Douglas had outlived his usefulness and was no longer "fitted to hold his present position of responsibility."[69]

The secretary of state agreed. In his letter to the acting governor of Nigeria, he directed that Douglas should be relieved of his position forthwith.

> I need scarcely observe that it has caused me considerable surprise that letters such as these, deliberately insulting in their tone, and disclosing an attitude of disloyalty towards the administration under which Mr. Douglas is serving, could

have been written by any officer of the standing of a 2nd class Resident and the only conclusion that I can draw from their perusal is that Mr. Douglas is not fitted to hold his present position of responsibility.

I have had some hesitation whether I should not direct you to take steps to frame a charge against Mr. Douglas for investigation before the Executive Council. But, in view of his long service in Nigeria, I am prepared to offer him the option of retiring from the service on the pension which he has earned. I should be glad if you would so inform him and invite him to apply to retire from his appointment under the Nigerian Government. Should he fail to do so, he should be brought before the Executive Council. In the circumstances it would seem advisable that Mr. Douglas should return to England as soon as . . . arrangement can be made for the performance of his duties, his resignation to take effect from the expiration of any leave for which he may be eligible.[70]

Contents of this letter were transmitted to Douglas who expressed shock and bewilderment at the hostile reaction of the authorities. Faced with a fait accompli, he therefore tendered his resignation on May 5, 1919, in a tone reflecting anguish and remorse. "I would like to say that in writing the letters referred to in the opening paragraph of your letter," he wrote to the acting governor, "I had not the slightest intention of being in any way insulting nor was my attitude intendingly disloyal to the Administration and I regret that His Lordship has taken that view." Yet, he felt convinced that his letter was "a legitimate expression of opinion."[71] Upon finally retiring on July 20, 1920, Douglas went to Northern Rhodesia (Zambia), where he later died on May 24, 1926 at the age of fifty-two.

Interestingly enough, Lord Lugard's friends in England confronted him with the "disgraceful" conditions of service in Nigeria during his administration. At a dinner party held in honor of Lugard's retirement on March 20, 1919, for instance, Sir Edwin Speed, formerly chief justice of Nigeria, upbraided Lugard for the seemingly low salaries in the Nigerian service. While praising Lugard for his remarkable work in Africa generally, he sharply criticized his "parsimony with personnel" which he insisted was responsible for the widespread discontent in the Nigerian public service. Whereas Lugard seemed unperturbed by the poor salaries being paid to his subordinates, Cecil Rhodes, said Sir Edwin, "would never have had ill-paid men about him." In an obvious reference to the Colonial Office, Sir Edwin suggested that "the conditions of service and the terms of service [in Nigeria must] be made sufficiently attractive" so as to attract capable men and thus restore confidence in the Nigerian colonial service.[72]

Uncharacteristically, Lugard conceded that things were not as good as they ought to have been during his governorship and pleaded with the officials still in Nigeria not to despair. "To those who are still in harness," he exhorted, "I would say: Do not let any petty thought obscure the high privilege you enjoy. The results of your work are your reward, of which no man can deprive you. Slow promotion, inadequate recognition, must not discourage you, for you live in the cradle of time; you are fashioning the destinies of a great country; your work will live when your critics are dumb, and you will look back and wonder that in a work so great such lesser things could ever seem to have mattered at all."[73]

Lugard's statements at the dinner party, however, provoked a flurry of angry protests from disgruntled officials in Nigeria. In a rejoinder, these officials not only assailed Lugard's reference to "lesser things," but also took exception to his claim of justice in his administration. Following is the account as published in *Truth* under the caption "Nigerian Officials Meaningly Treated."

At the dinner at which he was entertained last week on the occasion of his retirement from the post of Governor-General of Nigeria, Sir Frederick Lugard spoke of the application of British principles of justice as the ideal of the Administration. This remark must be particularly edifying to the Nigerian officials who were coming home in the *Abasso* when she was torpedoed in April, 1917. Many passengers were drowned, and the survivors lost everything they had on board. There were among them officials from the Gold Coast as well as from Nigeria, all travelling on duty and under orders. Within three weeks the Gold Coast men were paid £80 each for the compensation for the loss of their personal effects. The Nigerian Government would not grant its officials a penny, leaving them to bear losses amounting in some instances to £200 or £300. Last summer the Nigerian Government announced a scale of compensation for officials who might be torpedoed after June, 1918, but it refused to make any retrospective payments. Months later it came out that some of those who were on board the *Abasso* had after all received compensation from the Government. The precisely similar claims of others were, however, again rejected. Whatever it may do in Nigeria, the Administration seems to have shown precious little regard for principles of justice in the handling of this matter.[74]

This rejoinder at least serves to underscore Douglas's claim that "the majority of officials" in Nigeria were unhappy under Lugard. But as we have argued throughout, Douglas alone had the courage to puncture the complacency of the Nigerian administration that prided itself as the symbol of success in colonial Africa.[75]

4. CHRISTIANITY
AND SOCIAL CHANGE

THE BEGINNING

It was not until after the "pacification" of the Owerri District that missionary congregations began to stake out claims in the area. The earliest missionaries in Owerri came from Onitsha. The first Christian mission to arrive was the Church Missionary Society (CMS) which had been at Onitsha since 1857. It established its mission station at Egbu, three miles from Owerri, in 1906. It was followed some years later by the Roman Catholic Mission (RCM) under the direction of Irish Holy Ghost Fathers. In later years other church denominations like the Baptists, Methodists, the African Church, and the Salvation Army joined in the missionary enterprise. The coming of the missionaries, as we shall soon see, brought far-reaching changes in the entire society.

In April 1905 Archdeacon Thomas John Dennis and Alphonsus Chukwuma Onyeabo (later the first Anglican bishop of Owerri) visited Owerri from Onitsha. Their primary aim was to survey the possibility of establishing a CMS mission station and to use the station as the center for the translation of the Bible into Union Igbo. Upon arriving at Owerri they were received by Douglas, the district commissioner. But for fear of being identified as part of the government, Dennis and his companion decided to live among the local people. So for the next six days they were at Owerri, the missionaries stayed at the home of Mr. Igwigbe of Amawom village, a man whom Dennis described as "an old man and very deaf" but of great influence among his people. While here, Dennis and Onyeabo were visited by crowds of people including traditional leaders from outside Owerri Town. The chiefs and the elders, according to Dennis, were "uniformly friendly" and genuinely interested in the proposal to establish a mission station in the town. Their acceptance of the missionaries, however, seems to have been predicated on the understanding that a school would be established for the education of their sons. According to Dennis, many of the chiefs were very eager to send their sons to school. Some of them, he said, even wanted him to take their sons to Onitsha. One Elekwachi Okoroafor of Umuodu village is said to have been particularly interested in having his sons educated. Had Dennis wanted to oblige them, as he said, "I could have brought home a small army of boys" from Owerri.[1]

From Owerri, Dennis and Onyeabo visited the neighboring towns of Egbu, Awaka, Uratta, Naze, Nekede, and even as far as Mgbirichi. As in Owerri Town, the people in these places seemed favorably disposed to the missionaries. In keeping with the traditional sense of Igbo generosity, the visitors were showered with gifts of yams, fowls, palm wine, and foodstuffs. A keen observer, Dennis seemed perplexed why in all their travels no one offered them kola nuts, the Igbo symbol of hospitality and social acceptance: "It does not seem to be the custom in and around Owerri to offer kolanut to visitors in token of welcome and friendship. Yams, eggs, coker-nuts [coconuts], palm wine and occasionally gin were offered us wherever we went, but not one single kolanut." Dennis also noticed some differences in the speech patterns at Owerri and Onitsha. "Salutations too are different. Instead of 'Ndo' or 'Nnua' [welcome] and 'Dalu' or 'Deme' [thank you] so common around Onitsha and Asaba the word 'Ndewo' is used."[2]

All in all Dennis felt satisfied that the Owerri District would be an ideal territory for evangelistic and translational work. With special reference to the latter, the Owerri area seemed particularly suited inasmuch as "the purest Igbo, untouched by other border speech" was spoken there. However, both Dennis and Bishop Herbert Tugwell (who visited Owerri in November 1905) ruled out Owerri Town as an ideal missionary center. Their reason was that Owerri was occupied by the government and the soldiers. Their presence, it was feared, would militate against missionary evangelism since the local people would assume that the government and the missionaries were one and the same thing. Nekede was also rejected partly because of its being a military camp and partly because of its unimposing appearance. "I was not in any way impressed with the town or its neighbourhood as the centre for Mission work," wrote the Anglican bishop, who was at Nekede on November 13, 1905. Another reason given for the rejection of Nekede was that it was too far south from Owerri, being in the direction the CMS had not considered advancing. For all intents and purposes, said Bishop Tugwell, Nekede might as well be left to the Niger Delta Pastorate Church operating from Bonny.[3]

Having rejected both Owerri and Nekede, the missionaries selected Egbu as their center of operation. The choice was largely based on Egbu's strategic location in a region with high population density. Its abundant supply of good and clear water, the network of roads linking it with neighboring towns, and the virtual absence of soldiers contributed to the selection. To both Dennis and Tugwell, the Owerri District, "teeming with human life," was undoubtedly the most ideal place for missionary work. "The possibilities of the future," observed the bishop, "defy conjecture, but I am quite prepared from what I have seen to predict a great movement amongst the people."[4] This prediction proved accurate, for the subsequent mass movement toward Christianity and Western education in the Owerri area remains unparalleled anywhere else in modern Nigeria. Interestingly enough, when Bishop Tugwell left Owerri in November 1905, he took six boys with him for training as carpenters and sawyers at the Onitsha Industrial Mission. The identity of these boys remains a mystery.

On September 27, 1906 the CMS eventually occupied Egbu. The missionaries were temporarily housed by Chief Egbukole Okoroagbara, a man of considerable influence in the town. It was at his compound that early missionary proselytization began. Crowds gathered almost daily to listen to the preaching of Archdeacon Dennis and his companion. In due course land was granted to the missionaries at the site known as *Ọhia Ọjọọ*, or "bad bush," where social outcasts were disposed of. By early 1907 a makeshift church-school had been erected. But the missionaries had a few unfamiliar experiences as we learn from the account of Dennis's sister Frances (later Mrs. Hensley): "My hut was infested with rats, which came out at night on the rampage; and every morning I had to knock away the white ants [*sic*] tunnels from the roof supports and walls. The rats were particularly vicious with the boys. They bit their feet while they were asleep, and I was assured that the rats blew upon the part they wished to gnaw and deadened the feeling."[5]

CONVERSIONS, PROBLEMS, AND SOCIAL CHANGE

Early attempts at converting the masses in Owerri proved painfully difficult and disappointing. Although anxious crowds often gathered at the mission and listened to the missionary propaganda, none of the men and women who came showed any sign of giving up the religion of their ancestors. After all, they did not actually understand what Christianity was all about. As a matter of fact large crowds came to the mission because the missionary preaching was strange to them. And, as we learn from Dennis's sister Frances, the Anglican woman missionary, when the people were asked to embrace Christianity, they raised serious objection and demanded to be told why they should abjure their own traditional ways.[6]

Certainly, missionary criticism of "pagan" customs, particularly the condemnation of polygamy, militated against conversions. To the men as well as to the women, a polygamous household was an index of social well-being. In the Igbo scheme of things, to be rich is to have many wives and many children, and only a poor man was expected to marry only one wife. Women also prided themselves on being the wives of polygamists, for to be the only wife was an indication that her husband was poor. A former missionary, the Reverend G. T. Basden, wrote that, "Polygamy [among the Igbo] is favoured and fostered equally by men and women; in some respects the latter are the chief supporters of the system. . . . The ambition of every Ibo man is to become a polygamist, and he adds to the number of his wives as circumstances permit. They are an indication of social standing, and to some extent signs of affluence; in any case they are counted as sound investments."[7]

Having many wives, which by implication meant also having many children, afforded the Igbo man an enormous reservoir of labor for farming purposes. His wealth and prestige therefore were enhanced. Moreover, the extended network of relationships which resulted from marrying from many places enhanced the diplomatic influence of the polygamist. Indeed, given the many social, political, economic, and even psychological values of polygamy, it is easy to understand why men and women generally resented the strictures which the missionaries cast on the time-honored institution. To ask a man to abandon all his wives except one in order to become a Christian was tantamount to stripping him of his social status and prestige. Consequently most polygamists stayed away from the church and remained firmly convinced that the recommendation of marrying only one wife as the ideal Christian norm was entirely foreign in Africa. Monogamy, they insisted, was "not God's Law [made] for man's benefit." But missionary criticism and intolerance of polygamy remained unabated until very recently. Today it seems the church is modifying its stand on the admission of polygamists into the church. This is particularly true of Protestant Christian men who have married more than one wife but are generous donors to the church. Would the churches cast them by the wayside? In fact, some Protestant theologians have suggested that polygamists should not only be admitted to the church but should also be allowed to receive Holy Communion as well. In this way the indigenization of Christianity in Africa would become a reality.[8]

In addition to polygamy there were other factors that prevented people from embracing Christianity. To the majority of the people the new religion appeared utterly irrelevant. *"Ejim 'church' eme mini?"* many asked. In other words, of what particular value was Christianity to the majority of the populace? And because, in fact, traditional Igbo religion compared very favorably with Christianity, most elders advised the missionaries to simply preach to the children. "We are too old to change," they often told the missionaries. Over time, converts were made. It has ironically become fashionable today to be called a Christian, particularly among the women who now far outnumber the men in almost every denominational congregation.

The first baptisms at Egbu took place in 1907. Four early converts were Mbata Uwakwe who was christened James, Ohale who was given the name John, and two mission boys from Asaba and Onitsha districts—John Eluemenam (of Umunede) and Timothy Ide (of Obio). Here is an eyewitness account of the event: "The first Ebu public baptism was a tremendous event. It was also the first harvest thanksgiving. The church was decorated with ferns and flowers from the bush, and palm leaves, paw-paw and yams. More than 430 people came, and there was not room for them all in the Church."[9] To the exuberant Archdeacon Dennis, this day of first baptisms was a momentous occasion. The very presence of such a large number of people seemed to him a most encouraging sign of success and an indication that Egbu people were receptive to change.

A year later eight more people were baptized. They included Uwakwe's wife (Rebecca) and his infant daughter Chiaka (Rachel). The six others were young boys: Daniel Onwunebula, Paul Egejuru, James Onyewuotu, John Osuji, Jacob Ibeawuchi, and Paul Unwenma. There was strong opposition from the boys' parents. Paul Unwenma, for example, is said to have been warned not to associate with the missionaries. When he defied his father he was severely beaten up and chased out of his home. According to Dennis's sister, "His father had explained . . . that he looked to his son to continue his house after him, for he would inherit all he possessed at his departure. He must marry many wives, and become a great chief—a worthy successor to him." Evidently Paul's father was disappointed and consequently drove him away. He was harbored at the mission by David Eze, one of the evangelists. And he remained there "working for his food"[10] until his father relented and took him home.

The rate of conversion was very slow. It was not until 1910, for example, that the first converts were secured from Awaka, Emii, and Owerri town. In April of that year six young men from Awaka were baptized at Egbu. And in June and December, respectively, eight youths from Emii and two others from Owerri were baptized. Even then Christianity does not appear to have removed the hold which traditional religious beliefs had on the converts. At Awaka, for example, where a church bell was stolen in 1913, the church adherents with the tacit support of their mission teacher, Isaiah Jibuno, invited a Hausa man to make medicine which would make it possible for them to recover the bell. This naturally infuriated the CMS authorities and led to the station teacher being disciplined.[11]

At Egbu also an important change occurred in 1910. An old man said to have been a person of some substance was baptized. This was an event of enormous significance because, as we have so far indicated, the older generation had remained markedly indifferent to the new religion. We have no clues as to what must have induced this old man to embrace Christianity, nor do we even know his name. However, it was evident to the missionaries that a new era had dawned. For as the missionaries themselves conceded, it was almost unthinkable for the head of a household or even a chief to abandon his traditional religion and accept Christianity. Certainly those who did so paid heavily for it: "It is difficult for one unacquainted with heathenism to realise what it means for a chief to renounce and destroy all his idolatrous symbols. It cuts him off from the social life of his friends, for nearly all social functions centre around some superstitious practice; it exposes him to taunts more difficult for a native to bear, and it raises up enemies among those who have been his best friends."[12]

Scholars have debated the many reasons which prompted Africans to embrace Christianity, but we shall not go into them here.[13] However, on the level of generalizations it may be said that most of the early converts were either slaves who expected a new social status from Christianity, or children who seemed infatuated with the new religious message. The latter of course viewed association with the church as the surest means of acquiring education. There were also adults who had experienced various forms of hardship and misfortune in their lives and hoped that a switch to the new religion might improve their situations. There were of course others who were genuinely moved by the new teaching. Whatever the reasons might have been, it was clear that a revolutionary era had dawned, for it was the Christian revolution which shook the very foundation of traditional society. It was largely Christianity which, as Chinua Achebe put it, caused Igbo society to "fall apart."[14]

One of the consequences of Christian conversion was the inevitable split in the ideological unity of the society. Not only was there now a division in religious persuasion, but conversions fostered sociological splintering of social units, thereby accentuating forces of social and political conflict. And, as the church adherents identified with the values of their mentors (Europeans), they began inexorably to turn their backs to Omenala (customary practice). Also, as the ranks of the Christians swelled, so also did violations of societal codes of conduct rise. Misguided schoolboys and fanatical converts often threw caution to the wind. For example, they fished at the Otamiri River at prohibited times and places, and they defiled shrines, the temples of local deities, by removing objects of sacrifice (such as eggs and money) placed at the shrines. In several instances the Christians even refused to participate in community projects, claiming that these were pagan and heathenish customs. From all appearances, the Christians had constituted themselves a state within the state. Thus these Christian zealots were not only perceived as social irritants but also as dangerous elements to be disciplined. The annoyance of the elders, the custodians of tradition and morality, was intense. "The elders are continually lamenting the falling away of old . . . customs", reported one CMS missionary, "and the way in which 'the Book' as the preaching of the gospel is called, is spoiling [their society]."[15] Attempts were therefore made to discipline the Christians either by legislation or by imposing sanctions. To the missionaries, of course, such measures smacked of persecution, despite which, however, many of the Christians stood remarkably firm.

Christianity has obviously disturbed the traditional order of society. Much of its impact is unquestionably negative and destructive. On the other hand, it must be said that some of the changes brought about by the missionaries were worthwhile and beneficial. For example, consider the practices of twin murder and slave immolation (human sacrifice) which prevailed in the precolonial days. In Igbo society as a whole, giving birth to twins was considered an abomination (*aru*). Such babies were either put in earthen pots and thrown away or exposed to the elements and allowed to die. Mothers of twins were either banished or had to be cleansed before they were reintegrated into the community. They bore a social stigma forever. Such practices were not only repugnant to the missionaries, but reprehensible and inhuman. Hence they declared frontal war against twin murder and human sacrifice.

Instead of allowing the twin babies to die of exposure, missionaries took these unfortunate victims from their mothers and nurtured them at the missions. At Egbu and Emekuku this rescue operation gave rise to the establishment of hospices or orphanages for which both the CMS and the RCM became famous. The crèches were in fact the foundation upon which the Egbu medical center and Emekuku hospital were built. The *Ogige nwanyi Beke* at Egbu in particular attracted mothers from far afield who brought their children for medical treatment and physical examinations. This quasi-medical center was originally conceived as the counterpart of the CMS Iyi-enu hospital at Ogidi (1907), but it never developed into a full-fledged hospital. The Emekuku crèche, however, grew into a major medical institution by 1935. Both establishments also served as important centers of conversion. As the women came for medical care, they left with doses of religious instruction.

Missionary intervention was also responsible for ending the ancient custom of throwing cult slaves (*osu*) into the Otamiri River. Traditionally, slaves were dedicated to the river spirit and, upon their death, were thrown into the river. Some slaves were even cast into the river alive as part of human sacrifice. To the missionaries, these methods of disposing with slaves were both unhygienic and cruel and therefore had to be abolished. The drive toward the abrogation of the custom was prompted by the discovery in 1908 of four dead bodies which had been thrown into the river. Since the missionaries and others drank the water from the supposedly polluted river, it was thought that "to allow [the custom] to continue meant illness and almost certain death" to those who drank the water. To stop the throwing of corpses into the river, the missionaries employed both persuasion and threat. Chief Egbukole was therefore summoned by the missionaries and warned that unless his people put an end to the throwing of corpses into the river, the matter would be referred to the government officials at Owerri. Faced with that threat, the chiefs took prompt measures to avoid confrontation with the government.

> The next day all the chiefs came for the palaver. Tom [i.e., Archdeacon Dennis] talked to them about the seriousness and danger of such a bad custom. They were most anxious not to have trouble with the Owerri officials and promised to do all that was necessary. A special burial place was found well away from the water and the remains [of corpses in the river] were removed. After this was done the men of the two towns [Egbu and Naze] . . . cleared all the bush right round the source. . . . So ended a bad custom of many generations.[16]

Obviously, the Christian missionaries were now a force to be reckoned with, especially in the sphere of social change. For through missionary intervention such practices like twin murder and human sacrifice were abolished. Yet it was not only these and other social evils that the missionaries sought to eradicate. They seemed determined to uproot almost totally the African or traditional culture and replace it with the so-called Christian civilization, whatever that meant. Hence Christianity became a foreign religious experience—"colonial evangelism," as T. O. Beidelman aptly described it—and, as James Ngugi remarked, a religion which "took no account of a people's way of life . . . would only maim a man's soul."[17]

A great deal has been written about the missionary encounter with African culture and society—much of it understandably critical.[18] However, it is not our intention here to dwell on this issue from the point of view of whether what was done was right or wrong. Our interest is to approach the missionary encounter with traditional African culture from the perspective of social change, namely, the replacement of the African way of life with Western civilization. For example, by introducing Western medicine the missionaries undermined the influence of the dibia (priest, diviner, healer, medicineman, etc.). By condemning twin murder and the religious precepts that sustained it, the missionaries invariably challenged traditional customs and beliefs. And to bring about change in the area of twin murder and motherhood, women were co-opted as partners in social change. For, argued the missionaries, unless women were freed from the shackles of tradition, modernization of society in the image of the West would not be realized. Hence, as in Onitsha and Asaba, women's training homes were established in the Owerri area, first at Egbu and at Emekuku, to train women in child care, modern housekeeping, sewing, needlework, and cooking. In almost every case, however, the primary interest was to train the women as future wives of male converts. Thus the women received good doses of Christian doctrine at the training homes, and most of them were later baptized. Through these women social change would occur. For example, the girls trained at the institutions became the new "mothers" of twins and orphans rescued by the missionaries. And as we shall see, hospices for the orphans, twins, and the sick became not only centers of medical care, but also the nuclei of modern hospitals.

The Egbu center, known as the Women's Training Home, was founded in 1907 and placed under the direction of Frances M. Dennis, Archdeacon Dennis's sister. She was a trained nurse and had been in charge of a similar institution at Idumeje Ogboko in the Asaba District. The home was known locally as *Ogige nwanyi Beke,* European Women's Home. Because of the amount of work involved here, more European women missionaries were requested from England in 1908, but the London authorities would not oblige. For purely financial reasons, the authorities said, it was impossible "to appoint at the present time a recruit to join Miss F. M. Dennis at Egbu, Owerri." The missionaries were thus asked to make "the best arrangements they could with the existing staff." By 1909 the center had about fifteen girls. Demand for more European women workers continued, but little was done. To the regret of the London authorities, Frances Dennis resigned in 1909 after three years' work at Egbu interlaced with some progress and some frustration. Writing later of her experiences in the Igbo mission she remarked, "I think those years . . . were epoch making years . . . and the women were most blessed by the changes taking place."[19]

Another CMS home was established at Emii and was managed by Kate Beswick and E. A. Hornby. Here as at Egbu, girls were trained as future wives of converts. But it was never a flourishing home as such. Despite repeated appeals for more funds and assurances that Emii was an ideal place for women's training, the authorities in London decided to close the home. By 1919 the Emii home was merged with the Egbu home. Other centers had been proposed for Nekede, Ezeoke, Atta, and elsewhere, but these never went beyond the planning stage.

A rival institution known as St. Anne's Centre was established at Emekuku by the Roman Catholic Holy Rosary Sisters in 1937. Unlike the Egbu home which was designed for young girls (*umu agbǫǫ*), St. Anne's Centre was for more mature women and known locally as *Umuibiriachi*. As might be expected, this institution was founded by the Roman Catholics as a countermeasure against Protestant preponderant influence among the women. Here is Bishop Joseph Shanahan's explanation for establishing the convent: "There are sixty Protestant missionary women at work in the vicariate of Southern Nigeria. This is a serious danger for our Catholic girls who have no Sisters to form them in the ways of Catholic girlhood and womenhood. Our newly converted women have no other type of Christian womanhood before their eyes than representatives of Protestantism in all varieties."[20] By 1938 the Emekuku convent had over three hundred women, some of whom had run away from their homes. A recent study of this convent reveals that some of the women in the institution had been encouraged by the Catholic Sisters to run away from their "pagan" homes shortly after their conversion to Christianity. So the convent actually became both a house of refuge as well as a training institution. As in the Egbu home women were provided some basic vocational training. Through the "weapon of the needle"[21] (knitting and sewing), the Catholics and Protestants thus succeeded in winning over a number of local women, especially those who could not attend regular schools.

THE SPREAD OF CHRISTIANITY

With regard to the Egbu mission, we should emphasize here that the Egbu church (All Saints Church) was the premier Protestant church in the area and the center from which teams of evangelists trekked to many towns and villages preaching the gospel message. It was through their efforts that many local churches outside Egbu came into being. In fact, the role of these evangelists in the growth of Christianity can hardly be overemphasized. Of these zealous and dedicated men, a European missionary woman at Egbu has written, "The Evangelists were splendid and very keen, and were making the Gospel known in all the region around." The evangelists, also known as African "auxiliaries," were in fact missionaries in every sense of the word. For Roman Catholic Bishop Shanahan, every African teacher/ catechist was a missionary, and they were taught to regard themselves as such.[22]

At Owerri proper, the first CMS church was founded in 1909 and grew into the present Christ Church. It does not appear that Christianity had any particular attraction for the people at the time. According to the missionary at Egbu, the church was established here in response to appeals from alien residents who had previously attended Sunday services at Egbu.

> Quite a number of Government officials, stationed at Owerri, were natives of the Gold Coast [Ghana], Sierra Leone and Jamaica. They made request that a Christian service should be held on the Sabbath, saying they would build a church and supply everything necessary. We were thankful to have the request and Tom assured them that he would send them an Evangelist to take such a Service if they would build the church, preferably off Government grounds, so that anyone who wished could come.[23]

Thus through the work of evangelists, many churches sprang up in places such as Emii (1908), Awaka (1909), Umuoba Uratta (1910), and Umuorii Uratta (1911). In subsequent years permanent churches were opened at Nekede, Naze, Owelu and Owalla in Uratta (1914), Mbieri, Ogwa, Nguru, Ahiara, and elsewhere. In most of these areas local deputations to the authorities at Egbu led to the foundation of churches. Such was the case of St. Barnabas Church, Umudim, near Nkwerre.

> Early in the year 1920 it was unanimously agreed that a Church-Teacher should be appointed to Umudim as a prelude to the setting up of a CMS church in the town. . . . Subscriptions were asked for from the town and a fairly large sum of money was collected by Chiefs Igboejesi Akubuiro and Nwachukwuezi Chioma. . . . This money was handed over to the Rev. Alphonso C. Onyeabo [at Egbu] to assist in the stationing of a Church Teacher at Umudim. . . . Mr. Onyeabo felt unable to receive the delegation because they had not come up with any of the chiefs. . . . At the close of the year 1920 a second delegation from Umudim visited Egbu. All the Umudim Chiefs had been consulted. . . . The result of this meeting with the Rev. Alphonso Onyeabo was the decision to station a Church Teacher at Umudim in January 1921.[24]

Much earlier, in 1907, a similar deputation from Ogwa in Mbaitoli resulted in the opening of a CMS station at Abazu Ogwa in 1910. The British missionary woman who led a team of evangelists to Ogwa informs us that shortly after her arrival at Egbu from Asaba, "chiefs came from Ogwa begging us to visit their town. It was about 18 miles from Ebu; carriers had been brought to carry the hammock and my loads, and they were so insistent that Tom [her brother] thought we should go. All the evangelists went with me." Even before their arrival, a camp had already been set up in front of the head chief's compound and on Sunday the missionary propaganda began. "We sat under trees in the market place and began singing, when a big crowd gathered. The chiefs brought their seats, snuff and palm wine, settling themselves as if they meant to stay for some time. After we had sung three hymns to give them time to compose themselves we began. Eze was the spokesman; he gave the Message very simply and they listened quietly."[25]

But the missionary's preaching that Christianity would insure everlasting life and the exhortation that people should abandon their traditional religion did not go unchallenged. "They repeated sentences of the Message delivered and asked questions," recalled Frances Hensley (née Dennis), "expecting us to answer their objections to giving up their father's ways." In a characteristic Igbo pragmatic approach to life, the chiefs called the missionary's bluff by offering to "give us eight people who would come with us, give all they had, and we should give them everlasting life. If it worked well they would follow" the new way. Unable to meet the demand, the evangelists brought the "long palaver" to an end and thus left the chiefs and others unconvinced of the superiority of the new religion to their own. As to the literal interpretation of the promise of everlasting life, Mrs. Hensley remarked, "What they really wanted was to escape death: life to them was most precious . . . and suicide was a very rare thing" in their culture.[26] After four days' stay, the evangelists returned to Egbu, confident that Protestant presence in the area would be only a matter of time.

The expectation came through in 1910 with the establishment of a CMS church at Abazu Ogwa. This was followed a year later with the opening of other stations at Umuhu Atta (1911), Uzoagba (1911), Umunjam Mbieri (1913), Obazu Mbieri (1914), and Umuegbe Ogwa (1916), all in the Mbaitoli-Ikeduru clans. Missionary forays were also made in the Orlu, Okigwe, and Mbaise areas. In Mbaise the chief centers were Ife Ezinihitte (1913), Amumara (1915), and Ihitteafoukwu (1918). Between 1913 and 1920 a chain of stations had thus been established in the Owerri hinterland, also known as Isuama. In the Nsu region of the present Mbano Local Government Area, "every village chief was obsessed by the craze to have a church [and school] within Mbano," evidence of the emulative principle (*ezi amuru*) in Igbo society.[27]

Certainly, the role played by Igbo catechists must be considered in explaining the growth of Christianity in the old Owerri Division, as elsewhere in Igboland. Many of them are by no means prominent men today, but their names are immortalized in the history of Christianity in the region. For years many of them devoted themselves to the dissemination of the gospel, offering advice and guidance to converts and catechumens and teaching the rudiments of reading and writing to young school and church enthusiasts. At Umuorii Uratta, for example, few Protestants would forget the contributions of mission agents like Emmanuel Etochie of Egbu and Emmanuel Ejiaku, Sr., of Umuorii Uratta in the growth of the local church. Nor would Roman Catholics forget such names as Pius Amanze of Emekuku and Sylvanus Nnadi of Awaka. These two in particular became almost institutions at the Catholic mission at Emekuku.

Some of the catechists at one time or another rose to assume important positions in the church. I have interviewed dozens of these, and the story of their experiences is fascinating. But limitations of space and time would not permit a full treatment of these people here (see appendix B). One of the pioneer catechists who was instrumental in the development of churches in the Owerri area deserves some mention, however. Alphonsus Chukwuma Onyeabo, born at Onitsha in 1879, was educated at Onitsha, Asaba, and at St. Andrew's College, Ọyọ. In 1908 he was sent to the Awka Training College in preparation for his ordination as a deacon. On August 22, 1909 he was ordained deacon at Christ Church, Onitsha. After an unpleasant experience at the Onitsha church in 1912,[28] Onyeabo was sent to the Egbu mission. In 1914 he was finally admitted to the priesthood. In 1937 he became assistant bishop on the Niger with residence at Aba. Later the residence was moved to Egbu, where it remains to this day. Bishop Onyeabo retired from active service in 1948 and died in 1953.

From 1912 until his retirement in 1948, Onyeabo was a powerful influence at Egbu and in the entire district. By 1912 he and the other missionaries had launched an aggressive expansion scheme, their aim being to occupy as many towns and villages as possible. As a result, a network of church-schools was established in many areas within the Egbu District. Because of his affable manner and devotion to duty he cultivated the friendship of non-Christians who often provided funds and labor for the development of the churches. In 1916 he assumed the leadership of the Egbu mission, having succeeded the Reverend Fred G. Payne, the West Indian missionary, as the superintendent of the mission which was then known as the Southern District. Like the Roman Catholic stalwart, Bishop Shanahan, Bishop Onyeabo pushed the growth of church and school in the whole of Owerri Division and elsewhere. European contemporaries as well as Africans respected him. When he died in 1953, the London *Times* said of him: "He was a wise administrator and counsellor to Africans and Europeans alike, and had a deep knowledge and understanding of his own people, among whom he had great authority."[29]

THE ESTABLISHMENT AND CONSOLIDATION OF THE ROMAN CATHOLIC MISSION

Until 1912 the Protestant church (CMS) dominated the mission field in the Owerri Division. From that date, however, its preponderant influence was effectively challenged by the Roman Catholic missionaries. The resultant interdenominational competition and rivalry significantly quickened the pace of Christianization. Moreover, the coming of the Roman Catholics accelerated the pace of social change as reflected in the establishment of schools, hospitals, maternity centers, and Christian societies. On the other hand, the struggle for dominance between the Catholic and the Protestant missions generated an atmosphere of intolerance among the different religious bodies. It also fostered conflict among the church adherents themselves. This religious cleavage inevitably impaired the political unity of many village-groups. Consider this example from Awaka, which is by no means a unique case.

> . . . prior to the arrival of the British and missionary activities, the villages of Umuodu and Nde-egbelu cooperated as brothers and fought through thick and thin to survive the intra-town wars. But with the advent of missionary activities, a majority of Umuodu people were converted to the Protestant faith while a majority of Nde-egbelu became Catholic converts. These villages ever since have hardly agreed on any major town development project such as building a community school, town hall, or even a village market.[30]

Roman Catholic missionary activity in the Owerri area began officially in 1912. Prior to this date, however, Roman Catholic priests had visited Owerri and its environs. As early as 1899, Father Joseph Pawlas had visited Oguta from Onitsha. Also, Father Leon Lejeune, then the Catholic prefect at Onitsha, is said to have visited Oguta in 1901. Then in 1911 Father Krafft visited Owerri from Calabar, apparently in response to a request from Owerri chiefs. According to Father Lena, then the Roman Catholic prefect at Calabar,

> Some chiefs from Owerri, a great town 230 kilometres from Calabar, had sent deputation upon deputation, requesting us to establish a mission at Owerri. Fr. Krafft was, therefore, sent to see the chiefs. He travelled first by boat, then by bicycle and eventually arrived at Owerri. He returned to Calabar by the same route. This very year [1912], too, Fr. [Joseph] Feral made the same journey and stopped for three weeks at Owerri to study the environment with the aim of starting a new station.

It would indeed appear from Father Lena's account that the "discovery" of Owerri coincided with the desperate Roman Catholic search for a land route from Calabar to Onitsha. Said Father Lena in 1912, "For a long time at Calabar, the need for a quicker and easier communication with Onitsha, the headquarters of the Prefecture, was badly felt. To travel to Calabar from Onitsha, one had to journey for 15 days by boat and at great expense, even though the distance was relatively short. A determination was, therefore, made to find a land route. An opportunity to try out this project arose last year."[31]

Following Father Krafft's reconnoitering visit, Father Joseph Feral (1878–1929), who first came to Onitsha in 1904 from France, left Calabar on March 14, 1912 and arrived at Owerri on March 20, 1912 via Itu, Ikot-Ekpene, and Aba. He stayed at the home of Chief Emeto of Umuodu, and from there he visited the neighboring towns—Naze, Nekede, Ihiagwa, Ulakwo, Egbu, Awaka, Agbala, Emii, Amorie, Emekuku, and others. With the possible exception of Chief Nze Nwaokoroacha of Umuọrọrọnjọ Owerri, who is said to have been very pro-CMS, all the chiefs in the Owerri zone seemed favorably disposed to the Roman Catholics. Hence Father Feral wrote in his diary, "I have not found a single person who does not want to welcome us," adding that "all the chiefs support us" and have promised "to send their children to [our] school." Chief Nkwazema of Nekede, we are told, seemed particularly eager to have the Catholic missionaries settle in his town, perhaps because of the "unprogressive" character of the CMS station there. (The CMS authorities in fact had intended to abandon this "unprogressive station," but relented by 1915 partly because of Roman Catholic aggressiveness.)[32]

Overall, Father Feral seemed pleased with the warm reception accorded him at Owerri. It is important to emphasize, however, that local interest in the Roman Catholics was not because of the Catholic religion per se. Rather, it was the prospect that the Roman Catholics would open schools for the boys who were eager to go to school. Said Father Feral, "The children are very numerous with nothing to do." The children, it seemed, had nothing to do because the Anglican mission in the town reportedly was on the verge of collapse. "At the village of Umuọrọrọnjọ," noted Father Feral, "there is a CMS church which has been deserted since my arrival in Owerri." The government school (discussed later) which was also chronically cramped for space appeared incapable of accommodating the large number of boys eager to receive English education. Indeed, as Father Feral confirmed, the chiefs and elders tended to prefer English education to vernacular education. Thus, education acted as a magnet in predisposing the chiefs and elders toward the Catholics because they were "the ones that teach the English language,"[33] in contrast to the CMS which provided vernacular education.

Yet colonial oppression and exploitation were equally important reasons why the chiefs and elders welcomed the missionaries at this time. It must be noted that the advent of the missionaries coincided with the era of British "pacification," a euphemism for aggressive military conquest of the Owerri hinterland, as well as the period of colonial exploitation. That the missionaries therefore were perceived as the mediators of peace all across Igboland is clearly reflected in this report by a CMS missionary at Egbu.

The work of the District is difficult owing to the peculiar ideas which prevail as to what our work is. An outsider might be inclined to marvel at the demand for the Gospel and the request for teachers on every side. I have had eight towns in one week asking for Teachers, and one "Local Helper" reports 3000 at one Sunday service, but I fear that a great deal of the wanting a teacher is to escape Government [military action and] work, or be freed from the exertions of the chiefs, which at present many in this part imagine will follow their association with us.[34]

Having laid the groundwork for future Roman Catholic presence, Father Feral left for Calabar on April 20, 1912. In July he returned to Owerri in the company of Joseph Delaney, an Irish layman, and was granted a piece of land at Umuodu by Chief Emeto. Despite professions of support from the Owerri chiefs, Father Feral had some unsavory things to say about them. For example, he characterized Chief Njemanze as being "quite old, . . . a ruffian . . . who asks only for money." As for Chief Nze Nwaokorocha of Umuọrọrọnjọ, he was "neither very marvellous nor honest," even though he promised "that all the children from his village will support us." Of the other chiefs Father Feral wrote,

Emeto, whom I knew from the very first day, is nothing but debauched and corrupt, who only summoned us for his own ends—the royal crown—and seems to want everything for himself: the honour of having called us, the glory of doing all the work himself with the people from his village, and then the reward, that is to say to be placed at the head and above all the other chiefs. However, he has much energy and will use it I think to make us succeed in Owerri. "He can do everything, he has everything, everything belongs to him, he can make himself obeyed by everyone." This is almost true in his village for he knows how to bluff and he succeeds. Uche, the chief of Umoeche, is a good old man who truly supports us. He came to see me several times and always assured me he would send all his children to school and to work.

Ukebu [the chief of Umuoyima] is a good man too but he cannot do much, being, I think, the faithful servant of Emeto. He, however, always sends someone to work.[35]

Although the initial Roman Catholic missionary activity was at Owerri, the missionaries finally settled at Emekuku. The reasons for abandoning

Owerri are yet unclear. However, it is said that Chief Oparaocha Ekwe of Ulakwo enticed the missionaries to his town. But, as at Owerri, their stay there was short-lived, principally because the chief was angered by the missionary's strident attacks on polygamy. Being a polygamist himself, the chief is said to have unsuccessfully appealed to Father Feral to desist from attacking polygamists. Perhaps as a result of his clash with the chief, Father Feral was harassed by thieves (the church bell is said to have been stolen). Consequently Father Feral and his companion moved to Awaka, a nearby town.[36] From here the Catholics finally settled at Emekuku.

The history of the Catholic church in the present Imo State actually revolves around Emekuku. Chief Obi Ejeshi of Emekuku, then a prominent chief, is said to have been the force behind the permanent settlement of the Catholic mission at Emekuku. According to popular legend, Chief Obi lured Father Feral from Awaka to his town on the suggestion that Emekuku was a more strategic center, as well as being more populous, than Awaka. Besides, Chief Obi is said to have promised to make the Catholic church the only church in the town. Thus Chief Obi's famous "Awaka small, Emekuku plenty" argument, coupled with the promise to make Emekuku the sole preserve of the RCM, seems to have persuaded the Catholic missionaries to move to Emekuku. The coming of the Roman Catholic missionaries to Emekuku in 1912 appears to have fulfilled Chief Obi's ambition to make his town "grow up." For, as it has been said, Chief Obi had a great admiration for Egbu and Onitsha where "wonderful developments" had taken place through the presence of the Christian missionaries. Hence he reportedly invited the CMS to open a church-school at his town. But for reasons that are yet unknown, the CMS authorities are said to have refused, and the chief became determined to attract the Roman Catholics.[37]

Whatever the case, RCM presence at Emekuku became a reality when on July 16, 1912, on the feast of Our Lady of Mount Carmel (a Catholic feast devoted to Mary), a Catholic mission station was established. It was named accordingly Our Lady of Mount Carmel. By 1914 a permanent site had been chosen and missionary houses built. Chief Obi, of course, kept his end of the bargain; he decreed that henceforth all Emekuku people should embrace Roman Catholicism and that all Emekuku school children should desist from attending the CMS school at Egbu. "Chief Obi took it as a matter of priority to make sure that the missionaries did not lack [a] congregation. He made a law that any Emekuku [person] who went to the Church Missionary Society at Egbu would be severely dealt with. He took it upon himself to take charge of guarding the road leading to Egbu through Awaka. This fierce and despotic ruler had a special whip with which he dished out lashes to those who defied him."[38]

The Reverend Father J. B. Jordan, an Irish missionary whose account on this subject has remained the standard reference until recently, argued that the pioneer Catholic missionaries were fiercely opposed by Emekuku men but welcomed by the women. Only because of the intervention of the women, he argued, was it possible for the Catholic mission to be established at Emekuku. This account, however, has been strongly challenged. Chief Obi's son and successor, for example, told this writer in 1975 that Father Jordan's statement was a "sheer fabrication," adding, "I do not know how and where he got that idea; it is not true, and I told him so myself." Chief Amadi Obi seemed irritated by what he perceived as a deliberate attempt to deny his father's critical role in bringing the missionaries to Emekuku. Apocryphal or not, Father Jordan's story is even cited today as an illustration of women's political power in modern African politics.[39]

Like Egbu, Emekuku henceforth became the headquarters of Roman Catholic missionary enterprise in the Owerri Province. And, as will be shown later, the growth of Roman Catholicism here accelerated the pace of Western civilization and invariably the decay of traditional African religion, customs, and way of life. Bishop Shanahan put it succinctly in these words in 1921: "We continue to witness the collapse of paganism. It is a unique occasion for the church to save the youths and with it the country and its future. . . . Paganism is now a thing for the aged. The youth want to identify with the new world which they find around them. It would be useless for them to remain outside it. The door to this new world is the school."[40]

Protestant response to the Roman Catholic presence was markedly hostile. As a matter of fact, ever since the Catholic missionaries came to Onitsha in 1885, relations with the Anglicans had been acrimonious largely because the Protestants regarded the Roman Catholics as "intruders"—hence the mutual antagonism between the two denominations.[41] The nervousness of the Anglican missionaries may be understood from this report about the arrival of the Roman Catholics in 1912: "A new danger threatens this district in the arrival of the Roman Catholics," warned the Reverend Cecil Brown, then secretary of the executive committee of the Niger Mission. In his alarmist fashion, he raised the problem of the "pernicious" influence of the Catholic missionaries "who are opening in or near our already occupied stations" at Awaka, Emii, Ulakwo, Naze, and other places. Continued Reverend Brown, "Now is the time for immediate action" to forestall the "ruthless competition" of the Roman Catholics, "whose resources often seem unlimited." But, as will become apparent later, the Catholics appeared unstoppable. In Bishop Shanahan's boastful words, "They cannot prevent us" (*Non proevalebunt*).[42]

The growth of the Catholic church in the Owerri area during the early phase (1912–32) was rather dramatic. This was the period when Bishop

Shanahan directed RCM operations from Onitsha. Several factors were responsible for the growth. First, by the time the Catholic missionaries arrived, the quest for education here had become intense. Towns and villages wanted schools, and whichever denomination provided them won admiration. In several instances the RCM provided the schools and/or sent teachers to run them. In the confident words of Bishop Shanahan, "*Now* is the opportune time to double all the effort, when many of the towns are crying out for schools and the people are opening their hearts to us." Thus, while the Catholics effectively staffed their schools, the Anglicans lost ground because of lack of human resources. "Everywhere," complained the Reverend G. T. Basden, "the natives see progress except in the CMS," and "when we tell them we have no men to send out, they frankly do not believe us." Because of the constant loss of ground to the Catholics, he concluded ruefully, "our confidence has been rudely shaken."[43]

Indeed, the remarkable Catholic growth during this period was largely due to the mission's pragmatic policy of evangelization through the school. As Bishop Shanahan and his colleagues fully recognized, the Igbo seemed generally lukewarm or even overtly hostile to Christianity per se. But "when the pretext [for our coming] is to build a school," Shanahan conceded in 1912, "the access to the village or to the town is made easier for us." He added: "To the extent that the school succeeded, paganism would crumble, and as the children of today will become the men of tomorrow, the success would be enduring."[44] Education was therefore the powerful weapon for missionary evangelization.

There were yet many other factors that explain the spectacular movement toward the Catholic church during the early phase of its presence. Of these the recruitment of a large number of African catechists must be regarded as crucial. Reliable figures are hard to obtain, but by 1912 there were no less than 132 Catholic catechists in all of Igboland. By 1920, when Shanahan was consecrated a bishop, the number had risen to about 928. In the Owerri sector alone there were by 1920 a total of 150 station catechists and two Catholic priests (Fathers Dan Walsh and Cornelius Liddane) superintending several churches and handling thousands of adherents. Evidently, two priests alone could not have effected the so-called miracle of grace. The catechists, though poorly paid and not particularly well educated, were not only "the corner-stone of the African Church," but without a doubt they were "the leaders of the new Christian nuclei and it was they who had to interpret the faith at the growing points of the church." They were, in Father Shanahan's words, "the pillars" of the church and "the real apostles of the people." He added, "There would be no Church in the country today if they had not done their work so well. They never spared themselves, and every one of them was a catechist, as well as a teacher. We cannot number the vast multitude of souls that have gone to heaven through their hands."[45]

THE ERA OF EXPANSION

It was Father Feral, as already noted, who laid the foundation of the Catholic church in Emekuku. It was under him too that Roman Catholicism spread to the immediate environs. Before he was transferred to Holy Trinity, Onitsha in 1913, for example, he had established several Catholic mission outposts—mainly schools—in places like Emii, Awaka, Agbala, Ogbaku, and Añara Osu in Mbano. The rapid pace of expansion continued under his immediate successors—Fathers Paul Delisle and Dan Walsh. For all practical purposes, it was Father Walsh who consolidated Roman Catholic presence at Emekuku (1913–19), as symbolized by the conversion of the first Christians (about nineteen of them) on July 16, 1914. The second batch of converts in 1915 included such prominent names as J. K. Nzerem,[46] formerly Member of the British Empire, now chief, member of the Knights of St. Mulumba and recipient of the Nigerian "Order on the Niger" (OON). It was under Father Walsh also that the RCM established mission stations in town after town in the Isuama area, including towns in the present Mbaise, Mbaitoli, and Mbano local government areas, as well as in the Orlu-Okigwe zones. Of particular importance were the outstations of Ogbaku (1912; parish in 1948), Umuagwu Uzoagba (1912–13), Ihitte Ezinihitte (1913), Nguru (1914), Port Harcourt (1916), Ahiara (1916; parish in 1932), Obosima (1916; parish in 1938), St. Paul's Owerri (1916; parish in 1955), Ekwereazu (1918), Nsu (1918; parish in 1933), Onicha Ezinihitte (1918), and Aba (1916; parish in 1923).

The growth of the Catholic church here was also linked to the role of the Catholic nuns. As earlier indicated, the CMS had utilized women missionaries as doctors, nurses, and vocational teachers. But their impact on the church was not as far-reaching as those of the Catholic nuns. The earliest Catholic women missionaries, the Sisters of St. Cluny, arrived at Onitsha in 1889. But being French, they spoke neither English nor Igbo and so were considered ineffective in missionary evangelization. Father Shanahan, who replaced the French superior on the Lower Niger in 1905, actually contended that the large sums of money that were spent on their behalf could have been better used in training African catechists. So in 1919 the nuns were withdrawn. In 1930, however, the Irish Sisters of the Holy Rosary under Sister Mary Brigid arrived at Emekuku to take care of the sick, twins, and orphans, and to teach. In 1931 a boarding school for girls was opened. There were fifteen girls initially, which included three Emekuku girls whose sons are now Catholic priests—Mrs. Euna Agu, Mrs. Elizabeth Obi, and Mrs. Grace Obinna. By 1932 the school had its first indigenous African teacher, Cecilia N. Onwuzulike (later Mrs. Nweze) from Ozubulu.[47] Thus with the coming of the Irish Sisters the era of female education dawned in the Catholic education system in the Owerri Division.

Interestingly enough, Bishop Shanahan, the education enthusiast, had a very dim view of female education prior to the arrival of the Irish Sisters. By 1920, for instance, he had argued that it was "not good . . . at present" to expose girls to Western education. "It is better for them to remain as housewives," he insisted, "simple women, humble and submissive." Evidently influenced by experience at Onitsha, he argued that, "Often their acquaintance with the school, especially in the convent, has made them detribalized."[48] By "detribalized," of course, the bishop meant that missionary education (indoctrination) had indeed alienated Africans from their cultural heritage and thus made them the deracinated.

With Emekuku as the nucleus, Roman Catholic institutions for girls sprouted in various parts of the division, chief among them being the Holy Rosary schools at Ogbor Nguru (1934), Oru Ahiara, Okigwe (1948), Orlu (1951), Amaigbo (1955), Umuna (1955), Owerri (1959). In time, too, girls' teacher training colleges, secondary schools, and domestic science centers were established. The earliest colleges included Mount Carmel Teacher Training College, Emekuku; Immaculate Heart College, Umuokirika; Girls' Teacher Training College (TTC), Uboma; Holy Rosary TTC, Umuahia; Domestic Science Center, Ehime; St. Joseph's TTC, Aba; and Owerri Girls' Secondary School, Owerri. Although the Irish Sisters of the Holy Rosary dominated girls' Catholic institutions, they were not the only female religious orders. For example, by 1937 the Congregation of the Immaculate Heart Sisters had been founded, the first indigenous religious order for women in Eastern Nigeria. It was this order that took over the management of many of the girls' Catholic institutions after the Nigerian Civil War, following the expulsion of expatriate missionaries from the then East Central State in 1970. With the coming of the Irish Sisters and the opening of girls' schools, the Roman Catholic drive for influence had indeed received added momentum.

In addition to the foregoing, mention should be made of the internal problems that faced the CMS between 1912 and 1915, which helped the Roman Catholics to strike forcefully into Anglican strongholds. By 1912 the CMS Niger Mission as a whole was in dire financial straits. It also suffered from shortage of staff, both European and African. For the Egbu mission in particular the shortage of funds and staff was rather critical. Just at the time that the Catholics were "intruding" everywhere, the CMS missionaries lacked the human resources to occupy the scores of new stations that had been opened. Requests to the CMS authorities for assistance failed. Not only were the missionaries told that funds and staff were unavailable, but also they were strongly advised to curtail expansion schemes.[49] Because the CMS was also contemplating handing the Egbu mission to the Niger Delta Pastorate (an arm of the CMS), future expansion was not to be attempted until the issue was settled.

When the negotiations about the transfer of Egbu mission to the NDP failed in 1914, authorization was finally given to expansion schemes. Yet, shortage of human resources continued to limit the growth of the mission, and by 1915 the problem had assumed crisis proportions. Many churches remained for a long time without teachers. To the Protestant missionaries things seemed "to be going backward rather than forward," and there was even serious thought about abandoning several stations for lack of progress and shortage of staff. In a number of stations there were reports that "class members have lapsed to the Romanists." Indeed, "the dark clouds of 1915" hung heavily over both the local missionaries and the London authorities. "The crying need of workers overlies all other questions of policy," declared the CMS secretary in London, "and weighs like a never-ending nightmare upon the Committee." Interestingly enough, Father Shanahan faced a similar crisis, as reflected in this hyperbolic statement, following his futile appeal to Rome in 1912.

> I shall never forget the feeling that crept through my soul like paralysis as I came to the conclusion that human help for my mission was not forthcoming. I thought of the millions of thrones that would remain unoccupied in heaven for ever because of the pitiable inadequacy of human instruments. Yet one had to bow before the inscrutable wisdom of God. I know his voice was coming to me through His Vicar on Earth. Even if my journey to Europe was a ghastly failure to all appearances, could not God look after His black children in some way best known to Himself . . . ?[50]

Despite his frustration and evident soreness of heart, the indomitable Shanahan urged his priests to pursue the expansion scheme with relentless resolve. At Emekuku, Father Walsh, said to be one of the "best and well-trained missionaries," accepted the challenge with great enthusiasm and zeal. The result was that the RCM made dramatic gains in several directions, particularly in the Orlu-Nsu-Etiti zones as well as in the Mbaitoli areas, thanks in part to Protestant internal problems and local dissensions. In places like Agbaghara Nsu, Umudim (Nkwerre/Isu), Umunoha, Ǫgwa,

Mbieri, and Ugiri (in Mbano), to mention but a few, local disagreements among CMS members or with local political authorities led to mass defections to the RCM. The dramatic defection of Protestants to Roman Catholicism at Urualla in Orlu, recounted in a recent study by Dr. Isaac D. E. Anyabuike, is interesting and deserves quoting at some length.

> In Urualla Ideator area of Orlu in 1921 there was a cultural wrestling match. The C.M.S. church teacher (agent in charge) was Hezekiah Uzoodu of Umunya [sic]. He refused that any of his members would participate in what he called a heathen festival but many members including the Church Committee attended the wrestling match. The agent reported the matter to the then Superintendent Reverend James E. Ibeneme. The pastor ordered all members of the Committee to be flogged by his Clerk (Moses). This was an unprecedented type of humiliation. The affected members including Matthias Umealukwu, Joseph Isuatu, Jone [sic] Uduji, Abraham Nwangwu and the others deflected [sic] from the C.M.S. to St. John's Roman Catholic Church.[51]

Another example at Akokwa, also in Orlu, revolved around local politics and apparent Roman Catholic benevolence. To quote Dr. Anyabuike once more: "The Roman Catholic Mission in Akokwa was a reaction against the C.M.S. because the C.M.S. could not concede leadership to some members like George Njaka. Njaka and his group went to Adazi and Father Bindorf [Bubendorf] allowed them the establishment of a Catholic mission in 1922. The Reverend Father made house to house visits preaching and blessing and giving out presents such as medals, chaplets, heads of tobacco, clothes and a kind of wine then known as 'njenje'[gin]. Very many influential people . . . became enticed by the Rev. Father's goodwill and became members of the Church."[52]

INTERDENOMINATIONAL CONFLICTS

As noted earlier, the coming of the various missionary societies stirred interdenominational jealousies and bitter strife. Protestants of different denominations quarrelled among themselves, each aspiring to undermine the influence of the other so as to appear more influential. In several places this interdenominational struggle for dominance bred an atmosphere of intolerance leading to occasional fights among the different Christian adherents. At Naze, Obinze, Ife, and Itu (the last two in Mbaise), as well as in many other places, there were reports of violence being perpetrated against rival missions. At Naze, for example, the few Roman Catholic adherents were attacked in 1913 by the Protestants who objected to the Roman Catholic presence in the town. In Obinze too, where the CMS preceded the other sects, trouble erupted when the Baptist mission from the delta arrived around 1915. The Baptist propagandists were beaten up by the Anglicans and chased out of the town, only to return a few years later. Thereafter the Baptist mission became a factor to reckon with in the modern development of Obinze. For in 1942 the Reverend Amakiri of the Baptist Mission at Buguma opened the first standard four school (equivalent to fourth grade in the United States) in the town. From a purely local perspective, this was significant because Obinze people had sought for some time to have a standard four school in the town; but neither the CMS nor the RCM was in a position to satisfy the people's desire. Prior to the opening of this school, Obinze children attended the CMS school at Avu, but Avu people are said to have constantly harassed and at times molested Obinze pupils. So the establishment of a standard four school here tended to free Obinze school children from the harassment of their neighbor, Avu. Some years later, the school was raised to standard six, thereby raising the social status of Obinze vis-à-vis its neighbors. About 1963 the Baptists, under the sponsorship of the American Baptist Mission, established a girls' teacher training college which since 1970 has been converted to a girls' secondary school.[53]

There was, of course, as a Protestant missionary once said, "occasional ebullition of ill feeling between the Roman Catholics and our people" elsewhere in the Owerri District. Commenting in 1919 on this "lack of Christian spirit" among the missionary societies, the local district officer observed: "It is unfortunate that the Church of England and the Roman Catholic Mission are antagonistic competitors who are both expanding with undue haste merely in order to stake out claims in every village even although [*sic*] they have neither the European or [*sic*] native Staffs available to adequately instruct or guide their great flocks of nominal adherents and pupils of all ages."[54] Nowhere perhaps was this interdenominational conflict more pronounced than in the Mbaise and Ikeduru clans, as the Catholic-Protestant controversy in Ife, Atta, and Itu would suggest. This conflict, which attracted the attention of the district officer at Owerri as well as of the resident, first erupted at Ife in 1933. The root of the conflict was the apparent intrusion of the Roman Catholics at Ife, a town which the Anglicans considered their exclusive domain. In 1932 the Roman Catholic Mission established a church at Ife, a CMS stronghold since 1913. This Catholic presence outraged the local Protestants. The defection of former Protestants to Roman Catholicism further aggravated the already-strained relations between the two groups. Attempts were thus made by the Protestants to liquidate the Catholic presence in the town, a move that had as its pretext the punishment of a few Catholics alleged to have committed social and commercial offenses in the town.

At Ife, there were some Catholic boys from Nguru, Ahiara, and Ezinihitte who were employed by traders from Okrika. These boys were alleged to have "defiled" Ife women and to have also cheated them "in the prices of produce." They were also accused of maliciously destroying raffia palms (*ngwọ*) belonging to Ife people. Under pressure from the Protestants and Ife elders, the Okrika traders dismissed the boys from their service. Determined of course to remove the Catholic incubus from Ife, the Protestants induced the elders to expel the so-called stranger Catholics from Ife.[55]

The expulsion of the Catholics from Ife aroused the anger of the Roman Catholic priest at Emekuku, the Reverend Father R. Foreman. Moreover, the action infuriated Ezinihitte, Nguru, and Ahiara people. As they sought ways to retaliate, Father Foreman was consulted, and he allegedly suggested that the three towns involved should henceforth boycott Ife market, the intention being to cripple the Ife produce market. Thus, instead of trading at Ife, the people of Nguru, Ahiara, and Ezinihitte opened their own produce markets at Ogbor Nguru, Umunama, and Itu respectively. Father Foreman is said in fact to have pressured personally the United African Company (UAC) at Umuahia to open the produce market at Umunama Ahiara.[56]

Because of the organized boycott and the consequent decline of Ife market, Ife elders referred the matter to the district officer, E. H. C. Dickenson. When the DO brought the matter to Father Foreman's attention, the latter strongly defended the action taken against Ife. "The hasty dismissal of these boys," he wrote to the DO, "was an insult" to Nguru, Ahiara, and Ezinihitte, "and . . . their passive resistance to such an act was a just retaliation, well merited by Ife town." He further informed the DO that he could not understand why the Protestants at Ife should harass Roman Catholics, whereas "In Nguru, Ahiara, Amuzi and Ekwereazu, there are C.M.S. churches which have never been troubled, although . . . the Catholic party holds certainly a very large majority" in these places. Furthermore, he directed the DO's attention to the seething Catholic and Protestant animosity in the area.[57]

According to Father Foreman, both Catholic and Protestant members in the Mbaise clan held regular secret meetings at which strategies were planned to deal with the opponents. As a result of this sectarian intolerance, violence often erupted between the two forces. In an attempt to quell the disturbances that often ensued, Father Foreman claimed to have advised the Roman Catholics not to hold any more private strategy meetings. But, said Father Foreman, while the Catholics had stopped holding such meetings, the Protestants continued to do so. In a letter to the DO on

November 12, 1933 Father Foreman stated: "I have just returned from Nguru this morning, where I was beseiged by crowds of our members. Nguru and Ahiara seem to be upset because I have ordered them to a no meeting diet, whereas the other side are [*sic*] still allowed to hold their own meetings, plotting and planning ways and means, fair or foul, as to how they can do the Catholics in." He then asked the DO whether in the interest of fairness the Catholics should desist from holding meetings while their adversaries continued to do so. He also alleged that Roman Catholics were being denied justice at the Itu Native Court because of the malice of the Protestant court clerk. In some cases, he insisted, even the police, who were Protestants, cooperated with the court clerk in prosecuting Roman Catholics unjustly. In support of his allegation, he cited a recent land case at the Ahiara court involving the people of Ogwuama. According to Father Foreman, the court clerk, evidently out of sheer prejudice, overruled the decision of the court favoring Ogwuama Catholics. In the light of these events, said Father Foreman, "the feeling as regards both Itu and Ahiara Court[s] is that no Catholics ought ever to present himself [*sic*] there as he is sure to find himself on the wrong side. This is certainly not a level state of affairs."[58]

Father Foreman's anger at the Protestants may be further appreciated from the tone of his letters to the district officer. As the Catholic and Protestant controversy continued, some eight Roman Catholic youths were accused of molesting people on the road to Ife. Action was brought against them at the Itu court. Once again, Father Foreman was irritated upon hearing of the incident and so sought to intervene on their behalf. In his letter to Dickenson, he claimed that the Protestants were determined to bring harm to his followers. "It appears that when you came to Itu last week, all the C.M.S. were at the Court including the Pastor and Teachers. When I asked in Nguru this morning why our people did not go, I was told I myself prevented them by my ordering them not to cause trouble. No doubt had they gone, there would have been a disturbance." When the case was tried at the Itu court, the Catholic youths were found guilty. But since the DO was satisfied that the boys' alleged misconduct was not "very grave,"[59] they were simply bound over on their own recognizance and asked "to keep the Peace for six months," that is, to be on good behavior.

Father Foreman remained indignant. He alleged that the court clerk and other Protestants had actually conspired against the Catholics and so "raked up" false allegations against them. This point was sharply disputed by the DO, who felt that the Catholic priest was undoubtedly "misguided" in his suggestion. "I cannot accept his suggestion," the DO explained to the resident, "that the case against the eight boys was a conspiracy organized by the Court Clerk at Itu, as the finding of the Court refutes this." He went on to say, "I have seen the Court Clerk who tells me that he has only once been to Ife in the past two months, and that was to attend a Communion service. This may or may not be so, but I have heard no evidence to support Father Foreman's hearsay allegation, that the Clerk presided at an anti-Catholic meeting. I have, however, warned the Clerk that he must take no part whatsoever in any party meeting or discussion on the subject."[60]

Whatever assurances of fairplay the DO might have given him, Father Foreman remained indignant, believing that his Catholic members had been unjustly treated perhaps because of their apparent passivity. Consequently he felt the Roman Catholics should henceforth confront their adversaries no matter what the consequences: "Since things are going as they are, I am sorry, but I am not going to hold such a restraining influence on our people, which is lessening my authority in Ahiara and Nguru."[61]

It does not appear there was any further serious disturbance at Ife or at any other station, obviously because of the intervention of the district officer. When he later visited the area, he warned both Christians and non-Christians that any one found guilty of illegal action would be severely punished in the court. He also appealed to both the Catholic and Protestant authorities to eschew religious bitterness and intolerance inasmuch as the government's policy on religion was one of "complete toleration." And he warned that any further disturbances in Ife or elsewhere which stemmed from religious antagonism would never be countenanced. His stern warnings seem to have contributed to the lessening of tensions. In fact, he claimed that both the Protestant bishop and Father Foreman had assured him that they would cooperate in bringing about better relations between their two missions. In conclusion, he informed the resident that there was no more cause for anxiety: "At present the situation appears satisfactory, and for the past ten days there have been no further reports of lawlessness. Father Foreman has stated that he has now no object in establishing a Church at Ife, and there is no more open hostility between the Missions. But Nguru and Ahiara respectively, who had boys driven out of Ife, still nurse considerable resentment, and it is unlikely that their people will again trade at Ife for some time."[62]

The Catholic-Protestant rivalry and antagonism invariably spilled over into Mbaise social and political life. In other words, religious affiliations promoted social discord and thus strained clan or intergroup relationships—hence the appeal from progressive Mbaise elements to eschew denominational prejudice and hatred. Sectarian conflicts, writes Professor D. Ibe Nwoga, have for so long militated against political unity and social progress of Mbaise. And he adds, "If we do not unite because of, or in spite of, our religious inclinations, we will be swept aside in the wave of national forward progression."[63] Similarly Dr. Cletus E. Emezi has raised the alarm of denominational discord undermining social and political development in his hometown, Awaka.[64] Indeed, religious differences have almost irreparably undermined the social and political cohesion of practically all Nigerian societies.

As in the Mbaise case, religious rivalry promoted social and political disunity in the Ikeduru clan. Of particular interest were the religious conflicts between the Anglicans and the Catholics in Ugiri and Amaimo in 1937. This is how the DO reported the events there.

> It is deplorable that rivalry between the Church Missionary Society and the Roman Catholic Mission has been the cause of several displays of anything but Christian spirit. In the Ikeduru area visits to Amaimo in November were made by Administrative Officers in an attempt to preserve peace. There was much bickering in November and December though actual blows were not resorted to between people of that village [*sic*] and Ugiri. Church Missionary Society Christians of Ugiri who wished to obstruct the Roman Catholic Members of Amaimo from building a Church in Amaimo, managed to stir the townspeople of Ugiri into a land dispute frame of mind, and got them to say that people from Amaimo should not collect sand for their building from the stream near Ugiri.[65]

Catholic-Protestant conflicts also erupted at Atta in 1935, again because of outright jealousy and intolerance of religious coexistence. According to official accounts, the CMS-RCM dispute began here when the Catholic mission established "a large compound on one side of the motor road" opposite the CMS compound "and put up some substantial buildings" there. Afraid of being overshadowed, the Protestants reportedly laid claim to the land, arguing that because it did not belong to the Roman Catholics they had no right to build on the site. Heated verbal arguments lead to physical violence between the two forces which ultimately resulted in another long-drawn litigation in the native and magistrate courts.[66] Although neither court nor oral evidence is available, we may assume that the case was resolved in RCM's favor, since the building was not abandoned.

Similar sectarian conflicts were reported in several other places including Eziama Ikeduru and Amaeze in the Owerri court area. At both places, the Roman Catholics seem to have been the culprits. In the Eziama case, for instance, the district officer reported:

> The Church Missionary Society members are not the only ones who cause trouble. At the Eziama quarter of Oparanadim where the Church Missionary Society was earlier established, a fight took place on the 19th of May [1937] between the members of the two Missions in which 5 or 6 [persons] were badly wounded and taken to Owerri Hospital in an Ambulance. The matter was investigated by Mr. O. V. Lee, Assistant District Officer, who found that the Roman Catholic Mis-

sion members had been endeavouring to establish themselves at Eziama by use of "shock tactics," in spite of the fact that they already had a Church only a mile away.

And at Amaeze it was reported that in February 1937 "the Roman Catholic Mission members tried to seize the property of people of that village who refused to subscribe to their school." Resistance ensued, resulting once more in physical fighting and legal action. About thirty-one people were subsequently prosecuted in court for fighting. The majority of them were fined £2 each for the breach of peace. "There were also other petty disputes between members of these two Missionary bodies which did not give rise to fights," concluded the DO.[67]

COMPETITIVE CONVERSIONS

Clearly, competition and rivalry coupled with occasional outbursts of violence characterized Roman Catholic and Protestant relations in the Owerri Division. By the 1950s the struggle for dominance had reached its zenith as each mission desperately sought to maximize its gains. The ensuing struggle—indeed, scramble for "souls"—led to a spectacular rise in what might be called the new rural conversion of the mid-1950s.

To secure as many converts as possible each mission adopted practical and aggressive strategies, including the relaxation of church rules regarding baptism. The Catholics, for example, mobilized the Legion of Mary Society as an active evangelistic organ. By 1956 there were no less than 370 presidia in the Owerri diocese with a membership of over six thousand. This was a formidable proselytizing force indeed. In village after village one found members of the Legion of Mary, mostly women, teaching children, men, and women the basic doctrines and prayers of the Catholic church. Baptisms followed after a short period of instruction. In fact, many of these converts had very little grasp of the essence of Christianity, partly because of the hasty baptisms. Consequently, in times of crises when prayers to the Christian God failed to achieve their purpose, disenchantment with Christianity prevailed and, as Father A. Aghaizu once put it, "the fragile faith goes to bits"—a second conversion became necessary. Nevertheless, the contribution of the Legion of Mary in rural conversion was significant.[68]

The CMS on their part mobilized the student evangelists, whose white uniforms and canvas shoes provided an interesting spectacle. Sunday after Sunday, they poured into the villages and attracted instant attention by their melodious songs. Prayers were followed with Bible reading and explanations. How many converts were secured thereafter is hard to say. But judging from the number of anxious inquirers—and they were considerable—it can be said that many were indeed baptized. To make things easier, the CMS at this time relaxed its rules requiring catechumens to have a reading knowledge of the Bible prior to their being baptized. This requirement generally delayed many converts. At this time of competitive conversion, relaxation of the rules paid off handsomely.

Details of the new upsurge in rural conversions remain to be systematically investigated. However, two factors seem to have been crucial: first, missionary disenchantment with Christians in the urban centers; and second, the concern of the missions about the new education policy adopted by the East Regional Government. We can only treat these issues rather superficially for lack of sufficient data.

With respect to the urban question, it should be pointed out that by 1914 the growth of the new colonial townships had spurred vigorous missionary activity in these centers. The rural migration into the townships actually helped to stimulate the missionary enterprise there. But by the 1920s and 1930s disillusionment set in because of rapid social change. No longer viewing the townships as beachheads of civiliation, the Christian missionaries began to see them as the "hotbeds of corruption" characterized by promiscuous life-styles. According to the Catholic hierarchy, the townships had become deplorable centers for the "wholesome perversion of baptized school boys" and girls. It was this alleged moral decay in the cities that prompted the warning to Catholic priests to take "exceptional care" before admitting young men to the sacrament of baptism "in all of [these] corrupt centres."[69]

Official Roman Catholic attitude toward this problem is reflected in a 1924 circular: "There is serious reason for entertaining the gravest doubts about the good intentions of boys living in . . . townships," thus warning Catholic priests in the townships against indiscriminate admission of boys and girls to the church. Consequently, it seemed prudent to redirect missionary energies to the rural areas where, according to the Catholic hierarchy, "the dangers of perversion . . . are sufficiently remote."[70] As the Protestants adopted a similar rural policy, the feverish stampede for the souls of the African villagers became inevitable.

But there were equally interesting political underpinnings to the competitive conversions of the 1950s. Just as the social changes in the townships had spurred missionary response, so also did changes in the political sphere bestir the missions to action. In Nigeria generally and Eastern Nigeria in particular the 1950s were the years of political ferment. The African quest for a new "political kingdom" and cultural autonomy tended to frighten the

European missionaries. In Eastern Nigeria, for example, where the nationalist elite sought the reorganization of society via a new education system,
the missionaries interpreted nationalist sentiments as antichurch movements—or worse, secularization of society. Thus arose the aggressive missionary crusade in the rural areas, ostensibly to "proclaim the Word." In
the words of the Reverend John V. Taylor, "At a time when men are mov-
ing into deep tides of emotion, grappling with complicated problems in the
midst of rising tensions, and laying out the foundations of future nations,
the Church is more than ever needed to proclaim the Word . . . to dem-
onstrate the embracing fellowship for the healing of nations."[71] But for all
practical purposes the new religious movement appeared to be a crusade
against nationalist aspirations.

For the Nigerian nationalist leaders, a revamped educational system offered the best insurance for economic and national development. Hence in
the Eastern Region, where by 1954 the indigenous political elite had taken
control of education, a revitalized educational system was seen as "the
mainspring of all national action." The government therefore sought to
reduce the heavy influence of religion on education, as explicitly stated in
the 1956 education law: "We shall, if we deem it necessary, introduce legislation to ensure that no child is penalized in any way on religious grounds,
and that the religious atmosphere of all assisted schools is free and comfortable to all."[72] Moreover, greater emphasis was to be placed on science and
vocational education. The impending nationalization of schools (viewed
by the churches as secularization), "the curtailing of our rights to open new
schools" (in Father Jordan's words), the de-emphasis of religion in schools,
and other issues that fall outside the scope of this study precipitated what
Father Jordan has characterized as "serious differences" between church
and state during the 1950s. Not only did the missions collectively oppose
the new education laws, but also they loudly decried the "diminution of
missionary influence" in education—hence the campaign to win new allies
through rural conversions. It was in fact the mobilization of a strong
"Christian" opinion against the alleged secularization policy of the
nationalist leaders that resulted in the humiliating defeat of the minister for
education at the elections in 1957. Thus the church-state conflicts of the
1950s and early 1960s foreshadowed the nationalization of schools in Nigeria after the civil war, a measure the missions have continued to resist.[73]

5. EDUCATION AND SOCIETY

E ducation is regarded today as the most effective instrument for social and economic development. For this reason African governments, including that in Nigeria, have invested a great deal of their income in all branches of education. In Imo State, where the education revolution has now taken a firm hold, schools and colleges today absorb a large proportion of the state's expenditure. It is estimated (1979) that about 40 percent of the state's income is devoted to education. Without a doubt state governments as well as communities have now fully recognized the importance and necessity of Western education. For individuals and communities, it provides a way of escape from chronic poverty and underdevelopment. "Without education," an elder told me recently, "we shall remain in darkness all our lives." Another informant put it in more practical terms: "Unless we educate our boys and girls we cannot free ourselves from the grip of poverty. It is through education that we shall ensure our self-improvement. A town without schools is nothing."[1] It is no wonder that schools have mushroomed everywhere in Imo State. Here, for instance, primary school enrollment has risen sharply since the end of the Nigerian Civil War (1970). According to 1979 figures, there are about 1.2 million schoolchildren enrolled in the 1,925 primary schools in the state. Secondary school attendance is even larger. Over two million students are now attending secondary schools.[2]

The recognition of education as a factor in national development is not really new. Many Igbo communities seem to have been aware of this since the turn of the nineteenth century.[3] And by the early decades of this century many communities in the Owerri area certainly had appreciated the advantages of Western education. Consequently, as we shall see in this chapter, Owerri chiefs and elders responded enthusiastically to government proposals to establish a school in the town.

THE OWERRI GOVERNMENT SCHOOL

The first primary school in Owerri was founded in 1905 by the British colonial government. As noted earlier, Governor Egerton visited Owerri from April 12 to 14, 1905. After his routine inspection of the facilities at the headquarters and "a most delightful bath" at the Nworie River, the governor held a meeting with some Owerri chiefs. At this meeting he proposed the opening of a primary school in the town. The overture was welcomed enthusiastically by the chiefs and elders, and their interest was actually followed by action. The governor was assured that a schoolhouse would be built and that a house would also be provided for the schoolmaster. Given the genuine interest exhibited by the chiefs and the firm assurance of local support, the governor therefore recommended that a government school should be built at Owerri without undue delay: "There should be a Government School at Owerri. The population is large and the children are unusually intelligent and willing to learn. A large number of them are employed on the station as servants to the Europeans and the native soldiers."[4]

Work on the school commenced shortly thereafter, and on December 14, 1905 it was officially opened. It would have started much earlier but for the lack of a qualified schoolteacher. By the time it was opened, an African from the Gold Coast (Ghana) had been employed as the first headmaster of the school. So, with an initial enrollment of about sixty boys, the first primary school in Owerri thus came into being. Owerri was now among the few places in Southern Nigeria where a government school had been founded by 1905.

Like others elsewhere the school was designed for the sons of chiefs. According to Lord Frederick Lugard, the first governor-general of Nigeria, the main objective of these government schools was "to train boys to meet the demand for government clerks and junior employees," even though they were not to be excluded from taking employment with commercial firms.[5] Accordingly, emphasis was placed on teaching reading, writing, and arithmetic. Other parts of the curriculum included English language, nature study, hygiene, sanitation, and manual labor, with special attention given to moral and character training. For a long time, the school remained closed to girls. It is not immediately clear from the records when girls were first admitted, but 3 girls are reported to have been at the school in 1917. By 1923 the number had risen to 17 out of a total school population of 298. Gradually female presence at the school increased as did the overall school enrollment. There were 252 boys and 58 girls in 1934; 270 boys and 60 girls in 1935; 270 boys and 51 girls in 1936. By 1938, when the school was raised to the status of a middle school, there were about 400 schoolchildren and 16 teachers.

We do not know for sure who the early pupils at the school were. Nor is it clear who the first girls were. But it is clear from the scanty statistics available to us that girls were conspicuously absent during the early phase of formal schooling in the area. As for the boys, some of the prominent men in Owerri who held important government jobs attended the government school. Some even continued their studies at another government school at Bonny and elsewhere. Johnson Osuji Njemanze, for example, who rose to the position of inspector of police, attended the Owerri Government School and later at Bonny Government School. Chief Amadi Obi of Emekuku was also a graduate of the Owerri school, as were Sydney O. Akalonu of Ulakwo and Johnson Okoro of Egbu. These were, of course, sons of chiefs, who later rose to prominence. As a police officer, J. O. Njemanze was a highly respected man. He was often commended for his zeal, courage, and intelligence. During the 1914 insurrection at Obrette in the former Aba Division, where British forces were overwhelmed by local forces, Inspector Njemanze (No. 267) was specially commended for his bravery and for thwarting the strategies of the rebels. In recognition of his outstanding performance at Obrette, he was awarded the King's Police Medal in 1916. When his father died in 1920, he was asked to succeed him, but he refused, preferring his police work to chieftaincy. Later, however, he was appointed chief and remained as such until his death in 1965. Chief Amadi Obi also had a distinguished career. He served as a native court clerk from 1915 to 1935. Upon his retirement, he succeeded his father as the chief of Emekuku, a position he held until 1978.[6]

With respect to the Owerri Government School, it is important to stress that it was very popular right from its inception. It was supported morally and financially by the chiefs and others. Chiefs are said to have contributed the amount of £48 for general administrative expenses when the school first opened. School fees yielded another £21:17:6½d. In later years the financial burden devolved on the Owerri Native Administration. So even though the government was instrumental in the establishment of the school, it was neither free nor was it in any way supported with funds from England. On the contrary, the local people bore the responsibility of maintaining the school by providing labor and funds. As a rule, the government insisted on the payment of fees by the pupils, and in some cases school fees had to be paid in advance. According to the government directive, "Where there is failure to pay the pupil shall be excluded from school." School managers and inspectors were instructed to carry out the order as strictly as possible.[7] Of course, similar practices obtained in mission schools.

THE IMPACT OF "STRANGERS" ON EDUCATION

It is rather ironic that nearly everywhere in Nigeria, and in Igboland in particular, European colonial rule was hated. Yet when it came to the question of Western education, chiefs and their people were enthusiastic—in fact, eager—to send their sons to school. As the district officer at Owerri said in 1919, chiefs welcomed proposals for schools partly because having a school in their particular villages not only enhanced their authority, but also brought pride and prestige to the village.[8] But our interest here is to determine why chiefs and elders at Owerri welcomed the proposal to have a school in the town in 1905. This is not an easy task since the recorded evidence is scarce. However, it is well to remember that apart from the few Europeans at Owerri there were many Africans from different countries. There were, for example, traders and government employees from the Gold Coast (Ghana), Sierra Leone, the West Indies, Bonny, Onitsha, and Yorubaland. All these were strangers. By reason of their rudimentary education, they tended to assume airs of superiority over the local people. Besides, both the court clerk (Isaiah Yellow) and the interpreter (Samuel Jumbo) are said to have often "ill-treated some chiefs." These two officials in particular were accused of being arrogant, irritatingly imperious, and overbearing. And like their counterparts elsewhere, they were corrupt and exploitative. The court clerk, for example, is said to have at times flogged some chiefs and imposed fines on people without due process of law. In essence, the strangers used their positions, derived from Western education, to exploit the local people. Agonized by these flagrant cases of extortion and abuse of power, the chiefs and elders sought ways and means of ending their colonial subordination. Realizing that education gave the strangers considerable advantage over them, they became eager to have a school where their own children would be educated and "in days to come" perhaps replace the strangers. Their replacement, it was hoped, would remove the tyranny of fellow Africans. Seen from this context, education was thus perceived as a vital weapon of liberation from colonial oppression.[9]

Yet there were other interrelated sets of forces that catalyzed interest in education. Once again, the court clerk and the interpreter provided some stimulus. In the new colonial order, both the court clerk and the interpreter wielded considerable influence in the society. Besides, they were looked upon as rich and powerful, the source of their supposed wealth and power deriving from their education, especially their knowledge of the English language. Given their relative wealth and power vis-à-vis the local people, it seemed natural enough that parents would see them as symbols of the new age. If their sons were sent to school, it was possible that they too would become rich and powerful like the court clerk and the interpreter. Bishop Shanahan reinforced this when he wrote:

> The black interpreter was able to make big money because he had learnt enough books to speak English; the black court clerk could juggle with their cases without interference, for he could write what suited him and not what they wanted him to write. And would it not be better for them [parents] to stop wasting their money in bribing the interpreter and the clerk in the hope of winning their cases? Why not use the money to build a school and pay a teacher in their towns? Then one day their own children would know enough to be interpreters and clerks and police men and court messengers. They would [no longer] be at the mercy of . . . outsiders.[10]

It is interesting to note that similar circumstances elsewhere provoked almost identical responses. At Ohaffia, for example, the catalyst for bringing in a mission school was a series of unpopular court clerks who ill-treated the people. The court clerk at Elu, Mr. Vincent (alias "Ajagharigwe"), was particularly oppressive. And so to remove the immediate tyranny, Ohaffia responded in Igbo pragmatic fashion. Here is the story as told by Eke Kalu, "a man of consequence in Ohaffia," but formerly a slave at Bonny.

> There was one C.N.C. [clerk of the native court], a Sierra Leonean, by name Vincent. He very much ill-treated the Ohaffia people. On one occasion he locked several of them in the prison yard for a very trivial cause. They broke out from the prison and were intent upon beating the C.N.C. when the latter instantly reported the situation to Major Cobham, who very quickly despatched a posse of policemen to his rescue. Much was the fine imposed upon the culprits. After this experience the Ohaffia people appealed to me for a way out of such torture occasioned by fellow blackman. I therefore began to lecture them on the necessity of educating their [own] children by establishing and supporting schools.[11]

A delegation was thereafter sent to the Presbyterian mission about 1908 to establish a school at Elu. In 1910, one Onuoha Kalu of Abiriba, who had been a student at the Hope Waddell Institute, started the first church-school in the town.

CHIEFS AND EDUCATION

For many years the Owerri Government School at Owerri was plagued with shortage of staff and inadequate accommodations. Repeated appeals for expansion received little or no action. But when the governor visited Owerri in 1925 a delegation of chiefs, businessmen, and others demanded, among other things, that the school should be expanded in order to accommodate as many children as possible. Of concern to them also was the shortage in teaching staff, which they said should be augmented to ensure better education for the children. Moreover, they pleaded that the government should provide clerical employment to the school graduates. And in view of the declining employment opportunities in this area, the government was asked to add a technical branch to the school to provide technical and vocational training for the boys. In essence, the petitioners called upon the government to adjust its education policies to changing times and the needs of the society.

Of equal concern to the people was the apparent low standard of education at the school, which they claimed was responsible for the high rate of failures in the government clerical examination. Finally, an appeal was made for a secondary school. To impress upon the governor the necessity for such an institution here, the petitioners remarked that the absence of a secondary school at Owerri had forced parents from the area to send their sons to either Onitsha (Dennis Memorial Grammar School, founded 1925) or to Calabar (Hope Waddell Institute) for secondary education. This, they contended, was "inconvenient for the boys" and for the parents as well.[12]

In his reply, the governor flatly refused any consideration for a secondary school at Owerri: "SECONDARY SCHOOLS cost a great deal of money. At present there are only three Secondary Schools in the Southern Provinces of Nigeria, namely, Calabar, Lagos and Onitsha. There are places much further away from Onitsha than this place which have no Secondary Schools. It is not possible for every single place to have its own Secondary School." With respect to the quality of education and unemployment, the governor remarked, "It is not possible always to provide employment for SCHOOL CHILDREN. Any boy who wants to get into the Government Service has got to pass a Government Examination if they wish to do so, but I should like to see school boys go back to their farms and work—they cannot all be clerks." On the other requests, the governor remained silent. Sensing evidently that the petitioners were not satisfied with his replies, he concluded, "I have nothing more to say [to you]. Your grievances will always be attended to by the District Officer and the Resident."[13]

The governor's comment that schoolboys "cannot all be clerks" was echoed by other officials who wanted to dramatize the need for agricultural or vocational education. In an ideal situation, this makes some sense. But given the administration's pattern of employment at the time, it is difficult to see how farming as an occupation could have attracted the educated young men. For example, the government laid great emphasis on the training and hiring of clerks and paid higher salaries to those employed in clerical positions than to their counterparts in other occupations. Nor was farming actually regarded as a respectable occupation. Therefore as long as the government's reward system benefited those who held clerical jobs, it seemed nonsensical for the government to extol the dignity of labor and the virtues of vocational education. Besides, the exponents of the dignity of labor philosophy failed miserably to exemplify such attitudes in their own lives. Not until equal recognition was given to those in clerical and agricultural fields did agriculture as a field of study appeal to students.

When in the early 1960s there were proposals to establish farm settlements in the Eastern Region of Nigeria, it was suggested that standard six boys (primary school graduates) should be used at the settlements. There were objections from certain quarters. H. C. Swaisland, senior district officer and principal at the Institute of Administration in Enugu in 1961, believed, "If we really want to help agriculture through settlements we can only do so by recruiting those in their late-twenties and thirties who never left the village, who now have families and have no Standard 6 education. These are real farmers, and the mild dose of urbanization that can be reproduced in a settlement (e.g., a piped-water supply, better houses, better shops and, say a fortnightly mobile cinema show) will seem to them a real gain." Citing the case of English farmers, Swaisland went on: "The farm 'labourer' . . . has more satisfaction as a machine technician in mechanized farming—and therefore more status; he also has electricity and piped-water and a television set. He has most of what the town dweller has, without the panic rush each morning for the 8:15 to town."[14] For reasons which fall outside the purview of this study, the farm settlement scheme hardly went beyond the planning stage.

Let us return to the story of the government school. From about 1937 the government school at Owerri began to show signs of improvement. By then the enrollment had risen to over three hundred and the staff increased to about fifteen. It was in this year too that science subjects were first introduced and a laboratory was provided. Moreover, vocational education (carpentry) was provided. Above all, the school was elevated to class four status. The initial intake for the class was twelve. Local interest in the affairs of the school remained high. Parents generally attended school shows and commended the dramatic skill of the pupils. Government officials did so too, as we learn from the DO at Owerri: "Not the least praise-worthy is the scholar's dramatic skill, and the writer for one was particularly delighted not only to see at a school concert that the scholars dramatized superbly some of their own native folktales, but that these items were by far the most popular with the parents in the audience."[15]

In 1938 a change of name occurred. The school then became known as

Owerri Government Middle School, a name which reflected its elevation to middle four. The school enrollment also increased to about four hundred and the teaching staff rose to sixteen. E. Nkune, the headmaster, was singularly praised as "a hard and conscientious worker" under whom much of the progress had taken place. Although many of the old problems remained, such as shortage of staff and inadequate accommodations, it was reported that the Owerri Native Administration which had assumed financial responsibility for the school was proving equal to the task. Said the DO, "There are now, on the school compound, three blocks of classrooms, eleven teachers' quarters, a dormitory for twenty-eight boys, a laboratory and a carpenter's shop. All these buildings have been provided . . . by the generosity of the Owerri Native Administration which proposed to add to them very considerably in the future." However, the DO added: "The principal need at the moment is a well-qualified teacher of English and it is hoped that an Education Officer can be stationed at Owerri for at least a few consecutive months next year." Prompt attention was given to these concerns as the report of the senior education officer for 1939 reveals:

> There have been no outstanding events in Owerri Division during the year other than those connected with the Government Middle School. There two events of importance occurred. In the first place it was found possible to post a European Officer to the School for a period of four months. As a result the tone, spirit and general organization of the school have shown a marked improvement. Secondly plans covering a three-year building extension scheme have received approval, and the first year's work has now commenced.[16]

By the 1940s the school had become a full-fledged secondary school and remained very popular.

THE MISSIONS AND EDUCATION

Had education been left to the government alone, very few people would have had the opportunity to receive Western education, as government school statistics clearly show. In the Igbo country as a whole there were only eleven government schools by 1931. Indeed, it was the coming of the Christian missionaries that led to the spread of formal education practically everywhere in Nigeria. It was they, in fact, who made education quite popular. "Without them," many villagers today concede, "we would have been in the dark." "Whatever else may be said about the missionaries," an old man in his late eighties remarked recently, "they showed us the light. It is because of them that we have made so much progress."[17] He may have exaggerated the case somewhat. But effusions such as these clearly indicate the high regard men and women have for the missions in relation to education.

Clearly, it was the missions that opened schools in practically every village in the division. They made education accessible to both the freeborn and the slave and thus introduced a new force that transformed the society. For it was education more than any other factor which by and large created new opportunities for social advancement as well as new forms of social differentiation. Education was clearly the decisive factor that led to the rise of the new African elite whose political, social, and economic influence has remained dominant ever since. Conversely, "the education revolution which created a new elite also created social inequality—or, more precisely, enormously magnified . . . incipient social inequalities."[18]

The earliest mission school was opened at Egbu in 1907. As was true of the church building here, the local people went to extraordinary lengths to provide not only a schoolhouse but also funds for the running of the school. Thus before it opened, young children desirous of attending school offered to do extra work in one form or another in order to secure funds to pay their school fees. Because the practice of going to school was still relatively new, there were a few boys at first, forty-three in all. Of these, thirty-four were of local origin while the others came from neighboring towns. Theo Okeke from Onitsha was appointed teacher at Egbu in 1908.

Both oral and written evidence indicates that schooling was not popular at the early stages, especially for girls, because of cultural and sexual prejudices. Traditionally, women were seen as being less intelligent and less responsible than men. Equally important were the traditional expectations for adult female roles, women being viewed largely as childbearers. Besides, women were not supposed to compete with or challenge men in a male-dominated society. Consequently, education of women was generally discouraged at the early stages of missionary enterprise. This traditional attitude is clearly reflected in the reply given to the early missionaries by a Calabar chief. "They can no saby book," remarked the chief in typical West African pidgin English. And he added, "Suppose they saby book, they saucy boy. It no fit they pass boy." However, because both the government and the missions viewed the education of women as crucial for social transformation, they promoted it enthusiastically, even though the education they conceived was more vocational than academic. The report of a special committee of the Protestant missions on women's education in 1910 made this abundantly clear.

There can be no question at all that the education of women is very grave, quite as important as the education of men, and that educational training is quite as important in the case of women teachers. . . . While higher education may be less necessary in the case of women than men, and while care should be exercised not to offend unnecessarily traditional feelings respecting the place of women in society, yet in all plans for Christian education, women ought to receive equal consideration with men, and equal care should be exercised that the education provided for them is adapted to their needs.

As for the boys, parents were vehemently opposed to sending their first sons (*ọpara*) to school because it was through the school that the young generation became alienated from their traditional society. And since ọparas were expected to succeed their fathers as political and religious leaders in the family, going to school and as a result being converted to Christianity were tantamout to turning one's back to tradition; "there would be no one left to conserve our customs and our cult to the ancestors."[19]

In later years, to be sure, many of these people have regretted the lost opportunity occasioned by parental opposition. "Had I been allowed to go to school," my uncle once said to me, "I would have perhaps been as great [rich and powerful] as some of the politicians." Yet some people are disturbed by the negative impact of education and Christianity. "The movement of the young to the mission orbit was the prelude to our cultural disorientation," one social critic observed. "Where are we today?" he asked. *"Nkwu achana ọmu. A nwanyi na lụnụ diya."* (The unusual has happened; women nowadays tend to dominate their husbands.) Nevertheless, there was a dramatic change of attitude toward Western education as people recognized the advantages inherent in the new system of education. At first, going to school was thought to be for the outcast, *"nde efulefu,"* to borrow an expression from Chinua Achebe. But as these so-called social misfits began to assume new roles in the society, and as the freeborn began to experience some kind of withdrawal of status respect, a new movement toward the mission orbit occurred.[20] The free and the slave were now in school together; the school revolution was now in motion.

The missionaries, on the other hand, intensified and refined their recruitment strategies. Free clothes, free meals, and toys were made available to the young boys for the primary purpose of attracting them to school. In addition, occasional parades through the towns and villages were organized, and these had the effect of enticing many more boys to school. The missionaries had recognized that their religious propaganda had little impact on the adults. The children, said one missionary, "are our hope," and the school the best instrument for penetrating the society. In the words of a Roman Catholic priest, "Once the children enter our schools we get a grip on them that lasts for years," and by careful manipulation "one can get the parents" as well.[21] The school therefore became a powerful instrument of conversion and social change.

For a long time the Egbu school was the premier Protestant school in the area. It grew from a small one-room school into a major central school. Its popularity was such that the boys came from as far away as Arochukwu to attend. Before the arrival of the Roman Catholics, practically all who went to mission school did so at Egbu. Even when village schools sprouted in several places, the Egbu Central School remained the most important Protestant educational institution in the area. The Egbu Central School was indeed the school which most Protestant boys and girls aspired to attend until the emergence of Emekuku school.

One characteristic feature of Egbu school, however, was the preponderant presence of Onitsha elements. In both church and school the teachers were mainly from Onitsha. Onitsha's early access to mission education had naturally given it a unique advantage over many other Igbo communities. While many of the teachers and catechists were undoubtedly excellent, some were unquestionably incompetent. The Reverend Fred G. Payne, a West Indian missionary at Egbu, complained bitterly in 1913 that the Anglican authorities at Onitsha had for a long time made the Egbu mission "a dumping ground for tired and otherwise undesirable teachers." Official neglect and the incompetence of many of the teachers, he said, were among the causes for the retarded progress of the mission. Another British missionary echoed his frustration and charged that many of the teachers sent to Egbu were in fact no smarter than the pupils.[22]

Another important mission school in the area was the Roman Catholic school at Emekuku. No sooner was the town occupied in 1912 and a permanent residence established in 1914 than a primary school was opened. Like Egbu it attracted boys from far and near. In fact, until very recently both schools were the most famous in the division. For reasons that will soon become apparent, the Roman Catholics tended to dominate the field of education here as well as across all of Igboland. Consider, for example, these few statistics selected at random. In 1919 the CMS had a total of 93 nonassisted primary (or elementary) schools in the division with an average attendance of 3,500.2. The government had 1 assisted (i.e., grant-aided) primary school with an average attendance of 150. The RCM, on the other hand, had 1 assisted school (at Emekuku) and 136 nonassisted schools with an average attendance of 5,017.181. The figures in table 1 elaborate on this, but they are not necessarily accurate.[23]

Neither the government nor the missions had a well-conceived scheme of education. Each used education for its own purposes—the government for the training of clerks and artisans needed by the administration and com-

TABLE 1
Owerri Schools and Enrollment

Year	Agency	Number of schools	Number of children enrolled	
1923	Government	1	298	
	CMS	72	1,742	
	RCM	232	6,537	
1926	Government	1	360	
	CMS	88	2,895	
	RCM	279	4,118	
	Baptist	2	67	
	African Church	1	40	
1937	Government	1	366	
	CMS	55	4,334	(Egbu district alone)
	RCM	93	13,913	(Emekuku and Ahiara districts alone)

mercial firms, and the missionaries as a means of evangelization. "It is . . . at the school that the missionary can expose most conveniently the dogmas and the moral of Christian doctrine." Said a Catholic missionary, "It is there that the missionary can observe in all its fullness the precepts of our Lord; go and teach all nations." In essence, education was used by the missions to promote their special interests. As each mission set out to exploit the Igbo passion for education, competition for schools and influence ensued once more. And, because the people were prepared to receive any mission which brought schools—whether the Catholics or the Protestants—the struggle for maximum influence in the villages and towns intensified. Because of the conflicts that arose therefrom, the government attempted to intervene by issuing proclamations in respect to the occupation of territories. In 1922, for instance, it decreed that "no school worked under one Religious denomination should be allowed to be built within a radius of one mile of another under a different Religious denomination."[24]

Colonialism certainly spurred the demand for schools. The violence of conquest, the exactions of forced labor, and the apparent differential attitude of the government toward Christians and schoolchildren generated interest in education. To the local people, the missions appeared as allies as well as defenders against British militaristic imperialism. After experiencing disastrous clashes with the British soldiers, many towns and villages which hitherto had shown relative indifference to missionary overtures appealed to the missions for schools almost in a volte-face fashion. To these people it was "good policy" to parley with the colonial administration by establishing schools. In fact, in report after report both Catholic and Protestant missionaries acknowledged that the violence of conquest and the desire to escape British exploitation were partly responsible for the avid demand for schools.[25] Remember that the missionaries were extremely powerful in the colonial days. Should schoolboys be impressed into road work or seized to carry loads on a school day, the missionaries intervened promptly on behalf of their protégés. And should Christians be forced to work or carry loads on a Sunday, the missionaries also intervened. Christianity and education, it seemed, had conferred special privileges on a small segment of the society. Identification with the missions was seen then as an insurance against British exploitation and extortion.

Equally important was the intervention of missionaries in matters involving Christians and non-Christians. When in 1926, for example, a Christian young man from Nguru in Ngor was drafted as an "Mgbe man," the Reverend Father P. O'Connor, the parish priest at Emekuku, protested in a letter to the DO at Owerri, May 19, 1926:

> I have the honour to report to you that one of our baptised Christians of Amibo Nguru, in the Ngor Court Area, has been forcibly seized by the pagans of his town and carried into the Mbwe [Mgbe] house they are building down there. This boy, Thomas Eleazu by name, attended Services on Sunday morning at the Church in his town. On leaving church he was informed that these people had chosen him to work in the Mbwe house. On hearing this he started off for our Mission at Emekuku to tell me about it. These people followed him and overtook him at Emii about a mile from the Mission at Emekuku and tied him up and carried him back to . . . his own town. He is at present held there as a prisoner. On hearing this I sent a message to the Chief, Agocha of Nguru. Both he and the messenger went to the Mbwe house and were not allowed to see the boy. These people refused to let him go and used threatening language to the Chief and the messenger I sent.

Upon investigation, however, the DO discovered that Thomas Eleazu had not been forced to serve as an Mgbe man nor was he physically constrained to do anything against his will. "In view of these statements of the boy, "the DO informed Father O'Connor, "I am afraid that it is not possible to take any further action in the matter."[26] Clearly, being a Christian tended to confer privileges vis-à-vis non-Christians.

Many other factors helped to explain the enthusiastic acceptance of Western education. Of special significance is the character of Igbo society. In Igbo society competition and rivalry are part and parcel of the cultural ethos. Moreover, the people are highly achievement-oriented because the society places great emphasis on individual and group achievement. Hence "individual rivaled individual and social groups rivaled social groups." With reference to the Owerri area, various communities saw Egbu and Emekuku as paradigms of towns which had "grown up" or progressed because of their association with the missions. Both then became models for others to imitate or emulate. This emulative principle, which we may conveniently call *ezi amuru,* is well articulated in the saying *"Ihe ibe jiri maa mma (dimma) agbakwalam."* (May that which has conferred fame and prestige to others not bypass me.) Hence it is that, among the Igbo, and especially the Owerri Igbo, great premium is placed on individual and group achievement, and neither the individual nor the social group would like to remain unresponsive to forces of socioeconomic change for fear of becoming the laughing stock of others. As one man put it in 1956, "We can agree to yield to changes that bring about with them progress in society."[27] In its very idealized form, this Igbo disposition to "yield to change" is what is often referred to as Igbo wisdom or *Amamihe ndi Igbo.* To be sure, the missionaries did not fail to exploit the Igbo penchant for status mobility.

The popular demand for schools certainly created new opportunities as well as new problems for the missions. Gratified, no doubt, that the long-awaited era had dawned, "shown by the eager demand for the establishment of schools everywhere," the missions, however, found themselves increasingly unable to cope with the heavy demand for teachers. In the Egbu District, for example, the Reverend Onyeabo remarked in 1931, "The desire for learning has greatly increased and the question of meeting the demand for school teachers has become a problem," adding, "Let us hope that this open door will help to win the coming generation for Christ." The problem was even further aggravated by the demand for teachers who could teach the English language, not Igbo. "A teacher of a station who does not understand English," reported the CMS secretary, "is not valued. . . . I am frequently receiving appeals that a man who knows English may be substituted for the present teacher."[28]

With money in hand townspeople and villagers approached the different missionary organizations and asked for teachers of English who would teach their children to speak English and thus "deal on equal terms with people of other places who now have the exceptional position in the country because they can speak English." It is clear then that the English language had become a new desideratum without which one could hardly secure prestigious or remunerative employment. And as the government and the commercial firms emphasized its use, the Igbo people pursued it with extraordinary vigor. Is it any wonder, then, that the Igbo language was eclipsed by the English language in practically all schools?

It is easy to blame the missions for this, especially the Roman Catholics who hardly encouraged the study of the Igbo language except for religious purposes.[29] But one has to take into account the climate of opinion at the time. Igbo parents wanted teachers of English, not Igbo. They argued that their children spoke the language at home and that they did not send them to school to learn Igbo. They were mistaken, of course, and we are paying a heavy price for it today. The recent proposal to make the teaching of the Igbo language compulsory in all schools in Imo and Anambra states is certainly a step in the right direction.

Indeed, Roman Catholic schools thrived partly because English was the medium of instruction. The Catholics decided early enough to capitalize on the Igbo clamor for English education, and with the exception of the first two early grades, English was the medium of instruction. Their schools thus became extremely popular. In many cases Protestant schoolboys left their schools and went to Roman Catholic schools. Such incidents naturally embarrassed and infuriated the Protestants. Because the school was the forum for the teaching of the basic doctrines of the particular denominations, it meant that Protestants who went to Catholic schools would, as a matter of course, embrace Roman Catholicism. Moreover, because most of the CMS schools in the early years were actually infant schools where English was not taught at all, they could hardly compete with the Catholic schools. As the CMS bishop remarked in 1912, "The Romanists have practically captured education in the primary standards . . . whilst the CMS schools are mainly infant schools. Many of our children pass from these infant schools to the Roman schools as soon as they leave the substandards." Because the Catholics "give all the instruction in English," another Anglican lamented, the daily attendance of pupils in their schools "is three times as great as that in ours." The government also accorded due recognition to the Catholics. In 1919 the DO reported, "The only Mission School doing serious educational work is the assisted Roman Catholic School at Emekuku."[30]

For all practical purposes, Roman Catholic fame in the Owerri Division—in fact, in all of Igboland—lay primarily in its educational work. For this reason Bishop Shanahan remained uncompromising on the education question. It was said of him in 1929,

Bishop Shanahan governs his personnel with kindness. He is extremely large with his permissions and allows the missionaries very great independence in matters of discipline, administration and monetary control. . . . But as regards the method of instruction and evangelization, he tolerates no opinions. If a person dares utter a personal idea on the matter, the bishop regards it as a personal attack. He has a Vicar delegate who is regarded as a man of courage, but as this delegate made suggestions which did not agree with those of the bishop, he is completely ignored. He has a council, but since 1918, the council has never met for the same reasons.[31]

By the close of our period of study, the Catholics had clearly established their predominance in education. By the mid-1950s, for example, they controlled about 60 percent of the schools in Igboland. Education had thus given the Roman Catholics a decisive edge over the other denominations. Father Lena put it quite succinctly: "Anybody who condemns the school as a way to gain the people to our religion is to be blamed. The results are there which are very consoling and very encouraging. It is the way which has been chosen in our mission, it is good, it ought to be kept . . . on a footing as best as possible." Other than the CMS there was really no other mission in the old Owerri Division which achieved even half as much as the Roman Catholics in the field of education. "The Niger Delta Pastorate schools," observed the DO in 1919, "are in a deplorable condition. They obviously have no governing body which sends out capable men to direct and inspect the teachers (if they deserve that title) and their work."[32]

From the point of view of the Roman Catholics, education served a dual purpose. In the first place, it was the most expedient means of evangelization and a potent factor for the destruction of Igbo "paganism." On the other hand, it was through their education program that the Catholics succeeded in challenging the entrenched influence of the Protestants. Education was indeed "a powerful rampart against the Protestants."[33]

While admitting in 1945 that Protestant influence in the division was "still strong," the Roman Catholic bishop of Owerri and Onitsha vicariate claimed that the Protestants were nevertheless losing prestige "in many places" due partly to the latter's administrative "mismanagement" and partly because of their inability to undertake effective educational work. With regard to the matter of competition, the Catholic bishop boasted, "The Catholic Church increases at the expense of non-Catholic denominations." Bishop Charles Heerey, who was in charge of the Onitsha-Owerri vicariate (1932–48), put it even more pointedly in his 1949 report: "The Colonial Office in London praised highly our work in Education—The Protestants are falling far behind us in this respect, and so while the Catholic Church is gaining the Protestants are losing."[34]

In addition to the popularity they gained by offering English instruction, the Roman Catholics owed much of their impressive strides in the field of education to the substantial annual subsidies they received from the government. Starting in 1900, the government provided the missions with annual grants-in-aid. Even though the grants amounted to less than 10 percent of the total government expenditure by 1960, they were nevertheless a crucial factor in changing the direction of missionary education. The government grants, for example, enabled the Catholics to upgrade their schools in many areas; it enabled them also to employ a large number of teachers—both African and European. (In 1945 there were about four thousand teachers in the Onitsha-Owerri vicariate.) Moreover, this financial windfall made it possible for the mission to offer free education to many of its schoolchildren (and later college students). This resulted in many Roman Catholic schools being very popular because they attracted even Protestant schoolboys who equally benefited from Roman Catholic largess. By 1946 the Catholics admitted that "these grants have increased so substantially that the schools are no longer a financial burden" to the mission. Government grants also probably made it possible for the Catholics to establish agricultural schools—a development which the government expected would yield "important results." Reporting on the Catholic agricultural training school at Okpala which started in 1938, the DO stated, "Father Doyle who is in charge is a keen and trained agriculturist. More than ever is it important that primary education should have a decided agricultural bias."[35]

The Protestants were, of course, well aware that the rapid progress of the Catholics in the field of education derived from the substantial government grants, an astounding achievement that seemed ominous to them. "The Romanists are making great efforts to capture the [whole] country," the CMS secretary remarked in 1912, "through the establishment of schools which are largely subsidized by the Government grants."[36] In an obvious confession of weakness vis-à-vis the Catholics, the Anglican bishop notified the London authorities that "educationally our position on the Niger is far from being satisfactory, and I cannot say that there is any prospect for immediate improvement." To many of the CMS missionaries, this admission of weakness was not enough; strong steps ought to be taken to combat the "pernicious" influence of the Roman Catholics who, as Archdeacon Dennis feared, seem determined to "Romanize" not only the Igbo country but also the whole of Southern Nigeria. Thus, the Catholics needed to be stopped at all costs.[37]

Compared with the Roman Catholics, the CMS seemed to have lagged somewhat behind in the field of education up to the 1950s. Its problem, it now appears, stemmed from apparent penury and misguided policy. For too long the CMS refused to accept government grants on the grounds that such subsidies would involve government interference in mission education. In 1903 the government had issued a new education code which stipulated that: (1) English should be taught in all schools; (2) religious instruction should no longer be compulsory in schools; and (3) government grants would be provided on the basis of annual examination results. To enforce these regulations, school inspectors were appointed. While the Roman

Catholics agreed to give the code a try, the CMS Niger Mission, on the other hand, interpreted these government provisions as attempts to secularize mission education. Hence they attacked the provisions of the code and labelled the government's policy on education as utterly misguided and misdirected. From a purely pedagogical standpoint, the society contended, "Education conducted in a foreign tongue amongst utterly illiterate people cannot be productive of any real results." And from a purely self-interested standpoint, the authorities argued that should English supersede the vernacular in schools, then in a matter of "a few years, the bulk of our converts . . . would be unable to read the Bible in their own language." Moreover, the Anglicans contended that if the government policy on religious teaching were adopted, this would invariably mean the secularization of education and the destruction of "the Evangelistic character of our schools." Thus, to retain its vernacular education as well as to preserve the evangelistic character of its schools, the CMS refused to accept government grants. Consequently, of the fifty-five schools which the CMS controlled in the Owerri division in 1937, forty-three of them were simply vernacular schools.[38]

To fully appreciate the basis of the Anglican opposition to the teaching of the English language in schools, one has to clearly understand the new education policy of the Niger Mission since 1890. It was in that year that the African pioneers of the mission were ignominiously deposed and replaced with white missionaries. As a result of the humiliation, Bishop Adjayi Crowther, who had directed the mission since its foundation in 1857, died in December 1891, apparently of heartbreak.[39] Following the reorganization, the CMS adopted a new policy on education which, as it turned out, had clear racial overtones. The new education policy stipulated that vernacular education should replace English education in all schools under the mission. By 1895, in fact, Bishop Herbert Tugwell, now successor to Crowther, reported that "the vernacular has now supplanted English in all schools."[40] But the new policy was unpopular because the education it purported to provide was quite circumscribed and designed exclusively *for the African*. But Igbo parents made it abundantly clear to the authorities that such education was unacceptable since it tended to blunt the educational aspirations of their children. It was this system of "education for dominance" that the Igbo leader and former president of Nigeria, Dr. Nnamdi Azikiwe, described as "misdirected," because it was based on "erroneous" assumptions about Africans.[41]

By spurning government grants, the CMS found it quite difficult to upgrade its schools and lacked adequate resources to do so by itself. Hence the quality of education suffered. By 1915, for example, the CMS inspector of education presented a rather gloomy picture of the schools. Protestant schools, he said, were merely being "managed" insofar as there were neither adequate facilities nor sufficient personnel to ensure efficiency. As for classroom work in general, he reported that this was invariably "disappointing." Given the large number of pupils and the shortage of staff, the inspector concluded, "it is now a case of 'muddling' through with some hope that some good will come of the mass somehow, until such time as the staff is augmented . . . or there is a drastic cutting down by re-organization."[42]

Quite belatedly, the CMS adopted a change of policy by deciding to accept government grants. This was a particularly bitter pill to swallow, but the government had by 1914 allowed religion to be taught in schools as an integral part of the school curriculum. Besides, the CMS had also accepted education as an instrument of evangelization. This new attitude was reflected in Bishop A. W. Howells's address at the First Synod of the Diocese on the Niger in 1932. Said the Anglican bishop, "Some people there are who take objection to the work of education as being distinct from evangelistic work. Let us not forget that they are inseparable and that the one is the nursery of the other." Henceforth education and evangelization were blended into one. Ideology had thus given way to pragmatism. In the words of an Anglican scholar, "The CMS was [now] aware of public response to education and the Roman Catholic growing enthusiasm in establishing schools all over Isu-ama." If it wanted to compete, therefore, the CMS "had to intensify her efforts towards establishing its own schools." Indeed, remarked Dr. Anyabuike, "The CMS had woken up to the ingenious strategies and forceful evangelization of the Roman Catholics with the idea of schools as the best evangelistic strategy in a society which was not so much interested in the dry theology of salvation, life after death and judgment."[43]

Despite a change in policy and direction the CMS still seemed unable to cope with Roman Catholic aggressive expansionism. As the number of Roman Catholic schools increased, so also did the number of conversions to Roman Catholicism—hence the Anglican outburst of anger and frustration at "the increasing activities of the R.Cs." Said one Anglican missionary, "We are faced with a [serious] challenge" from the Roman Catholics, "whose material resources seem by far to exceed our own." While some Protestants argued for a head-on confrontation with the Roman Catholics, others seemed perhaps to be more cautious. Given the lack of adequate resources, reasoned the latter faction, the prudent policy should be "to find the ways and means of consolidating the ground already gained." Hence the consolidation policy of the CMS emphasized holding onto a few schools instead of engaging in unbridled expansion simply for the sake of competition with the Roman Catholics. "We have already lost so much ground," cautioned the Reverend Basden, "that it is doubtful whether the leeway can be made up now."[44] The striking difference in the Catholic and Protestant policy toward education has given rise to the myth that the CMS stood for "quality" while the RCM embraced the policy of "quantity before quality."

Anglican critics of their mission's policy of consolidation argued that the policy was misguided because it tended to put the Protestants at a great disadvantage vis-à-vis the Roman Catholics. After all, argued Eleazar O. Enemo in a lecture to Protestant teachers at Awka in 1950, aggressive Roman Catholic expansion "was a calculated, carefully planned and lengthily prepared offensive, directed by an expert strategist and an overwhelmingly powerful personality" for the sole purpose of outdistancing the Protestants. Given this reality, he asked, "What are we Anglicans doing?" In his view, the consolidation policy was a mistake; the Anglican authorities ought to have braced themselves for the Roman Catholic challenge. In other words, quantity and quality should have gone hand in hand. In his lecture of August 1950, he said, "There are many reasons for our decline. The first is that those who are in charge of policies are men and women of very lofty ideals that want only the very best schools and colleges. So they have been timid of opening new institutions until they are sure there are excellent hands to run them. Time will prove the wisdom of concentration on the few. I for one am all out for both quality and quantity together."[45]

The apparent "decline" of the CMS however, stemmed not from "lofty ideals" but from shortage of financial resources. That this was so may be illustrated from a critical examination of the predicament of the Owerri archdeaconry in the early 1950s. The archdeaconry, which was under the management of the Reverend H. O. Nweje (superintendent)—known popularly as "Holy" Nweje because of his seemingly austere and exemplary modest life—had a total of nine school districts. As will soon become apparent, the archdeaconry experienced financial difficulties in running the schools because of the sharp decline in government grants. Whereas the RCM witnessed a substantial increase in government grants during the 1940s and 1950s, the CMS, on the other hand, faced serious financial difficulties because of the decline of government grants. Thus the RCM expanded its educational work. Government grants, acknowledged the Catholic bishop in 1946, "have increased so substantially that the schools are no longer a financial burden."[46] Similarly, the Catholic education secretary admitted that "the vast majority of Catholic schools, both primary and secondary, receive a very considerable proportion of the local grants spent on education in the country." According to him, the education subsidy covered about 70 percent of school expenses. "The remaining thirty percent," he explained, "comes from school fees and various forms of organized contributions."[47]

In contrast, the CMS experienced an embarrassing decline of education grants during the period. Few Anglican school districts perhaps faced a greater financial decline than the Owerri archdeaconry. At both the Owerri Archdeaconry Finance Committee meeting and the Diocesan Education Board meeting held at Egbu in 1950 Anglican officials expressed concern over the increasing financial difficulties that faced the Owerri archdeaconry schools. In the words of the mission education secretary, the Owerri archdeaconry "came off very badly as compared with [RCM schools] in the matter of government grants." And, explained the Reverend F. A. Oruche, "the insufficiency of school grants . . . is the chief cause of many districts running into debt." Shortage of funds, it was further explained, accounted for the reason why the superintendent of the Owerri archdeaconry, the Reverend Nweje, "dipped into Archdeaconry [church] funds," amounting to about £1,019:7:6½d.[48] Although Reverend Nweje's action provoked spirited debate at the finance committee meeting, he was nevertheless absolved from blame. In the opinion of the committee, "Holy" Nweje was the victim of circumstances. It was therefore unanimously resolved to "strongly" appeal to the Education Department for increased allocation of education funds to alleviate Owerri archdeaconry financial problems.[49]

Despite the consensus that the Owerri archdeaconry should have received "better treatment" from the government, Bishop E. T. Dimieari pointed out that "the Government is not to blame" for the archdeaconry's financial shortfall. Its economic predicament and those of other school districts, he explained, derived principally from noncompliance with government regulations. Said the bishop, "Our premature raising of schools [to senior primary] and the poor number [of pupils] on the roll" were the chief factors for the decline of education grants. He further explained that, insofar as most schools "are assisted in the junior primary," raising them prematurely to senior standards meant that they would be classified as "unassisted schools" and thus not funded. Unless government regulations were strictly adhered to, he warned, "poor or no grants at all would be the result for Anglican schools."[50]

The Owerri archdeaconry, echoed the education secretary, "needed to put its house in order" if it expected any improvement on government grants. The fact that "there were too many small schools with very poor attendance," he remarked, would continue to militate against securing increased government grants. And there was this ominous warning from the provincial education officer that unless the Anglican mission complied strictly with government regulations relating to staffing, enrollment, and classification, grants to even "assisted" schools might be withdrawn altogether.[51]

To deal with the financial crisis, the Owerri Archdeaconry Finance Committee proposed increasing school fees and considered imposing local contributions. These measures, it was argued, would probably bring relief to the underfunded archdeaconry. The advocates of imposing local assessments argued that these would make the local people feel that the schools "belonged to them" and so would make them willing to share "the financial burden of the schools." After a prolonged debate, the committee decided not to go in that direction. Instead it resolved that all future education and church projects should be frozen indefinitely until the financial resources of the archdeaconry substantially improved.[52] In real terms, the CMS consolidation policy was dictated by economic forces, not necessarily by "lofty ideals."

THE METHODIST ZION MISSION AND EDUCATION

This study on education would be incomplete without at least a brief examination of the Igbo initiative which was critically important in the expansion of Western education in the Owerri division and beyond. Of particular significance is the role played by Igbo leaders such as the late Reverend Moses Diala Opara (1915–65) of Mbieri, founder of the Zion mission at Obazu Mbieri. His schools provided alternative avenues for education to a substantial number of Nigerians who otherwise might not have had the opportunity for educational advancement. Though less endowed than the Roman Catholic and Anglican missions, the Zion mission nonetheless played an important role in the spread of Western education in many parts of Eastern Nigeria. Because very little is known of the history and role of this indigenous Nigerian mission, a brief sketch of its history is here provided, with emphasis on Reverend Opara's role in the field of education.

The Zion church at Obazu Mbieri was founded in 1942 by M. D. Opara. It was known at its inception as the African Methodist Evangelical Zion Church, but was officially registered in 1949 as the Christ Methodist Zion Church. Like churches of its genre in other parts of Africa, it was founded as a breakaway church, its founder having seceded from the CMS in 1941. Reasons for his secession from the CMS are still obscure, but available evidence suggests that his failure to gain admission to the CMS training college at Awka (Awka Training College) led to his resignation. According to Mbieri informants, the CMS local authorities at Egbu refused to recommend him for training as a higher elementary teacher despite the fact that he was "brilliant" and "a good teacher." Thus frustrated at being "passed over year after year" for training, Opara reportedly left the CMS and in March of 1942 founded his own church—the A.M.E. Zion Church.[53]

As it turned out, his resignation from the Anglican mission proved fortuitous, for not only did he ultimately obtain the academic laurels that eluded him while under the CMS, but he rose to national and international prominence thereafter. For example, in 1944 Opara sat for the Higher Elementary Certificate examination as an external candidate and passed in all the subjects except for two "optional" papers. Also, in 1946 he sat for and passed the Senior Cambridge Certificate examination.[54] Still eager to advance in the academic arena, Opara applied for the prestigious Senior Teachers' Certificate examination (now Grade One Teachers' Certificate) in 1948, but was turned down by the education department. "This examination," explained the director of education, "is restricted to Higher Elementary Certificated teachers only, who have taught for at least one and a half years since passing Higher Elementary. Mr. Opara is an uncertificated teacher, and cannot therefore be allowed to sit for the Senior Certificate" examination. By 1954 Reverend Opara had not only ultimately obtained the Higher Elementary Certificate, but he was also the recipient of honorary degrees from the United States—a bachelor of arts in theology and doctor of divinity. His evidently remarkable achievements earned him the coveted cognomen of "a self-made man," "a fighter," "the achiever," and "the man with a . . . vision."[55]

Before we examine the role of the Zion mission in the sphere of education, let us first look at its struggles for existence. Throughout its life (1942–85) the Zion mission had experienced a variety of difficulties, including local hostility, interdenominational prejudice and persecution, as well as acute shortage of resources. At Mbieri, for instance, the Zion church was initially laughed at because its church house was built with local grass (*opu*). Hence it was derisively called *Church nwa opu,* that is, the "grass church." In addition, its admission of polygamists and "backsliders" from the Catholic and Protestant churches tended to tarnish its image as a serious religious organization.[56] It must be remembered that the more traditional churches, such as the RCM and the CMS, refused to admit polygamists as bona fide church members. In any case, local indifference toward the nascent church proved very ephemeral. In fact, negative local opinion about the Zion church changed soon after it was recognized that the mission symbolized social progress, especially via the school and the health clinic. Indeed, it is for this reason that Reverend Opara continues to be remembered as "the fighter" who brought social and economic development to Mbieri.

If local prejudice was short-lived, denominational hostility, opposition, and even persecution proved to be more enduring. In Reverend Opara's words, "Our staunch enemies, the Catholics and the modernists are deadly against our divine . . . evangelistic work and progress." Furthermore, he complained that because members of these churches "are in positions of power in this country," they continually "victimized our institutions," especially Zion schools, by refusing to accord them government approval and financial subsidies. Yet, despite the "deadly" opposition from its enemies, the Zion mission weathered the storm. In the confident words of Reverend Opara, "We [had to] defend ourselves to the last man for our religion, God being our helper."[57] Thus through many struggles the Zion mission emerged as a force to reckon with, but partly because of foreign assistance from the United States of America.

It would be too much of a diversion to chronicle all of Opara's heroic struggles to make the Zion mission a veritable religious and educational institution. Hence, only selected aspects of its history are treated here, especially those that shed some light on the mission's contributions in the field of education.

The "grass church," as already noted, served a dual purpose—as church and school. From 1942 to 1944 the school operated as a Bible school. But in 1944 it was approved as a regular primary school and thus attracted more students. By then too a maternity center had been established, thus making the nascent mission the focus of attention at Mbieri. In time, the Zion school and maternity center helped change the attitude of the local people toward the Zion mission. Indeed, to many people these establishments symbolized social development (*mmepe*) and so were objects of local pride. Finally, when the Zion commercial-secondary school (1948) and St. Catherine's College (1956), a two-year teacher training institution for girls, were established, Obazu Mbieri had become an enviable town. So not only were lands granted to the Zion mission free of charge, but letters of congratulations came to Reverend Opara from different quarters. This letter from B. U. Anyasodo is typical.

I noted your activities to enlighten our folks at home in the modern way of life [wrote Anyasodo from Port Harcourt]. In fact I am proud that you are doing your best to let our people share from your learnings abroad. It is not every body that will appreciate your remittances for the town, and even many may turn to sabotage them; I am only assuring you that time will kill all such diabolical movements because the time we sincerely devote to public duties, has its own reward.[58]

Similar letters of praise and appreciation also came from as far away as Isiekenesi in Orlu where a Zion school (St. Peter's Methodist Zion School) and a maternity center had been established. Here at Isiekenesi the Reverend Opara was the great liberator, having "made us to be free from the hand of our opponents, the CMS." For Jonathan Amaefule of Isiekenesi, the wonderful work being done by the Zion mission deserved special praise—hence his letter of appreciation to Reverend Opara "for all the good work" he had done and was still doing "for our town." He wrote,

It will surprise you to hear that some of our Roman Catholic members are [even] giving more and better account of your services and achievements with admiration. I can assure you, sir, that it was a . . . Roman Catholic who volunteered to afford . . . £50 for the proposed Maternity. . . . All our communities both at home and abroad were praying hard for the betterment of Zion Mission in town . . . , especially when we heard [about the] failures of Oruche and company . . . [to] sabotage your laboured and God established Organization.[59]

Reverend Opara, of course, had his detractors, as the two letters clearly indicate—hence his expression of joy and appreciation for the above compliments. To Anyasodo, for example, he wrote that he was "overwhelmed with joy" at the receipt of his letter, adding, "I will do my very best to struggle on" despite the fact that "there are so many at Obazu who misunderstand me." And to Amaefule, Opara expressed special gratitude for his touching letter and assured him that he would do all in his power to help the town. But, said Opara, "it is very hard, you know, to subdue satanic people. Oruche is doing his worse [*sic*]. . . . Do not fear, all will be well. . . . We shall conquer Satan."[60]

Available oral and literary evidence suggests that Daniel U. Ajoku, then resident at Port Harcourt and Reverend Opara's kinsman, was probably Opara's greatest critic, or as Reverend Opara put it, chief among "my detractors." The details of their mutual antagonism falls outside the scope of this study. However, Ajoku's alleged hostility toward the Zion school at Obazu is interesting and relevant. By his own admission he was accused of plans to sabotage the Zion school. In reply he had this to say to Reverend Opara: "After long forebearance I am compelled to acquaint you in writing of the news which reached me from certain quarters, that you accused me of planning against your school in various ways. After due consideration I decided to write to you to ascertain if the news is true. I would be grateful if all your verbal saying to people about me were to be put in writing so that I may be fully informed of everything you might have said."[61] We have no evidence that Reverend Opara acknowledged this letter. Yet Ajoku minced no words in subsequently criticizing Opara for "forcefully assuming" the leadership of Mbieri through his educational institution. By "forcefully assuming the administration of my people," he wrote, "you have destroyed the entire discipline of my people which . . . I have tried to cultivate ever since my childhood." More significantly, Ajoku questioned Opara's claim of altruism. "Your primary object [sic]," he charged, was "to collect huge amounts of money from the mass illiterates at home and abroad for your own personal interests."[62]

Distracting though Ajoku's criticisms were, Reverend Opara seemed determined to pursue his "work for Africa," that is, his educational mission, at all costs. Thus, like the other missions, the Zion mission was besieged with requests to open schools and colleges in various towns. "Our people are in great need of those who will come to our place and establish a college of any type that will bring progress," wrote Elijah Emerenini of Orlu to Opara in 1961. And there was a letter from Uyo in Calabar province:

> There is a school at my place which is being run by the Catholic mission. The Rev. manager has been making vain promises to my people for many years and still yet the school is nowhere. He promised last year to raise the school up to standard four this year. At [sic] the surprise of our people our children who passed to standard four were taken to Ihe in Aro[chukwu] division. . . . Our people are really annoyed and want a manager who can take over the school and raise it up to standard four next year. . . . I want you to take up the school. . . . The natives will unfailingly wheel over to [your] mission without delay because they are not real[ly] full members of the Catholic mission.[63]

But the indiscriminate opening of schools here and there in parts of the Owerri Division and beyond resulted in inevitable overextension and the overstretching of scarce resources. Thus the poor standard of education in Zion schools, as will be shown later, can easily be traced to problems of inadequate resources—especially funds and qualified staff. Hence the resource question proved to be the critical factor that delayed the approval of Zion schools until the mid-1950s.

For an illustration, let us look at the history of the Zion school at Obazu Mbieri. Originally approved as a full-fledged elementary school in 1944, by 1947 it had been raised to standard six which made it eligible for the Nigerian First School Leaving Certificate. But student performance in the 1948 examination was very poor, largely because of the inadequate number of teachers. Out of the thirty-six students who took the examination, only ten were successful. Consequently the government felt compelled to reduce the school to standard five. In addition, the government threatened to close the school entirely because of general "inefficiency and breaches of [Education] Regulations." When Reverend Opara protested the poor results at the school, arguing that the best students had failed, the provincial education officer (PEO) retorted angrily, "You are extremely fortunate to have any certificates at all issued to you, in view of the deplorable paper set and the general administration of the examination." He added that the ten passes accorded the school were simply "a concession," not merit. "Your statement that none of the brilliant boys was in the pass list is, therefore, absurd."[64]

Indeed, Zion schools were chronically strapped for funds—hence the "appalling standard of work and the unsatisfactory conditions" that prevailed at the schools. It was for these reasons that education officers repeatedly refused to grant them approved status. For one thing, the Zion mission lacked qualified human resources and the finances necessary to run efficiently its twenty-three primary schools. "In those days," acknowledged the former school manager, "we simply managed" because trained teachers, particularly higher elementary teachers, "were extremely hard to get." Consequently lack of qualified staff, inadequate equipment, shortage of classroom space, as well as the low standard of work at the schools militated against their securing government approval and education grants. Said one school inspector, "None of [the] schools are of proved efficiency," and therefore none eligible for approval.[65]

Lack of approval, of course, meant that Zion schools could not receive government grants. Besides, the Zion mission was not even recognized as a voluntary agency, in contrast to the RCM and the CMS. The mission's desperate efforts to secure this status failed until 1954, meaning that no Zion schools received government grants until that date. But despite repeated refusals, Reverend Opara was not discouraged. "We need some help," he pleaded with the Ministry of Education, "to enable us to maintain our schools more efficiently." Arguing that none of the Zion schools could derive even "one-third of the yearly expenses from the school fees collected," he continued to request at least "a little special aid" so as to improve the efficiency of the schools. But the appeal was futile until the government began to provide the needed education subsidy in 1954.[66] Before then, however, Reverend Opara directed much of his energy to securing government approval for his schools. For only through official recognition could the schools attract government grants.

First and foremost, Opara requested that the Ministry of Education restore approved status of standard six to Obazu school. Regretably, unfavorable inspection results delayed the approval until 1954. For example, the PEO's inspection of Obazu school in 1950 showed evidence that not much had changed since 1948. The PEO thus felt compelled to reject the request for approval. "Unless and until the Manager can show willingness to cooperate with the [Education] Department to a greater extent than in the past," remarked the PEO, "I am not prepared to recommend that Christ Zion Methodist [school] be granted approved status." Subsequent inspections in 1951, 1952, and 1953 proved equally negative—hence this stern warning from the acting inspector-general of education in 1952:

> The standard of work shown by Obazu Mbieri Zion Methodist School in 1951 can only be described as appalling. This allied to the fact that the inspection report shows many unsatisfactory features, plus the fact that the school has been understaffed all the year and has had poor results have led me to take drastic action. . . . *The school is not approved for First School Leaving Certificate in 1952.* You have *no* permission to have Standard Six next year (1953) and should reduce the school to Std. 5. I am tired of the constant unsatisfactory conditions which prevail in your Voluntary Agency.[67]

Financial difficulties, approval problems, and low standards notwithstanding, Zion schools continued to exist, perhaps because of the infusion of funds from the United States, at least before the receipt of government grants in 1954. Material assistance from America was substantial. By 1953 about £11,400 had been sent to Reverend Opara from the American Evangelical Methodist Church (EMC) with headquarters at Altoona, Pennsylvania.[68] Reverend Opara's link with the EMC began in 1950 when he visited the United States and attended the EMC's annual conference at Shelbyville, Indiana. At the conference, Reverend Opara reportedly "brought word pictures of his life, and a challenge from the Bible. He closed with the challenge of evangelizing Nigeria." From that time the EMC authorities took special interest in his evangelistic and educational endeavors in Nigeria. And, not only did the EMC send material assistance, but also they sent American personnel to help in furthering the evangelistic work. By the time of his death in 1965, American funds and personnel had helped to make the Zion mission a viable proposition. [69] Despite the struggles, Zion schools certainly provided educational opportunities to a very significant number of education-hungry Nigerians. Perhaps Reverend Opara's most enduring legacy in the sphere of education was not only the establishment of schools and colleges, but also his award of scholarships to students both at the primary and secondary school levels. Free education was also granted to students at the Zion teacher training college.

Some students even received scholarships for university education overseas, especially in America. All of these Opara did because he was, in his own words, "a nationalist and a humanitarian by blood." To Reverend Opara, it seems, education was both the most expeditious means of self-improvement as well as a vital weapon for colonial liberation. Hence education figured prominently in what he regarded as "my work for Africa."

By thus offering free education to Nigerians, especially to the less privileged class, Opara believed he was making an important contribution toward "deliver[ing] our nation" from ignorance and colonial bondage.[70] In essence, education was to him part and parcel of the decolonization process. This epitaph says it perhaps more eloquently:

> Rev. Opara was not selfish. He believed in the education of everybody. This was what forced him to establish schools and colleges. To encourage this liberal education for all, he gave . . . primary[,] secondary and university scholarships to hundreds of people. Rev. Opara never liked the African [to be] rated a second class citizen anywhere [in the world].[71]

In the annals of modern education in Nigeria, and particularly Eastern Nigeria, the name of Reverend M. D. Opara will always be remembered—even though his schools have, like all other mission schools, been taken over by the present government of Imo State.

SECONDARY EDUCATION

In the field of primary education the record of the missions was clearly impressive. In 1966, for example, there were about six thousand schools in Eastern Nigeria with a school population of over 1.2 million. With the exception of only a few government or council schools, all of these schools were controlled by the missionary bodies. Despite their obviously outstanding achievements in the field of primary education,[72] the missions, however, failed to provide early secondary school education to hundreds and thousands of avid primary school graduates whose insatiable quest for advanced education was fully recognized by the missions themselves. In the Owerri area and in fact all over Igboland secondary education came relatively late. In Yorubaland, for example, grammar school education had been provided by the missions since 1859.[73] It was not until 1925 that the first secondary school was opened in Igboland by the CMS—after sixty-eight years of missionary activity. The RCM followed in 1933, after forty-eight years of educational work. As for the government, there were only two government schools in the Eastern Region, at Owerri and Umuahia. Thus, until the 1950s the provision of secondary education was appallingly inadequate.

Judging by the slowness at which higher education was introduced in Nigeria as a whole, it is difficult to escape from the conclusion that the missions and the colonial government had really no serious commitment to advanced or higher education in the country. Even when the missions "essayed to give education that went beyond the elementary level, their preference was for training institutions whose highest products would be either teacher-catechists or catechists pure and simple. In either case the priesthood would be their ultimate ambition." The Asaba Training Institution, which was opened in 1895 (closed in 1900) by the CMS, was one example of such postprimary institutions whose main goal was to train schoolteachers and catechists. The CMS Awka Training College (1904) and the Roman Catholic Training College at Igbariam (1913) were other examples. The latter was closed down in 1918 and a new teachers' training center was not opened until 1928—St. Charles College at Onitsha. In fact, by 1911 the CMS Niger Mission had adopted a policy which in effect limited opportunities for advanced education. In its Executive Committee Meeting resolution of that year, the Niger Mission endorsed the view that all "advanced education [should] be limited to Training Colleges where candidates accepted for CMS (or Native Pastorate) work were received for preparation as Evangelists, Teachers and Pastors."[74]

While financial problems may have contributed to the delay in the provision of secondary education, it would be shortsighted, however, to ignore European racial prejudice as an important factor to the equation. In the view of some missionaries, advanced or academic education (secondary education), which demands more than average intelligence, was far beyond the capability of the African. In fact, in the Igbo case there were those missionaries—not many, but a vocal minority—who contended that advanced education was not for the Igbo "type." The Reverend S. R. Smith, for example, who was the secretary of the CMS Niger Mission at Onitsha, dismissed the necessity for introducing secular advanced education among the Igbo on the grounds, as he said, that "these people are not suitable for a high mental development." Not only did Smith reflect the prevailing European ideology of racial superiority, he also openly admitted that even though he was supposedly a Christian, he did not endorse the concept of racial equality. Nor was he a social leveller for that matter. That the ideology of the mental inferiority of the African influenced missionary education policy in Africa is a fact that has now been amply demonstrated. It is instructive to note, however, that there were many well-meaning missionaries who did not allow the virus of racism to poison their judgments of Africans and, more specifically, the Igbo people. Father Shanahan, for example, found Igbo schoolchildren as capable of any educational endeavor as their European counterparts. "These good Black boys are intelligent, full of life and good will. It is marvellous how fast they learn." Compared with English schoolchildren in terms of speed of learning, another British missionary conceded that Igbo boys would almost certainly "put some of our English children to shame."[75]

Naturally, Africans found European labels of "mental inferiority of the Negro" offensive and bereft of any scientific validity. It hurt them and tended to make them lose confidence in themselves. But there were African stalwarts who challenged the very basis of European claim to racial superiority.[76] In an obvious reaction against this outmoded European ideology, Dr. Ben N. Azikiwe, who by his own academic achievements in America exploded the myth of African mental inferiority, advised Mazi Mbonu Ojike in 1939:

> There is no achievement which
> Is possible to human beings which
> Is not possible to Africans. . . .
> Therefore go forth, thou
> Son of Africa, and return
> Home laden with the
> Golden Fleece.[77]

Discussion about opening a secondary school in Igboland dates to the early 1900s. In 1901, for example, Archdeacon Dennis, a serious student of Igbo language and a fervent education enthusiast, recommended to the CMS that a secondary school should be opened at Onitsha. Struggling very much against the tide of official opinion in the CMS circles, he suggested that English should be an important part of the school curriculum. A secondary school, he said, was absolutely essential in order to satisfy the avid demand for higher education by the Igbo people. The school, he also believed, would enable the CMS to retain its prestige vis-à-vis the Catholics, who by that date had established a high school at Onitsha (probably a technical or vocational school). Until 1913 the CMS demurred.[78] In 1909 the Roman Catholics had proposed the building of two secondary schools, one at Onitsha for the Igbo people and the other at Calabar for the Efiks. Again, this was partly in response to the increasing demand for more advanced education and partly as a response to the government policy on secular and literary education. The project did not, however, go beyond the talking stage ostensibly because of the lack of funds. Renewed appeals for funds in 1914 were based on grounds that if the RCM did not open any secondary schools "all the young children of the country will go to the heretics."[79] But this argument did not move the authorities of the Holy Ghost Fathers in Paris to action until after 1925.

By 1913 there was a new climate of opinion within the CMS regarding the teaching of the English language in schools and the need for a secondary school. Faced with Roman Catholic aggressive expansion in education and the defection of Protestants to Catholic schools, the CMS eventually relented and introduced English as the medium of instruction in schools. It was also agreed that the standard of education at the central school at Onitsha should be raised "to that of a secondary school." Even then, the evangelistic raison d'être of the mission was emphasized. "From such a school it is hoped that a larger number of young men will pass out to become missionaries to their own people."[80] Plans were thus made for raising funds for the proposed secondary school, estimated to cost about £5,000. For years, however, the authorities procrastinated, and no concrete steps were taken to translate the proposal into a reality. Frustrated by the delaying tactics of the authorities in London, the missionaries in Nigeria resolved to shelve the project in 1915 because neither the personnel nor funds for erecting the schoolbuilding had been forthcoming from the home office.[81]

In 1917, however, Archdeacon Dennis, the most fervent advocate of the secondary school, died. Shortly after, a serious effort was made to translate his dreams into reality. (Dennis, who had achieved fame as a result of his translation of the Bible into Union Igbo, died prematurely at the age of forty-eight. He and his wife were returning to England when, unfortunately, his ship was torpedoed by the Germans on August 2, 1917.) At the meeting of the local Executive Committee of the Niger Mission in February 1918 it was resolved "that a fund be opened with the object of perpetuating the memory of Archdeacon Dennis." Such a fund was to be used to further education in the mission. Eventually the committee agreed that the proposed Onitsha Grammar School should be dedicated to the memory of Archdeacon Dennis.[82] It was henceforth known as the Dennis Memorial Grammar School.

The school had to wait until 1925 before it was officially opened. Before then a serious fund-raising campaign was launched in 1920. Suggestions to appeal to the government for financial assistance were rejected on grounds of policy.[83] But recognizing the urgency for a secondary school, the Igbo people responded to the appeal fund with amazing alacrity. Individuals as well as church groups contributed very generously. In the end, the Igbo people contributed more than three-quarters of the total cost. The Igbos, said Bishop B. Lasbrey in obvious expression of gratitude, "have provided by far the largest part of the cost of this [School], the first secondary school in their country." Out of the total cost of £4,000 the Igbo people contributed more than £3,000.[84] On January 25, 1925 the Dennis Memorial Grammar School was opened. The initial enrollment was forty-six day students and nineteen boarders. The era of secondary education in Igboland had now arrived. Since then the passion for secondary education has spread rapidly. Today, "a town without a secondary school is nothing," said an Owerri elder.[85]

While the opening of the grammar school was obviously a source of pride to both the CMS and the Igbo people, it was an embarrassment to the Roman Catholic missionaries. To them it seemed that their premier position in the field of education was being seriously challenged by the Protestants. Given the insatiable hunger for advanced education among the Igbos, the Catholics argued, Catholic adherents would almost invariably seek admission to the Protestant college. And, since students naturally embraced the religion of the particular denomination which controlled the school, Roman Catholics would therefore be lost to the Protestants. The idea of Catholics going to non-Catholic institutions was summarily condemned by the Catholic authorities. To prevent the possibility of Catholics ever going to Protestant institutions (which included the government college at Umuahia established in 1925), the Catholic bishop at Onitsha petitioned his overseas sponsors for funds to establish Catholic secondary schools in order to safeguard "our children" from Protestant influences.[86] It is not exactly clear what now prompted the Congregation of the Holy Ghost Fathers in Paris to provide funds, since similar appeals had been made as far back as 1909. In any case, funds were provided and in 1932 Christ the King College was opened at Onitsha, the first Roman Catholic secondary school in Igboland. This was followed in 1935 by the establishment of the College of Immaculate Conception at Enugu. The race for preeminence in higher education among the missionary societies had now begun.

The avid demand for institutions of higher learning by the Igbos and their neighbors actually intensified from the 1930s. Both the government and the Christian missions were called upon to provide advanced education for the ever-growing number of children with standard six certificates. The clamor for advanced education was partly utilitarian. A secondary education was viewed as the surest way of escaping menial jobs and unremunerative occupations. As F. Ferguson (DO) once remarked, "The Owerri youth has a marked dis-inclination for domestic occupation" and so aspires after good education as the most expedient means of securing better employment. Besides, advanced education broadened the intellectual horizon of the African and thus freed him from an inferiority complex vis-à-vis the European colonial officials. "Give a boy a good secondary education," said a member of the Igbo Union organization in 1920, "and he can rise to any height in the world without being dragged down by the dead weight of inferiority complex."[87]

Given the incessant local demand for postprimary education and the urgent need for teachers as well, the different missionary societies began to establish institutions of higher learning in several sections of Igboland. But we should not lose sight of the prestige factor here. It would appear indeed that the prestige and influence of a particular denomination rose in proportion to the number of educational institutions it controlled. Considerations of influence and prestige certainly influenced the actions of the missionaries. There was no doubt, for example, that the overriding ambition of the Roman Catholic missionaries during the 1940s and 1950s, when postprimary institutions were being established in various areas, was for the Catholic church to become "the strongest single educational influence" in Nigeria. The Protestants also viewed the establishment of colleges as a symbol of prestige and influence. Reacting to the Roman Catholic establishment of girls' colleges in various parts of the country, the CMS bishop felt his church could ill afford to be behind in the provision of educational opportunities for girls. Said Bishop Lasbrey in 1938: "Girls' schools are of vital importance right now. . . . Educated Christian men need educated Christian wives to preside over their homes and help make them truly Christian. The Roman Catholics are realising this and are building girls' schools in many places; we cannot afford to be behind."[88]

Indeed, it was this competitive spirit among the missionary bodies that partly accounts for the spread of advanced education in the whole of Owerri Province and elsewhere. In fact, the Roman Catholic ambition to gain educational ascendency over its rivals seems to have provided the impulse to build as many colleges as possible, since graduates from these colleges would become the future political leaders and, it was hoped, would promote the interests of the church to which they were affiliated. The Reverend Father J. P. Jordan certainly had this in mind when he wrote in 1960: "The proportion of Catholics among politicians, doctors, lawyers, University graduates and administrators is not as high as it ought to be. This is a legacy from the past. . . . The Protestant Missions secured an advantage of almost a quarter of a century in secondary education. This gave them a dangerous degree of control at the top, both in and out of Government."[89]

The desire to gain prestige in Nigeria probably influenced the Roman Catholic proposal to build a Catholic university in the country. The Catholic authorities had talked for some years about the need for a Catholic university. Initially it was thought that the institution would prevent prospective Catholic students from going to either Europe or America where they could be exposed to non-Catholic influences. On the other hand, the establishment of a Catholic university would significantly enhance the advancement of Roman Catholicism in Nigeria.[90] But for various reasons which are not dealt with here, the proposal was shelved until 1955. Interest in the proposed university revived in that year presumably because of the decision of the government of the Eastern Region to establish a state university at Nsukka. Thereupon the Roman Catholics seriously considered preempting the government. Rome even promised to provide substantial funds for the project. For a variety of reasons (beyond the scope of this study), the proposal for a Catholic university never materialized.[91] Since this pet scheme proved a total failure, the Catholic missionaries henceforth concentrated their efforts on secondary and teacher training education.

Despite the fact that Owerri Division had a larger Christian as well as a larger educated population than Onitsha Division,[92] most of the institutions of higher learning were located at the latter division. In fact, with the possible exception of the Roman Catholic Mount Carmel College at Emekuku, a two-year teacher training college for girls which opened in 1943, none of the missions had any postprimary institutions in the Owerri area until 1948. To many people in the Owerri area it appeared that the missions actually treated Owerri Division unfairly. For the Roman Catholics in the Owerri area, it was poignantly clear that the Catholic authorities were quite negligent of the needs of the division, hence the petition to Rome in 1936 for the creation of Owerri bishopric which would ensure the separation of Owerri from Onitsha.[93] The petitioners evidently believed that the interest of the Catholics in the Owerri Province would be better served if Owerri was separated from Onitsha. Bishop Charles Heerey, who was in charge of the Onitsha and Owerri vicariate, viewed the separation movement as injurious and so remained firmly opposed to it. In his own words, "It would be a terrible blow . . . if Owerri were taken away from us. It is the most progressive part of the missionary world today. About two-thirds of our Christians and catechumens are in Owerri Province, and the future is brighter than ever. But we are not doing it justice with regard to staff."[94] Yet despite Heerey's admission of obvious injustice, people in the Owerri area seem to believe that the bishop was clearly anti-Owerri.[95] Happily, Rome proved quite receptive to the suggestion for separation, and so in 1948 Owerri was created as a separate diocese. Father Joseph Whelan, an Irish priest, was appointed as the new bishop of Owerri province.

The separation of Owerri from Onitsha heralded a new era in the history of higher education in the Owerri Division. Faced with a dire shortage of teachers and local clergy, Bishop Whelan almost immediately initiated the creation of an indigenous clergy for the diocese and also promoted the building of secondary schools and teacher training colleges. It is significant that it was in the first year of his episcopacy that several colleges were established. These included the Holy Ghost College, Owerri; Owerri Girls' Secondary School; Bishop Shanahan Training College, Orlu; St. Joseph's College, Aba; Stella Maris, Port Harcourt; and Holy Ghost College, Umuahia. The Protestants also began to build their own secondary schools and teacher training colleges, such as St. Augustine's Grammar School at

Nkwerre, the teachers' training college at Irete, as well as St. John's at Diobu. Private initiatives also played a role in the spread of secondary education in the Owerri area as in other places. In 1948, for example, Emmanuel College was opened at Owerri Town under the proprietorship of E. Eronini of Mbieri. In the same year, as already noted, Reverend Opara established the Zion Commercial School at Mbieri. From the 1950s institutions of higher learning proliferated. By the 1970s and 1980s there were hardly any towns in the present Owerri Local Government Area and indeed all over Imo State where there were no secondary schools or teacher training institutions.

Ironically, while postprimary education was introduced in this region of Nigeria relatively late, the people have succeeded by dint of hard work in catching up with their Nigerian neighbors who had a head start in higher education. Thus the Igbos, as an American scholar wrote in 1966, "are the energetic parvenus who in a few decades altered the established order, both by successfully challenging Yoruba supremacy in the professional and civil service elite and by leading the struggle for Nigerian nationalism which led to independence from Britain." This educational progress, almost "unparalleled in any other country,"[96] was made possible, certainly, by the Christian missions and by the Igbo people themselves. The Igbo philosophy of self-help has contributed significantly to the material progress of the people. Of course, the colonial government played a role in the advance of Western education. But as indicated earlier, if education had been left to the government alone, the education revolution in Eastern Nigeria, or in Igboland, would not have seen the light of day.

6. THE MISSIONS AND INDIGENOUS CLERGY

THE ERA OF BENIGN NEGLECT

From the preceding chapters, it is quite clear indeed that the Christian missions in Owerri and elsewhere in Nigeria had made significant progress in the field of education, as well as in the provision of hospitals and other social services. Yet, as Adrian Hastings points out, "while the churches had worked hard . . . on the development of schools and hospitals . . . they had done strangely little in most places to train a local clergy." In our area of study, the missions, particularly the Roman Catholic Mission, strangely did very little until about the 1950s and 1960s to develop a local clergy. In fact, before then very little serious attention was given to the training of African clergy. Thus, for all intents and purposes, the Roman Catholic church in Igboland was dominated by foreign missionaries, notably the Irish. Of the eighty-eight Catholic priests in the Onitsha-Owerri vicariate in 1947, for instance, only ten were Africans. Also, out of a total of eighty-two priests in the vicariate in 1952, only nine were indigenous. Elsewhere in Nigeria and, for that matter, Africa, statistics show overwhelming European dominance in the clerical or church personnel.[1]

Equally striking, as Hastings's researches have demonstrated, is the fact that there were few Africans in positions of leadership in the church prior to the 1950s. Thus, remarked Hastings, "it could easily look as if many missionaries did not want . . . clerical leaders to arise, or at least not to arise too soon or too far." Thus before 1950 "it was still unusual to find a church or diocese seriously planning the training of [indigenous] clergy to take over the . . . posts held by [European] missionaries."[2] In the Owerri division, as we shall soon see, there were no such plans to transfer ecclesiastical power to Africans. The Irish, who dominated the missionary field, hardly ever gave any serious thought to their being replaced by the Igbo. But history has its own dynamic—for the Nigerian Civil War (1967–70), as we shall see, made the almost unthinkable become a reality.

That the missions were slow to raise an indigenous clergy is now generally acknowledged even by the mission societies themselves. Writing on this
matter in 1963, the Catholic superior of the Society of African Missions
(SMA) in Nigeria observed, "We have little to be proud of in our record of
recruiting and training of Nigerian aspirants to the clerical and religious
life. The small proportion of indigenous priests and sisters tells its
story. . . . We should be highly embarrassed should a stranger judge the
work of the Nigerian Church by its achievement in this field." Surely, the
Catholic church as well as the other Protestant missions were judged by
their record of Africanization. For example, Sir Hugh Clifford, formerly
governor of Nigeria (1919–25), criticized the mission societies for their be-
lated effort to train African clergy. With special reference to the Roman
Catholic Mission, the governor correctly observed that "until quite recently" its authorities "steadfastly refused the ordination of its African
converts," thus making the mission's leadership predominantly European.[3]

Similarly, officials of the Catholic church who visited Nigeria in the
1920s and 1930s deplored the typically colonial character of the Nigerian
churches. The almost total absence of Igbo Catholic clergy in the mission
under the Holy Ghost Fathers was particularly hard to understand, given
that the Igbo area was, in Father J. P. Jordan's apt phrase, "the heart and
core" of Roman Catholicism in all of Nigeria. It therefore looked odd to
Father Joseph Soul of the Holy Ghost Fathers, who visited Nigeria in 1929
from France, that there were practically no local Catholic clergy here. The
Apostolic delegate, Archbishop David Matthews, who came to Nigeria in
1937, was equally astonished at the slow pace of Africanization in Nigeria
and West Africa in general. Comparing West and East Africa in terms of
the development of indigenous clergy, the archbishop expressed surprise
that West Africa, which "is more advanced in many ways" than East
Africa, seemed to lag "very much behind" the latter in the Africanization
process. By the time the archbishop visited Nigeria, it should be noted,
there were only three Igbo Catholic priests in the Onitsha and Owerri vicariate; none of them, incidentally, came from the Owerri Division. Yet, here
was the area where the missionaries had been crying for "more and more
priests to minister to the teeming, pious and zealous Catholic population."[4]

Because of the long tradition of Africanization in the Protestant
churches, particularly the Anglican church, this study will not deal with the
Protestant missions. Instead, our examination will focus almost exclusively on the Roman Catholic attitude toward the development of indigenous clergy. For the RCM in the Owerri Division as elsewhere in Nigeria was
characteristically colonial in orientation, its personnel and its liturgy being
essentially foreign. It was in this context that one Roman Catholic writer
described the Catholic church in Nigeria as being "as [foreign] as anything

could be under the blazing [African] sun."[5] Thus, not only was the liturgy foreign, but the mission personnel in the region remained predominantly European until 1970. By then all foreign missionaries in the newly created East Central State of Nigeria were expelled. Their departure, for all practical purposes, proved fortuitous. For on September 20, 1970, an Igbo priest, Father Mark Unegbu, was consecrated as the bishop of Owerri diocese. Since then, many more have been appointed, and there has been a dramatic rise in the number of local priests. For the first time, in fact, vigorous attempts have been made to indigenize the church not only in terms of personnel but also in making the church reflect the culture of the people. Thus its colonial character is being steadily altered.

Irish Missionaries and Racism

As already noted, the development of indigenous clergy was pretty slow. The fundamental question here is: why? In other words, why was it that despite "the crying need" for more priests to minister to the teeming Christian population the Irish missionaries seemed reluctant or unwilling actively to recruit and train a significant number of local priests to handle the pressing work? Explanations for this will become apparent as we discuss the attitude of the Irish toward their Igbo wards. But we should emphasize at this juncture that until very recent times the conspicuous absence of Igbo Catholic priests in the church was not necessarily due to a lack of Igbo interest in religious vocations. On the contrary, the desire "to learn priest" among Igbo young men dates back to the late nineteenth century. Strangely, as Governor Clifford observed, the Catholic authorities "steadfastly refused" to welcome them into the ministry. It was not until 1920, for example, that the first Catholic Igbo priest, the Reverend Father Paul O. Emecheta (1888–1948) of Ezi, was ordained in the former Asaba District. He was indeed the first Igbo Catholic clergy of the Society of African Missions (SMA). In 1930 the Holy Ghost Fathers produced their first Igbo Catholic priest, the Reverend Father John Cross Anyogu (later bishop of Enugu). Given, as already indicated, the dire shortage of missionaries in the Igbo country as a whole, the persistent and often angry demands for missionary reinforcements, and the ever-increasing Christian population, one would have expected the missionaries to consider the recruitment and training of a local clergy as a matter of top priority. This, it would appear, might have reduced the missionaries' heavy dependence on the home sponsors. On a more practical level, the use of local clergy would probably make the mission operation less expensive. After all, Africans were less expensive to maintain than Europeans. Furthermore, Africanization of the church would have possibly rendered Christianity less foreign and strange, at least from the point of view of church personnel and public relations. But these arguments seemed perhaps irrelevant to the missionaries. For rapid Africanization would have destroyed the missionaries' raison d'être for coming to Africa—that is, to dominate and to serve. Hence, few missionaries if any wanted the collapse of the colonial walls around them. In other words, there were no immediate plans on the part of the European missionaries to render themselves redundant through a vigorous policy of Africanization. Nor was it a popular idea for Europeans to serve under African leadership. For "however experienced and competent, an African would still be left technically subject to some newly arrived European."[6]

However, one must recognize, as the missionaries say, that missions lacked resources. As one missionary put it quaintly, one must eat before contemplating indigenous clergy. In other words, the problem of inadequate resources—financial and human—served as an excuse for the slow development of local clergy.[7] There seems to have been, however, a lack of commitment to active recruitment and training of Africans for the ministry. For when circumstances ultimately forced the missions to do so, the resources became available somehow. And there are other important reasons for the apparent reluctance to train local clergy in our area of study.

Available evidence suggests that the Irish Holy Ghost Fathers in Eastern Nigeria tended to regard the region as their sole missionary preserve. Hence they fought desperately to retain full control of the territory, not only by not training a large number of Igbo priests, but also by excluding other missionary organizations as well as missionaries from other nationalities. For example, the Irish missionaries perceived American, English, and French missionaries as intruders and thus unwelcome in the area. Even though the French were the missionary pioneers here, the Irish saw them generally as failures and troublemakers. Hence the anti-French sentiment that prevailed in the Igbo mission in Irish circles.[8] Similarly, British missionaries were castigated and declared unsuitable for Nigeria because, according to Bishop Heerey, they "do not suit Nigeria." They were therefore to be sent to places like Angola where they "might do well." And the popular stereotype of American missionaries was that they were too materialistic, arrogant, and even disobedient. "I think from what I have seen of them so far," wrote the Irish bishop, "that they are not made for the conversion of Africa. If only they settled down to hardship, mortification, unselfishness, obedience, and humility all would be well." Thus in contrast to the

Irish, continued the bishop, the Americans had indeed "a long way to travel before they get up to us." In a desperate move obviously to "Irishify" the Igbo territory, the bishop strongly urged his superiors to send him only Irish missionaries. "For God's sake," wrote the bishop to the Catholic authorities, "send us Irish Priests and send the others to Angola."[9]

Whereas the Irish considered Igboland their special missionary preserve, they strangely had negative attitudes toward the training of an indigenous clergy for the Igbo mission .The case of the late Bishop John C. Anyogu is perhaps typical. John Cross Anyogu, born at Onitsha, was the first Igbo Catholic priest east of the Niger River. He was also the first Igbo Catholic bishop (1957). In 1910 he applied to the Catholic authorities "to learn priest." Three years later he was sent to the Catholic seminary at Castlehead in England. After five years of study, Bishop Shanahan decided that Anyogu should finish his training in Ireland. He therefore requested that his countrymen accept Anyogu at the Holy Ghost Fathers seminary at Kimmage Manor, Dublin. Even though Shanahan promised to bear all the financial responsibility for Anyogu's maintenance, the Irish superior at Kimmage refused to admit him there purely on racial grounds. For this reason, Anyogu was sent to France, but was later brought back to Nigeria to continue his studies at the newly created seminary at Igbariam. He studied and taught there from 1924 and finally in 1930 was ordained priest.[10] Father Anyogu thus became the model for Igbo aspirants to the priesthood although, as already noted, Father Paul O. Emecheta had been ordained priest ten years earlier. Father Anyogu, however, was from east of the Niger where most of the Igbo priests originated.

Irish bigotry may be further illustrated from this other incident concerning two Igbo Catholic priests. In 1947 Bishop Heerey had proposed to send two Igbo priests to Ireland for further studies. They were Fathers Godfrey Okoye (later bishop of Enugu) and Moses Orakwudo. Both were to be stationed at the Holy Ghost Fathers seminary at Kimmage Manor. Bishop Heerey, as in the previous case, had written the superior general of the seminary to this effect. But, as in the case of John Anyogu, the superior refused to accept the two priests there. He argued among other things that "the faithful [in Ireland] would not want to receive holy communion from their hands," and that "Irish priests, except for a few," were not disposed to receive African priests in their churches. Equally enlightening is the fact that former Irish missionaries in Nigeria and elsewhere in Africa were reported to have "vigorously opposed" the coming of the two priests to Ireland. In fact, the Irish Provincial Council had no qualms about rejecting the admission of the two Igbo priests on the basis of their race. Here is how the issue was explained to the Catholic authorities in France: "The question is not as simple to us in Dublin as it might be for you in Paris. . . . At present the council responsible for the novitiate has resolutely refused to accept any black whatsoever, having been convinced that their acceptance would vitiate our propaganda in Ireland." The report concluded by stating that "no Irish administration which understands the actual circumstances and the feeling of the country would compromise the work of recruiting by such measures as proposed by Bishop Heerey."[11] As a consequence of this rejection, the two priests were sent elsewhere, as in the Anyogu case.

Naturally, this blatant racism of his countrymen was both embarrassing and painful to Bishop Heerey. Not surprisingly, he deplored the racist attitude of his compatriots at home. And he made it abundantly clear that what they had done was not only "shameful" but embarrassing. It seemed utterly incomprehensible to him, he remarked, that "African priests, who are our own formation, and are our cooperators in the Mission, are excluded from Kimmage!" Certainly, he went on, "this [is] shameful for a Missionary Congregation " to discriminate against Africans. Equally disappointed in this matter was the apostolic delegate to Nigeria, who correctly interpreted the Irish action as bound to "have a prejudicial effect on the admirable relationships between the Holy Ghost Fathers and their Nigerian flock."[12]

The Irish, of course, were part and parcel of European society, where racial prejudice and bigotry seemed endemic. Nor was racial prejudice toward Africans limited to those in Ireland per se. In fact, some of the missionaries in Nigeria were equally infected with the virus of racism. As any educated Igbo Roman Catholic would attest, Irish paternalism, racial bigotry, as well as sheer contempt for the African seemed rather pervasive. Educated Africans, for example, both clerical and lay, saw Irish missionaries as being imperious, overbearing, arrogant, and irritatingly contemptuous. In the words of Igbo priests interviewed by this writer in 1975, "Those of us who made it in those [colonial] days . . . must be said to have had the vocation" indeed.[13] They were referring, of course, not only to the difficulties they encountered during their clerical training, but also to the racist, paternalistic, and often disrespectful attitudes of their Irish superiors. In fact, African priests, teachers, and even catechists resented the disdainful attitudes of the Irish missionaries toward them, even though few ever expressed this openly.

European stereotypes of Africans as children, to be sure, seem to have conditioned the missionaries to treat Africans poorly. "Putting Africans down" or even physically assaulting them seemed of little consequence to Europeans. Thus, the case of Father John Fitzpatrick, formerly principal of Christ the King College at Onitsha, is typical. Father Fitzpatrick was notoriously known as a "Negro-hater" because of his rudeness to Africans.

He worked in the Owerri Division (presumably Emekuku) in the 1940s and is said to have treated Africans disrespectfully and at times referred to them as apes. Besides his contempt for the Africans, both clergy and lay alike, he is said to have been very overbearing—hence the general demand for his removal from the Owerri area. It is also said that his evident negrophobism galvanized an anti-European movement in the Owerri district. In the words of the local bishop, "The antagonism to the white man is growing daily. The Fathers and Sisters are being threatened in parts of Owerri where there always have been malcontents even among the Catholics. . . . The people are very restive and are watching for any *faux pas* on the part of the white man; and Fr. Fitzpatrick is one that gives them plenty of opportunities for observation."[14]

Although there were "demands from all sides for his removal," as the bishop acknowledged, Father Fitzpatrick was simply given "a final warning." This implied that unless he mended his ways his days in Owerri were numbered. But by allowing him to stay in the Owerri area "for another while," the bishop perhaps unwittingly fanned continued antiwhite sentiments in the region. However, some of the seemingly progressive missionaries have condemned shabby and disrespectful treatment of Africans. Said Father O'Connell in 1963:

We have badly managed aspects of our public relations. . . . Until quite lately priests in parishes had to [deal] only with the uneducated people. Some priests have not yet shaken off that stem from that situation—more unfortunately they have at times communicated these [contemptuous] attitudes to younger colleagues. Such men constantly upset the more educated section of the Catholic community, particularly teachers, through a lack of courtesy and consideration in their dealings with them.[15]

The practical solution to the apparently master-slave relationship between the European missionaries and the Africans would have been the replacement of the missionaries by Africans. But then there were no such considerations or movements either in the Catholic or in the Protestant missions. What the local people wanted, beginning in about the 1930s, was some kind of local representation in the church hierarchy. In other words, the demand was more for indigenous clergy than for church control— hence the pressure on the Catholic bishop at Onitsha for more sympathetic consideration of the needs of Owerri people. Not only were Catholics from Owerri frustrated by the lack of local clergy, but also they complained bitterly about the benign neglect of Owerri by the Catholic authorities at Onitsha. Hence the Oweri-Onitsha controversy dominated the affairs of the vicariate in the 1930s and 1940s.

THE ONITSHA-OWERRI QUESTION

Before embarking on the Catholic Owerri-Onitsha question, it might be useful to look at a similar development in the Protestant church. Anglicans in the Owerri area, for example, had for decades complained that the authorities at Onitsha seemed more interested in the development of the Onitsha mission than the Owerri mission. Thus CMS missionaries at Egbu protested the "dumping" of almost illiterate teachers from Onitsha at Owerri: "This district has for too long been the dumping ground for tired and otherwise undesirable teachers," protested the West Indian missionary at Egbu. It was this type of policy, he contended, that resulted in the relatively stunted growth of the district, a point of view that was shared by others. "It is true," affirmed the Reverend J. N. Cheetham, "that if we had several years ago decided to 'push' the work in the Ebu District it would have been much more developed than it is" today.[16] In essence, the missionaries at Owerri firmly believed that the CMS policymakers at Onitsha tended to concern themselves more with the interests of Onitsha than of Owerri.

Complaints about the benign neglect of Owerri's "crying needs" were not, of course, confined to the missionaries alone. The local people, in fact, protested vehemently the absence of postprimary institutions (secondary schools and teacher training colleges) in the area. For instance, when the Dennis Memorial Grammar School was built at Onithsa in 1925 and thus became the first Anglican secondary school in Igboland, Protestants in the Owerri area were aggrieved. Because the school was named after Archdeacon Dennis who founded the CMS mission at Egbu and spent most of his missionary years there, Anglicans from Owerri argued that the school should have been established at Owerri. It has been claimed, in fact, that the original plan was to have the school at Egbu. But this proposal, it has been said, was thwarted by Onitsha elements.[17] The authenticity of this argument remains to be investigated seriously.

Indeed, resentment against Onitsha "domination" in Owerri paralleled that of Irish domination and lately Mbaise domination of the church in the Owerri diocese. Thus there were cries for "sons of the soil"—meaning local clergy and teachers—to take over control of the schools and churches. As one Owerri informant observed, Bishop A. C. Anyeabo was from Onitsha. He came here as a catechist. The Reverend "Holy" Nweje, formerly archdeacon of Owerri, was from Onitsha. The school headmasters and most of the teachers at Egbu came from Onitsha. "Where are our own pastors and teachers?" It was this apparent Onitsha preponderance that led to the indigenization movement within the Protestant mission. Even in 1986, there was still agitation for a "native" bishop of Owerri, even though Bishop B. C. Nwankiti is from Imo State. But he hails from Atta, near Owerri. To Egbu Anglicans, therefore, it seems utterly incomprehensible that ever since 1906 when the CMS was established there, no son of Egbu has risen to the position of bishop.[18]

Just as the Protestants accused the authorities at Onitsha of unfair treatment of Owerri, so also did the Catholics charge the Catholic bishop at Onitsha with anti-Owerri policy. To the Catholics from Owerri (particularly those in the former Emekuku parish), Bishop Charles Heerey, then bishop (1932–48) of Onitsha and Owerri vicariate, seemed singularly anti-Owerri. His attitude, they argued, was clearly manifested in his allocation of social services such as schools and colleges. "Bishop Heerey did not seem to like us. He refused to give us any institutions of higher learning"[19]— hence the strong movement from the mid-1930s for the separation of Owerri from Onitsha. In other words, Owerri Catholics demanded their own separate bishop and diocese, believing that their special needs would be better served by a more sympathetic bishop.

The secessionist movement gained momentum after 1935. By that date, Calabar and Benue dioceses had been created, resulting in the partition of what was once the vicariate of Southern Nigeria into three—namely Benue, Calabar, and Onitsha-Owerri vicariates. Calabar province was then under the control of the Maynooth missionaries, better known as the St. Patrick's Foreign Missionary Society, made up essentially of secular priests.[20] The Irish missionaries who controlled the Onitsha-Owerri vicariate, on the other hand, were Spiritans, or more popularly, the Holy Ghost Fathers. And even though both congregations were Catholic, they nevertheless rivaled each other. Thus, the alleged territorial ambitions of the Seculars provoked extreme nervousness among the Spiritans. At a time when the Holy Ghost Fathers seemed to have fallen from grace in Rome, there was evident concern among them that Rome might assign more territories to their rivals—hence this nervous reaction from the bishop:

> The secular priests, especially the men at the head of the [secession] movement are extremely enthusiastic. They have their eyes set on the best part of the Vicariate, and the original document from his Eminence Cardinal Van Rossum had assigned them the best part [of the territory]. Without meaning any uncharitableness we should say they are very ambitious and covetous of the "lion's share" in the spoils. Rome will not hesitate to give them this lion's share if they have the lion's power—the men.[21]

As in the Calabar case, the movement toward the separation of Owerri from Onitsha caused considerable concern and opposition. The major reason for this, according to Bishop Heerey, was that Owerri Province, in Father Jordan's words, was invariably "the heart and core of Nigerian Catholicism," meaning that the province had the largest Catholic population in the whole of Nigeria. Furthermore, carving out Owerri from the vicariate would substantially delimit Onitsha's ecclesiastical authority. Bishop Heerey's anxiety over the possible creation of an Owerri vicariate was thus clearly reflected in his 1936 letter to Father Francis Griffin, the superior general of the Congregation of Holy Ghost Fathers: "I have just got an air mail letter from the Apostolic delegate [indicating] a further division of the Vicariate. The Owerri people wrote him about it. Since Calabar got its own Bishop they don't see why they shouldn't get theirs. So, if you don't send many Holy Ghost Fathers here, the rest of all Africa will be lost to the CSSP [Congregation of the Holy Spirit]." Not only did the bishop urge that Onitsha and Owerri should be "left united for some years yet," but also he expressed great apprehension that Owerri might in fact be assigned to another Catholic order. Indeed, said the bishop, "it would be a terrible blow" to the congregation "if Owerri were taken away from us" and given to another congregation. The "rumour," he went on, was that the Capuchin Fathers from Germany were about to come to Southern Nigeria. "If these Fathers apply to Rome or Monseigneur Hinsley," remarked the bishop, "I am afraid they will get their wish."[22] Hence, as Bishop Heerey intimated, the necessity for Irish missionary reinforcements had become doubly urgent.

Yet the request for a separate Owerri diocese continued. In 1947, for example, Catholics from the Owerri Province petitioned Rome again and demanded a separate episcopate, insisting that "the Bishop [Heerey] was cheating them intentionally" in the allocation of personnel and social services. But as in 1936 the bishop protested against the creation of an Owerri diocese. Again he argued that the possible loss of this "most progressive part of the missionary world" to another congregation would constitute a serious blow to the Spiritans. Added the bishop, "About two thirds of our Christians and catechumens are in Owerri Province, and the future is brighter than ever." Of course, he admitted, "we are *not* doing it [Owerri] justice with regard to staff."[23]

In spite of the bishop's opposition, however, Rome seemed determined to grant Owerri's request. Thus when the papal delegate visited West Africa again in 1947, Catholics from Owerri Province made a last-ditch effort to secure their own separate episcopate. Local unions at home and abroad petitioned Archbishop David Matthews and demanded not only a separate diocese and bishop, but also the establishment of secondary schools and teacher training institutions or colleges. According to one of the participants at the time, "His Lordship Bishop C. Heerey was holidaying in Ireland at that crucial time, and before he flew back, things had gone out of hand. Archbishop David Matthews ordered that six colleges [should] be opened in Owerri Province . . . with immediate effect."[24] More importantly, Owerri diocese was created in 1948, thus heralding the breakup of the Onitsha and Owerri union. Father J. B. Whelan, an Irishman then directing St. Paul's Seminary at Okpala, was appointed the new bishop of Owerri diocese. Thus began the Bishop Whelan era (1948–70) which, for our purposes, represented the decades of rapid development in both secular and clerical education.

Evidently "things had gone out of hand" for Bishop Heerey, insofar as he had been presented with a fait accompli. But contrary to his fears, Owerri remained under the management of the Holy Ghost Fathers. Perhaps more significantly, it was still placed under Irish control. But as we shall now see, a new era had begun, marked by significant progress in the development of a large corps of indigenous clergy. For by the 1950s and 1960s a number of seminaries were established and many more Igbo priests ordained. Indeed, the two decades or so that preceded the Nigerian Civil War witnessed the expansion of both secular and clerical education in Owerri and its hinterland, thus transforming the region from an apparently educational backwater vis-à-vis Onitsha into one of the most progressive areas of Nigeria. But not until after the civil war would it really be proper to talk of an educational explosion in what is now Imo State.

AFRICANIZATION AND INDIGENIZATION OF THE CHURCH

With reference to the development of indigenous clergy, the Whelan era laid the foundation for the ordination explosion of the 1970s and thus for the rapid Africanization and indigenization of the Catholic church in present Imo State. For by the 1950s and 1960s several seminary centers had sprung up in various parts of Owerri diocese, which then comprised the present dioceses of Owerri, Umuahia (1958), Port Harcourt (1962), Okigwe (1978), and Orlu (1980). Chief among the seminaries were the ones at Okpala (St. Peter Claver), Ikenanzizi, Obowo, Umuowa Orlu, Awomama, and others. It is also very significant that students from Owerri and its hinterland were now admitted to the seminaries in ever-increasing numbers. With respect to St. Peter Claver Seminary, a local priest has written, "Vocation to the priesthood was a new phenomenon in Igboland. . . . To induce and enhance a steady growth of entrants, boys were recruited from standard five of the primary school to do their last form of primary school studies in St. Finbars School, which was annexed to [St. Peter Claver] Seminary." Thus, as he added, St. Peter Claver at Okpala, which was established in 1951, has since the 1950s "produced more priests than many other Diocesan seminaries in Nigeria."[25]

Interestingly enough, the ordination explosion of the 1960s and 1970s,[26] which resulted in the rapid Africanization of the Catholic church in the region, had much to do with the guidelines provided by Rome. The papal encyclicals *Evangeli Praecones* of 1951 and *Fidei Donum* of 1957 actually stressed the need for more local priests as well as for more missionaries. The ordination of more Catholic priests, as Adrian Hastings has shown, inexorably led to "the sudden emergence of a black clerical voice with a sharp message of its own." Not only did the new priests, the "Young Turks," in Hastings's words, advocate the indigenization of the church, especially its liturgy, but more significantly they began the defense of African religion and philosophy. Of the revolutionary character of the new age Hastings writes:

> Around 1954 and 1955 there was a remarkable group of young black priests studying in Rome: Alexis Kagame from Rwanda, Vincent Mulago from Bukavu in the Congo, Robert Sastre and Bernardin Gantin from Dahomey, Joaquim Pinto de Andrade from Angola, Robert Dosseh from Togo, Jean Zoa from Cameroon. From their Roman Association of St. Augustine began to appear articles on all sorts of subjects and such as to prove very alarming in some missionary circles. A movement of Young Turks, in fact, had quite unexpectedly arrived. Joined by friends in Paris they produced in 1956 *Des prêtres noirs s'interrogent*, a book of wide-ranging and hard-hitting essays which was to have a very considerable impact. The same year Kagame's thesis, *La philosohie bantu-rwandaise de l'être*, was published in Brussels. Here was an articulate African response to Temples and the beginning of a debate on the nature of African religion and the proper relationship of Christianity to it which would soon, if belatedly, become a central Catholic preoccupation.[27]

In the Owerri Division, to be sure, the increasingly large number of local clergy during the 1960s and 1970s (over sixty priests were ordained) meant that sooner or later ecclesiastical authority would invariably pass from European to African hands. The assumption of local autonomy was actually accelerated by the Nigeria-Biafra war. For shortly after the war all foreign missionaries in the former Biafran area were expelled, leaving the local priests to take over control of the church. In 1970 therefore Bishop Mark Unegbu became the bishop of Owerri. Under his leadership, the diocese has witnessed a dramatic rise in the number of indigenous clergy. By 1970, for example, there were twenty-six indigenous priests in the diocese. By 1981 the number had risen to 129, an increase of over 400 percent. Since then two forces have been at work, namely, decolonization and indigenization of the Catholic church. The former implies the elimination of European missionary or colonial domination, while the latter is symbolized in the "making of the christian life the way of life of the people." Thus to the Igbo clergy, the end of foreign domination and the ongoing process of indigenization are reasons for self-gratification. In the words of a local priest, "The church is now our own. It is no longer a foreign mission. It is our own in local administration. It is ours in local ministration. It is ours in the sense of the infusion of [African] cultures and doctrinal concepts. It is now our own in language" as well.[28]

The emphasis on language is significant. Although many of the foreign missionaries were in Igboland for twenty or more years, hardly any of them could speak Igbo fluently. Nor could they even say mass in Igbo! All they were required to have was a rudimentary knowledge of the language to enable them to hear confession. Thus they were like artisans without tools, preaching sermons in English and relying on local catechists and village teachers as interpreters. In the cynical words of the Ugandian writer,

> The things they shout I do not understand,
> They shout anyhow. . . .
> A strange language they speak
> The Christian diviner—priests,
> And the white nuns
> Think the girls understand
> What they are saying,
> And are annoyed
> When they laugh.[29]

Like some of their colonial administrators, the Catholic missionaries rationalized their lack of a good knowledge of the language on grounds of pressure of work. "You have been overtaxed in your work for the eight or ten years past which has marked the extraordinary growth of the Mission," argued one missionary. Because of pressure of work, he insisted, it seemed almost impossible for anyone to have "sufficient time to learn the very difficult Igbo language fairly well." Nonetheless, he admitted, "To acquire a good working knowledge of it . . . is important."[30]

In conclusion, it is interesting to note that the replacement of the Europeans by Africans especially in the Igbo area was actually predicted some two decades or so before the event. A well-informed Roman Catholic observer of the African political scene remarked in 1953,

Judging by the present thriving of diocesan junior seminaries, I cannot imagine that in fifty years from today there will be a single Irish C.S.S.P. man ministering to souls in Nigeria. Nor can I foresee that there will be any need for men to come from the Irish Province in twenty-five years time, perhaps less. All this independent of political factors which may accelerate considerably the decline of European authority, clerical as well as lay, in Nigeria, and other parts of Africa.

Surely, the Nigerian Civil War considerably accelerated the demise of European ecclesiastical authority. Elsewhere in Africa, the great wind of political change has also generated what President Mobutu of Zaire has called the movement toward African "authenticity." Declared Mobutu: "We are now embarking on our cultural liberation, the reconquest of our African . . . soul. We men of black skin have had imposed on us the mentality of quite a different race. We must become once more authentic Africans, authentic blacks, authentic Zairians."[31]

Indeed, this manifestation of African nationalism has prompted Western mission societies to reevaluate their role in Africa and elsewhere. To quote from an American document as to "what lies ahead" in the 1980s:

The 1980s and 1990s will certainly turn out to be quite different from our expectations. Long-range planning of mission priorities and programs will become less inviting—and less popular than in past or present grand strategizing for the Christian conquest of the world. A missionary style of responsiveness, flexibility, and openness will prove most effective, testing fresh adventures and experiments in new modes and areas of work. Effective mission will usually take the form of response to opportunity—often spelled N-E-E-D—*especially as identified by local Christians* [emphasis added]. This venturing and responsive style will place heavy emphasis on [new] relationships, widening and stimulating partnerships. Heavy funding and staffing . . . will diminish for several reasons . . . [O]verseas churches will be uneasy with the dominance implicit in large unilateral subsidy [for where Euro-American money is used, there will, sooner or later, follow Euro-American control[32]] . . . This trend toward full [local] participation and self-determination reflects what might well be called a pervasive "radicalization" of the context for mission in the 1980s.

The document went on to emphasize the obligation of the missionaries to uphold the basic principles of social justice and respect for human rights. "All over the world peoples formerly caught in traditional patterns of inequality, dependence and exploitation have caught a vision of their human right to a significant say about the conditions of their life and a fair share of the resources which make life more secure and comfortable."[33]

It has in fact been suggested that missionary evangelism in Africa in the

1980s may now have become irrelevant, if not anachronistic. Thus Hastings writes, "One cannot help having the impression that by the [1980s] the foreign missionary had become, essentially, an irrelevance, or at least something vastly more marginal to African Christianity than he had ever been before."[34]

7. TRADITIONAL POLITICAL SYSTEM AND PATTERNS OF SOCIAL AND POLITICAL CHANGE

In chapter 1 we noted that the establishment of British rule gave rise to the creation of native courts and the appointment of warrant chiefs. These two novel institutions radically affected the traditional systems of law and authority. As a matter of fact, their impact is still being felt in Owerri today and, for that matter, in all of Imo State. Until well after the Second World War, the native court and warrant chief systems dominated the political history of Owerri. Their introduction, as we shall soon show, altered the patterns of indigenous administration and created political and social restlessness. In his annual report for 1938 the DO at Owerri lamented the preoccupation of administrative officials with the native courts and their problems. "As soon as anyone attempted an examination of Owerri political affairs," he said, "one's mind automatically turns to the Native Courts," adding that "it would be a healthier sign if this were not so, since the Courts have for too long loomed too large on the political horizon of the people." He continued, "The day when the officer writing [an annual] report can honestly say that the emphasis has been transferred from Court to Council will mark a big step forward in Owerri political history." Regrettably, he added, "the day has not yet come."[1] Because the native court loomed too large on Owerri political history, it is fitting that we should begin this chapter by examining the evolution of the native court system and its impact on Owerri history as a whole. But before we do so, it might be useful to examine briefly the patterns of traditional political administration. For a basic understanding of the indigenous system of government will help us to appreciate more fully the effects of the political transformation that took place in the colonial period. Since the literature on this subject is vast and easily available, only the major outlines of the traditional system are attempted here.

The traditional political system in the Owerri division is similar to that of most Igbo communities. In general, the family is the primary and smallest social and political unit. Here the oldest member, the *Qpara* (*Qkpara*), of the family or extended-family exercises a measure of authority: "The authority of the *okpara* is based largely on the fact that he is the intermediary between the family and the ancestors, and that to insult him is to insult the ancestors, on whose goodwill the members of the family are largely dependent." His function was multifarious: "He offers sacrifice for the welfare of the family, organizes the exploitation of family land, assigns kitchen-garden plots to wives, rations supplies in times of stress, helps members of the family who have got into difficulties, and bears a large part of marriage, funeral, and hospitality expenses. . . . In short, the head of the household is the material and spiritual guardian of the group, and in external matters assumes [political] responsibility for all, as far as he reasonably can."[2]

Also, as the holder of the family *Qfq* (stave; symbol of truth, authority, and honesty), the qpara represents the family at the village level. For beyond the family is the village (*Nchi*). Each village has it own assembly or council whose members comprise the family heads or holders of Qfq. This village assembly or council, also known as the council of elders (*Qha*), was responsible for the normal administration of the village, the maintenance of law and order, as well as the settlement of disputes among members of the village or community. Decisions on village affairs were arrived at by consensus after a prolonged and often heated debate. To an outsider unfamiliar with Igbo political culture, such meetings might give the appearance of lack of law and order. But public participation is the very essence of Igbo village democracy, meaning that every member of the village, including women and children, could attend the village meeting. And everyone was allowed to air his/her views. Indeed, no interested party would be debarred from attending a village council meeting. "An intelligent and lucid expression of opinion was listened to in silence, interrupted by grunts of approval, while a foolish or unpopular speaker was howled down."[3] In general, however, the elders' opinions predominated.

Beyond the village assembly was the town council. A town or village-group, in Igbo parlance, is a group of related villages who trace their origin from a common ancestor. Thus we have Uratta (the children of Atta), Owerri, Emekuku, Ogwa, Egbu, Naze, and so on. Each town then had its own town council, again composed of village elders (for example, Qha Uratta, Qha Owere). When cases of common interest arose, town councils were summoned. However, "a general meeting of all sections of a village-group was infrequent, being held only when it was necessary to take common action against some external enemy, to offer common sacrifice, to get rid of some 'abomination,' or to attempt to settle an internal dispute which, if allowed to continue would be likely to disrupt the community." In general then the village council or council of elders handled local political affairs. Hence Igbo democracy has been described as "Ọhacracy," or perhaps more accurately, gerontocracy. This means that executive and legislative authority lay in the hands of the elders, men of wisdom, influence, and intelligence. J. G. C. Allen provides this description of the council as it operated before the advent of colonialism.

> This body met in the central meeting place of the village (Ama uku) at regular intervals, generally once every native week of eight days, and discussed matters of administrative importance in the village. It gave orders for the cleaning of markets and paths, formulated regulations for the control of market prices and agriculture and dealt with all matters concerning the economic welfare of the community. On occasions it also dealt with minor judicial matters, since its functions were not limited to executive duties only.[4]

In their handling of village disputes, the elders often reinforced their authority by invoking the memory of the ancestors. This they did by using their Ọfọ as an instrument of social control or curse. For example, before rendering judgment between disputants, the holder of the senior Ọfọ would exclaim: "Our judgment is in accordance with custom and is one therefore by which you must abide. If you refuse to obey the decision may Ọfọ kill you." He would then strike the ground with his Ọfọ, and all the other elders would follow suit, adding, "*Eha!*" (Amen). A decision once made and announced was enforced by the weight of public opinion, and "where that failed by the invocation of . . . Ala [the Earth Goddess] against the disobedient person. This in the past was quite sufficient to enforce the decision and the idea of obstinate disobedience was evidently foreign to the ideas of the people."[5]

It would be grossly an error, of course, to assume that the elders had a monopoly of power and authority. For in republican Igbo society no single individual or social group actually monopolized power or authority. Instead, authority was in fact diffused. Thus "native" priests (*nde dibia*), secret societies (for example, *Ọkọnkọ*), age-grades, and others had their spheres of authority and influence. The age-grades (*Ebiri*), for instance, played an important part in the social life of the community. "In time of war they were of great assistance in the rapid mobilization of warriors, while in peace time each was allocated a different portion of the communal work [such as the cleaning of the compound, the roads leading to the market, farm, or stream]. In some areas also the young Age Grades were given the task of policing the village and of arresting male factors [*sic*]."[6] In essence, authority was shared among various social and religious groups.

Thus the question of someone assuming paramount authority over everybody did not arise in the Igbo traditional political system.

Of course, there were men of wealth who wielded considerable influence and authority. But as we shall see, they earned whatever influence and authority they exercised. And should they abuse their power, they not only lost the loyalty and allegiance of the people, but also they could be censured by the elders and the entire community and thus become personae non grata. It was therefore necessary for "a wealthy and powerful man to keep on good terms with his fellow citizens." Surely, in all societies, as Meek has pointed out, "the possession of wealth confers power." Hence in precolonial Igbo society a significant number of men with wealth (Qgaranya) assumed a measure of authority and influence in their communities. In the Owerri area, men such as Anumudu, Njemanze, Obi Ejeshi, and Oginye (of Umuegbe Ogwa) attained fame and prominence as Qgaranya. Of these men J. G. C. Allen, formerly a British colonial administrator, writes, "In the first place such a man would be a great slave-owner, while in addition he would generally undertake the more indigent among his townspeople, especially of such people that could be of use to him. Very often among his slaves were numbered those of his townspeople who had been convicted of some offence, and whose fines had been paid by him. Such people became his vassals until they had refunded to him the amount of the fine."[7]

Evidently rich men of the kind indicated above "pursued a definite policy of rendering assistance in order to gain ascendancy over the persons assisted." In addition, they generally provided assistance to their own people and others in time of war. A family or village which felt itself to be weak, for example, would seek the protection of men such as Njemanze and would thus pledge their allegiance to him. Sometimes his relationship was sealed by an oath whereby the rich man and his clients bind themselves as a fighting unit. In many instances these clients rendered him voluntary services. Through this patron-client relationship Njemanze's influence spread, as did fear of him, as some say. Besides, men of wealth and influence offered safe conduct to travellers or visitors, being well known to the people of other communities. Thus "any person claiming friendship with the great man could pass unmolested through any village in the neigbourhood." Also, rich men gained considerable influence by lending money to individuals at "enormous interest." Defaulters thus found themselves tied to the rich man. In Allen's words, "The power of a rich man in former times depended on the number of persons whom he could support." An Qgaranya who possessed a number of dependents was certainly in a position to enforce his commands, being "a man to be feared."[8]

Yet as already noted, the Qgaranya could not afford to be autocratic. On this issue Allen writes,

Disputes might be brought to him for settlement, but he would not proceed to judgment without first calling in a council of elders of proved intelligence. The details of village administration, also, he was content as a rule to leave to the elders, but he would not hesitate to interfere if their conduct was unsatisfactory. His influence over the people was probably due more to his talent of leadership and his knowledge of mob psychology than to brute force and the crushing effect of riches. It is probable that anything in the nature of despotism would not have been tolerated.[9]

NATIVE COURTS AND SOCIOPOLITICAL CHANGE

When the high commissioner, Sir Ralph Moor, and Chief Justice M. R. Menendez established the Owerri Native Court in 1903, very few if any of the local people understood the significance or implications of the court. Nor did they seem to care. For despite attempts by Douglas, the DC, to persuade people in the district to come to Owerri to settle their "palavers," the indigenes preferred to conduct their political and judicial affairs in accordance with native laws and customs. That the majority of the people at the early stages treated the native courts with disdainful indifference might be appreciated from the reply given to Douglas and "friendly chiefs." Douglas was told that the laws of the white man "are not our own" and that he should no longer attempt to impose his authority over the people. Even chiefs who attempted to enforce government orders were firmly told to go away and warned never to come back with messages from the white man. Thus, although the stiff resistance to patronize the courts ultimately turned into grudging acceptance over time, hostility toward the native courts was never totally removed. For during the First World War resentment against the alien institution was expressed in the destruction of court houses and attacks on court clerks and court messengers (especially those sent to issue court summonses) or even the chiefs themselves.[10]

In some communities, to be sure, laws were passed prohibiting people from attending the native courts. In 1917, for example, Umuapu court was boycotted, thus paralyzing the local government there. Police constables and court messengers sent to restore order were attacked and some of them injured. The government responded by sending a well-armed military patrol to the various towns that attended Umuapu court. The damage was considerable. According to the officer in command, E. Osborne, approximately 1,250 raffia palms ("Tombo trees,") and 2,500 plantain trees were destroyed. In addition, 20 cows and 16 goats were killed while 127 goats were captured and 10 yam stores (ọba) were totally destroyed. In the end seven towns were "visited" and severely punished for the "revolt against central authority"—the native court. These towns were Umuapu, Awara, Asa, Ohoba, Ikweride, Opete (Obite), and Umuokanne. Revolts such as the above and attacks on court messengers were often interpreted by the administration as not necessarily directed at the government per se but at the government agents whose "outrageous" assertions of authority over the people were resented. Thus, in reference to the attacks on court messengers, the DO observed,

> The causes of these tentative revolts against the authority seem frequently to have been some outrageous acts on the part of the Messenger and sometimes because the Court Messenger was not accompanied by a boy or representative of the chief of the town. The general tendency appears to be [that the people are] antagonistic to the chief and not the recognised central authority, the Native Court. The chief [is] being held responsible for the deeds of the latter.[11]

In fact, however, attacks on the courts or court messengers reflected deep dissatisfaction with the government as a whole.

As the foregoing account demonstrates, the people were determined to maintain their political and juridical independence. But the government was equally as determined to impose its authority on the conquered inhabitants. In effect, the government had determined to destroy the traditional order of things so as to build on the ruins. Thus, by the Native Court Proclamation of 1901 (modified in 1906 by the Native Court Ordinance), the government had decreed that "the only legal means of administering justice in [the Nigerian] territories are through a Commissioner's Court or Native Council." By implication, all other forms of adjudicating disputes in the different communities were now declared illegal. As a matter of fact, traditional systems of justice were regarded as obnoxious and so their continuation was viewed as constituting a breach of the peace.[12] Clearly, then, the government had made a frontal assault on traditional political and judicial institutions. It was through the native courts, on the other hand, that the government administered the country. By 1908 the provincial commissioner for the eastern provinces, W. Fosbery, was to report that "the extent to which they [Native Courts] are appreciated by the native population can be gauged by studying the number of cases which have been dealt with therein."[13] From the point of view of the Africans, however, the creation of the native courts heralded the era of social and political disintegration, the impact of which is still being felt.

Before the native courts reorganization of the 1930s, there were six native courts in the old Owerri Division. These were located at Owerri, Oguta,

Okpala, Ngor, Nguru, and Umuapu. The Owerri court, being the premier court and situated at the headquarters, was closely supervised by the district commissioner. In keeping with the Native Court Proclamation, the district commissioner acted as the ex-officio president of the court. The other courts were simply visited occasionally. The jurisdictional authority of the Owerri court was quite extensive and embraced the above court areas. The court membership of the courts was as follows in 1917: Owerri, 54; Oguta, 20; Okpala, 26; Ngor, 38; Nguru, 34; Umuapu, 14. Compared with some other courts in the eastern provinces, such as Ikot-Ekpene, the Owerri courts were relatively lower in status, being empowered to impose limited terms of imprisonment or fines. They could impose fines not exceeding £50 while those in the Ikot-Ekpene Division could impose heavier fines. "In my opinion," wrote the DO at Owerri in 1919, the Owerri courts "might well be placed on an equal footing with the Courts in the Ikot-Ekpene Division" because, as he put it, the Igbos "are at least as intelligent as the Ibibios in that part of the Southern Provinces."[14] By the end of 1919 the civil jurisdiction of the Owerri, Oguta, and Nguru courts had been raised. They were then classified as Grade B courts while Okpala, Ngor, and Umuapu courts remained as Minor Grade C courts. By 1935, however, they were all reclassified along with many others and were designated as Grade D courts.

In exercising the powers granted to them, the native courts tried both civil and criminal cases and imposed fines ranging from a few shillings to a maximum of £50. They also had the power to sentence criminals to various terms of imprisonment, often with the concurrence of the district commissioner. The colonial prison, a hated penal innovation, ultimately sounded the death knell of traditional forms of punishment for serious crimes. In Igbo society, observed J. G. C. Allen, a former administrator/anthropologist, "No recognized penal system existed, but the mode of punishment was based on the idea of compensation for a wrong done rather [than] of revenge on the perpetrator." Sending a person to prison in the early days of colonial rule was indeed tantamount to issuing him a death warrant. For many prisoners the food was bad, the environment was both unfamiliar and depressing, and the sheer confinement in a small dungeon robbed them of personal freedom and manhood. As one British official at the Colonial Office in London put it rather dramatically,

A man is taken from his village, from his family and kindred, from the only life which he knows, and confined to a prison cell. . . . The cell where he sleeps is provided with ventilation based on British ideas of fresh air. The result is often such that it would be more merciful to hang him at once. He pines at the loss of freedom; the unaccustomed food and sleeping arrangements cause disease—and he *dies*. To all intents and purposes he had been sentenced to death as surely as if he had been sentenced to hanging.[15]

In addition, imprisonment carried with it a social stigma. In precolonial days a man who committed a heinous offense could be reintegrated into society after the necessary purification rites or ceremonies had been performed. For the colonial prisoner, life was never again to be the same, for he lived at the periphery of society and was denied employment in the civil service and/or position of leadership in his own community.

In 1905 there were a total of 235 prisoners at the Owerri prison. To Governor Egerton, who visited the prisoners, this was a "regrettably large number," given the fact that the station had been in existence for barely three years. Some of the prisoners, he reported, were even chained together for "no apparent reason." He therefore instructed that they should be unchained. Many of these prisoners were either young men who had resisted road work, or captives of the military expeditions, or both. Moreover, they included hostages, especially elders, who were seized from various towns and villages with the aim of coercing the local people to comply with government orders and demands. By 1919 there were about 923 prisons at Owerri. Given the deplorable conditions under which they lived, many of these prisoners died, some from harsh treatment, from disease (especially dysentery), or from congestion and unsanitary surroundings. The cold and damp cells also caused pneumonia as a result of sleeping on cold floors, as blankets were not often supplied to the prisoners. But blankets were generally in short supply and, as the DO remarked in 1917, blankets for prisoners were "the most serious shortage" at the Owerri prison. Food was also inadequate, resulting naturally in prisoners being poorly fed. "Food," reported the DO, "is the most difficult part of the running of Owerri Prison. The country being over-populated and with a large number of people who do not cultivate crops themselves, thus yams, cassavas, greens are hard to obtain in any quantity."[16]

It should be noted too that accommodation was particularly bad, overcrowding being the chief feature of the prisons. The Owerri prison, for example, was officially "certified" to accommodate about 104 prisoners, but it contained no less than two hundred inmates. Yet the DO argued that "this is no hardship to the inmates" because they "are used to closer quarters in their homes"! He of course acknowledged that the situation was nonetheless "undesirable" and indicated that efforts had been made to improve the situation. "Three new cells have been built, certified to hold 11 each and should be in use in a few days time," he reported. To further ease the terrible overcrowding, it was proposed to send some prisoners to Port Harcourt prison. Unfortunately, the outbreak of chicken pox at the Owerri prison led to the transfers being prohibited. Besides, Port Harcourt prison itself was full to capacity. Interestingly enough, the officials seemed to view the mishap as somewhat beneficial. Admitting that the average number of prisoners at Owerri "has been over the allowed number" the DO, however, stated that "this increased number enabled a lot of work to be done which otherwise could not have been accomplished." Said E. Falk (DO), "The repair and construction of mud and mat buildings and the general sanitation, and maintenance of the Station will easily absorb the labour of two hundred men."[17]

In addition to imposing terms of imprisonment, the native courts also administered corporal punishment of which public flogging was the most detestable. Men and women were flogged, a practice unheard of before in Igbo society. To some policymakers, to be sure, flogging seemed far better than "the barbarity of the European punishment of imprisonment." The argument in favor of flogging seemed to be that imprisonment often resulted in the death of the prisoners. Yet the dangers inherent in flogging were equally serious. For example, the infliction of several strokes of the cane often left scars of permanent injury. Besides, "intractable ulcers" occasionally developed on the buttocks as a result of the "unhealed effects of floggings administered by the Native Courts." For these reasons some officials argued that flogging by the native courts should be abolished in Nigeria. Governor Hugh Clifford (1919–25), for example, was particularly critical of Hausa courts. In his view the administration of corporal punishment by the courts was not only "excessive" but equally "shocking." Clifford therefore questioned the wisdom of the government in deliberately investing "extensive powers" on the native courts and the chiefs. While objecting to the flogging of women, a practice that would have been intolerable in British society, the officials at the Colonial Office insisted that flogging as a form of punishment should be allowed in the native courts. Even though the officials agreed that the severity of the flogging should be minimized, they nevertheless argued that any attempt to abolish flogging at the courts would "damage the prestige" of the chiefs. Unless the power of the courts "has in fact been abused," minuted the colonial secretary, no effort should be made to deprive chiefs and courts of their power to punish the people by flogging. Instead of abolition, continued the colonial secretary, stricter supervision of the courts should be undertaken so as to correct any apparent abuses. Indeed, said the secretary, it is on the power of the courts to administer corporal punishment that the prestige of the chiefs "must largely depend." It would appear indeed that this defense of corporal punishment by the Colonial Office was simply an attempt at blunting open criticism of Frederick Lugard's policy of indirect rule. For the criticism of the courts and chiefs seemed to the officials an unwarranted affront on Lugard. Hence Governor Clifford and his subordinates were clearly made to understand that "the Secretary of State is definitely opposed to any departure from Sir F. Lugard's policy of taking every step to encourage indirect rule by giving local chiefs the maximum powers compatible with their abilities."[18]

By and large, Nigerians were induced to patronize the native courts rather than the traditional judicial institutions. In Igbo society the most immediate effect of the native court system was its impact on the traditional institutions for adjudicating disputes. In pregovernment days the village assembly, that is, the council of elders (Qha), the secret and titled societies, and oracles played significant roles in the administration of justice. The creation of the native courts, however, drastically curtailed the ability of these bodies to play their traditional juridical roles. Instead of complaints being sent to the Qha or to any other bodies, they were now sent to the courts or to the district commissioner. Commenting on the attitude of Owerri people toward the new political arrangement, the DO stated in 1919 that "with the exception of a few remote places near the divisional boundaries," Owerri people "have for the past few years been in the habit of bringing the most trifling complaints to the District Office."[19] Clearly, the native courts had driven the indigenous forms of administration underground.

Judging from the volume of cases heard at the native courts, it would appear indeed that the courts had become accepted in 1919. A few random examples may help to illustrate this. In 1916, for example, 5,741 cases were handled at the six divisional courts. Of this number, 2,228 were criminal cases and 3,513 civil. And for the first six months of 1917 (from January to June) the number of cases came to 3,588 while that of 1919 (July to December) was 4,643. In 1925, some 11,836 cases were heard; the number in 1926 was even larger, 11,937. Although there were a variety of cases, land cases are said to have loomed large in many of the court transactions, especially the Nguru court area.[20] (Refer to table 2 for additional illustration of numbers of court cases handled.) Without a doubt the native court system fostered a passion for litigation which invariably proved injurious to the body politic. Certainly, the multiplicity of cases at the courts reflects the degree of social and political disintegration, and the impact is still being felt.

Obviously, the ever-increasing volume of cases proved exceedingly burdensome to both the chiefs and the district officers. Faced with this rapidly increasing number of cases, the chiefs could not possibly give full attention to every individual case. Nor were they really disposed to do so. The majority of them, it seemed, were more interested in exploiting the opportunities

TABLE 2
Native Court Cases in the Owerri Division for the Half-year July 1, 1919–December 31, 1919

In the native court of	Number of persons convicted in criminal cases											Number of persons convicted in civil cases							Total criminal and civil cases
	Murder	Attempted murder	Manslaughter	Rape	Stealing with violence	Stealing	Malicious injury to property	Other offenses against native law & custom	Offenses against the NA order	Other offenses against ordinances & bylaws	Total criminal cases	Matrimonial	Land	Debts & other contracts	Trespass, assault & other wrongs	Liberation from slavery	Other cases	Total civil cases	
Umuakpo C	—	—	—	—	—	6	5	138	68	—	217	135	—	92	34	—	31	292	509
Owerri B	—	—	—	—	—	90	23	342	—	133	588	235	4	368	42	—	15	664	1,252
Oguta B	—	—	—	—	—	22	3	194	15	44	278	100	2	109	15	—	4	230	508
Nguru B	—	—	—	—	—	119	57	287	355	—	818	215	2	198	43	—	15	473	1,291
Okpala C	—	—	—	—	—	9	17	200	42	—	268	123	1	114	8	—	47	293	561
Ngor C	—	—	—	—	—	60	11	213	52	1	337	88	1	74	9	—	13	185	522
Half-year total	—	—	—	—	—	306	116	1,374	532	178	2,506	896	10	955	151	—	125	2,137	4,643

Source: NNAE: 48/19 OW DIST 9/5/10. Errors in addition in the original have been corrected here.

available to them for personal gain than in performing their duties to their people. The result was that many people who perhaps would have been found innocent were often convicted. In many instances, of course, the corrupt practices of the chiefs were responsible for the misdirection of justice. However, as DO E. Falk once pointed out, whenever it was discovered that the chiefs "were apparently too lazy to hear evidence available in individual cases, such cases were invariably referred back to them to complete the hearing." This referral policy, according to the DO, had the "good effect" of reducing the number of convicts furnished by the courts.[21] Of course, the DO had the power of overturning the judgments rendered by the chiefs.

It would appear, at least from the body of evidence at our disposal, that the practice of referring cases back to the courts was partly motivated by a genuine sense of justice and partly by personal interest. If the chiefs rendered more balanced judgment, it seemed possible that the need for appeals would be minimized. Considering that these appeals were numerous and proved extremely burdensome to the officials, it would be reasonable to speculate that the insistence on the chiefs rendering more acceptable judgments was to lighten the burden on the officers. For, as E. Falk (DO) pointed out, "Almost every Native who loses a case appeals to the District Officer who cannot possibly rehear every case *ab initio*, when it is considered that the number of cases dealt with in the Owerri Native Courts exceeds 300 per month."[22] That a considerable number of cases were reviewed by the DO is clear from the following quotation from Falk's 1919 report: "A large number of cases are reviewed by District Officers. This work coupled with that of acting as Legal Adviser to the people would by itself give a European Officer a fair day's work at Owerri. This is all to the good, but the misfortune is that one official [alone] cannot possibly give the individual the full attention he desires unless some other branch of work is to be neglected." In a related 1917 report on appeals, J. M. Pollen (DO) added an interesting phenomenon: the emergence of the so-called letter writers or petitioners. In his words, "There is a large sprinkling of literate natives in the Division now, petitioners and 'complainants' no longer come and tell their story before the D.O., but almost invariably hand in a letter. I am told £5 or even £10 is sometimes paid to a letter-writer, but no petitioner whom I have questioned has confessed to more than £1, and most have named a few shillings."[23]

Because of the unusual rise in court cases, the need for better-educated clerks became crucial. As the DO explained, "In an amorphous society such as Owerri the usefulness of the Courts depends largely on the efficiency of the Clerks" who would provide some "reasonably intelligent" record of court proceedings. Given the pace of social change and the expectation of the people, he said, it was imperative that any of the court clerks who were deemed inefficient "should be eliminated" forthwith. For, as he pointed out, "what might have been tolerable in the way of efficiency [some] years ago is no longer so today." The DO, however, commended the work of one Mr. Dapper at the Owerri court and Messrs. Pepple, Shaw, and Kallio for their very satisfactory work. "The remainder" of the clerks, he said, "have shown good conduct but are below the educational standard the situation [now] demands." One Mr. Braid was particularly referred to as being "notably weak." The 1926 report was significantly full of praise for the African clerks. "The fact that nearly 1,700 more cases were dealt with reflects very creditably on the native court clerks" in the division.[24]

Despite the burden the increasing volume of cases imposed, the officials seemed quite pleased with the local patronage of the courts. After all, the courts were the major sources of revenue for the local administration. The revenue, derived largely from court fees and fines, rose in proportion to the number of cases handled at the court. In his semiannual report for 1919, Falk informed his superiors that "the Courts continue to be by far the largest source of local revenue and total fines imposed show a net increase" over the previous year. F. Ferguson reported in the same vein in 1920 that "the Native Courts continue to be a source of Revenue and the receipts are well up to the standard of the past few years." "I regret," he added, that "I cannot chronicle definite improvement of their probity and justice." A few figures may be instructive. In 1916 the revenue from court fees alone amounted to £2,271:0:6d while the receipt from fines totalled £2,282:19:6d. The revenue from fees for 1917 (half-year) was £1,376:0:0d, and the receipt from fines was £1,940:0:0d. This impressive increase in state revenue, corresponding to the rise in the volume of court cases, established the need for additional personnel to maximize court profits. "It would pay to appoint more assistant Court Clerks," said Falk, "as it would lead to increase net receipts as more cases could be dealt with."[25]

This demand for court clerks tended to enhance the popularity of the office. But these semieducated clerks, whose salaries were relatively low, tended to enrich themselves from the court proceeds and from bribes taken from the people. Instances abound of these clerks pocketing court fees and fines. As cases at Ngor and Nguru revealed, court clerks often failed to enter into the cashbooks the correct amount of revenue collected. In some cases no entries were made at all. That the majority of the court clerks were corrupt is almost axiomatic. In any case, revelations of embezzlement and bribery not only damaged the reputation of court clerks but also often led to their prosecution and dismissal. Take the case of one Mr. Egbushie, the court clerk at Nguru in 1917. On March 27, 1917 he was tried and convicted of embezzlement, although the amount involved was never stated. However, this prosecution opened the floodgates of investigation for corruption and subsequent dismissals. Said the DO, "The conviction of Egbuchie [*sic*], the Clerk at Nguru, for embezzlement, . . . had effects which illustrate a type of case which is common in the Native Courts. A crop of actions and prosecutions followed, brought by his sympathizers against his prosecutors and their people; while one could not say that the charges or claims were false, it was evident that nothing would have been heard of them but for the prosecution of Egbuchie." The Egbushie incident helps to shed some light not only on official corruption but also on the pattern of revengeful litigation. Let us quote the DO once more: "In connection with this [case] it is to be noted that the native temperament prefers putting forward a counter-case to establishing his defence, even if he must serve a term in prison first; many of the cases that come before the Native Courts are more or less palpably counter-cases of this kind."[26]

THE WARRANT CHIEF SYSTEM AND OWERRI POLITICS

It was Sir Ralph Moor, as we pointed out earlier, who appointed the first chiefs at Owerri in 1902. Of these, Chief Njemanze, perhaps because of his wealth and force of character, emerged as the most influential and powerful chief of Owerri. At the beginning of British colonial rule, each of the five villages at Owerri town had its own chief. Chief Nwagbaraocha Anumudu of Umuọrọrọnjọ, for example, was a very influential chief as was Chief Emeto of Umuodu. Father Feral in 1912 portrayed Chief Emeto satirically as a man who "can do everything" because of his boastful attitude and assertiveness. "He can do everything, he has everything, everything belongs to him, he can make himself obeyed by everyone." Chief Njemanze, however, dominated Owerri politics until his death in 1920. He was the leading warrant chief of Owerri and was even appointed vice-president of the court, a position which conferred on him great prestige and power. He often presided over court sessions to the envy of other warrant chiefs. For all intents and purposes, he was the paramount chief of Owerri Nchi Ise. Upon his death, Chief Nkwazema of Nekede, who had been appointed chief on February 1, 1907, aspired to fill his position. In his petition to the governor in 1923, Chief Nkwazema asked to be recognized as the paramount head of the new Owerri Native Council, that is, the paramount chief of all the Oratta clan. He reminded the governor that for almost twenty-four years

he had been a loyal and dedicated friend of the government. His cooperation with the government, he said, should be appreciated from the fact that
"nearly in every battle I took part by supplying soldiers and food, carriers,
etc. with alacrity whenever the Military or Political Officers called upon me
to do so." He further stated that he had never had any trouble with the
government nor had he been negligent of his duties. Besides, he said, the
government should recognize his age as something in his favor. In his reply,
the lieutenant-governor appreciated Chief Nkwazema's long service and
loyalty but made it clear to him that "it is contrary to the present policy of
the Government to appoint any one as a paramount chief over other towns
with which he has no hereditary connection, and that I believe any such
appointment would be contrary to Ibo usuage and custom." The lieutenant-governor, however, agreed to grant him some special emblem of recognition which would be only personal to himself "and would not confer any
powers over other towns in the Division."[27] Chief Nkwazema was thus
bestowed with a special cap and stick which he used as a symbol of "roy-
alty" until his death in 1928.

Several other chiefs were appointed from other towns. Some of the more
prominent ones included Chief Ibekwe Mgbemgbe of Uratta (d. 1917),
Chief Nwankwere of Ihitte (d. 1917), Chief Njoku Nwansi of Akabo (d.
1920), Chief Onyejiako of Ogbaku, Chief Nwaturuocha of Nguru, Chief
Duru Abachi of Awa, Chief Egbukole of Egbu, Chief Emeaña of Naze,
Chief Oparaocha Ekwe of Ulakwo, and many others. Some of these chiefs
reportedly abused their power, and as a result their warrants were cancelled. Chief Onyejiako's warrant, for example, was cancelled in 1910 for
unlawful imprisonment of his subjects. Chief Nwaturuocha's and Chief
Abachi's warrants were also cancelled in the same year as well as Chief
Abbi's of Eziudo (in Mbaise) in 1917, for abuses of power.[28]

The warrants issued to the chiefs entitled them to sit in the native courts
from time to time to judge cases. The warrant also empowered each of the
chiefs to assume executive and judicial powers, both of which were rather
territorial in scope. Such assumption of executive and judicial powers ran
counter to Igbo traditional political system. For as pointed out earlier,
social fragmentation was a striking characteristic of Igbo society. There
was no tradition whatsoever, at least in the Owerri area, of any one man
being regarded as a paramount ruler over other persons or communities.
Admittedly, men of wealth (Ogaranya) commanded a measure of influence
but they never wielded executive power. Who ever heard of anyone issuing
orders to people in the towns or villages without the approval or consent of
the people? For the Ogaranya or anyone else to even pretend to exercise
executive or judicial power would provoke civil war.

Writing in 1937 on the accretion of political authority in the Igbo country, Dr. C. K. Meek remarked, "There has always been a tendency among the Ibos for energetic, ambitious and wealthy men to arrogate power and positions to themselves. It happened in pregovernment times, it happened under the old Native Court System, and we must not be surprised if it is still attempted." Yet, it would be a serious error indeed to equate the power of the Ọgaranya in precolonial Igbo society with the power of the warrant chief during the colonial era. The power or influence of the former was clearly limited by the check and balance system in Igbo political organization. The power of the latter, on the other hand, was virtually arbitrary; it was naked despotism unparalleled in Igbo political history. Whereas the Ọgaranya or anyone else could be removed from his position by the people, only the government could remove the warrant chief. Because the people did not "make" the warrant chief, "they could not bring him down."[29] By deliberately investing the warrant chiefs with executive and judicial powers the government encouraged the subversion of indigenous Igbo political administration.

It is well to remember that it was Sir Frederick Lugard who more or less caused the rapid disorganization of indigenous political administration. Following the amalgamation of the northern and southern provinces in 1914, Lugard not only "created" territorial chiefs but also invested them with enormous powers. In areas where there were no paramount chiefs, as in the Owerri area for instance, the DO was instructed to "encourage any Chief of influence and character to control a group of villages, with a view to making him Chief of a district later if he shows ability for the charge." By bestowing warrant chiefs with powers beyond their own villages, Lugard thus laid the foundation for persistent social and political unrest. For as it turned out, attempts by chiefs to exercise power beyond their own immediate villages often led to revolts. Said the DO at Owerri in 1919, "Revolts by outlying compounds . . . against the authority of the warrant holding chiefs occur occasionally." To the DO, Lugard's policy seemed clearly inappropriate. For "towns in Owerri are democratic and independent . . . and are not ready to acknowledge a [one man rule]." Since Lugard's instructions were nonetheless to be implemented, local officials attempted to allocate specific areas of authority to the chiefs. "Care was taken not to extend the powers so granted to chiefs over neighbouring towns to anything but business dealt with in my office," reported Falk. He went on to describe the efforts made to reduce the power and authority of the chiefs in the division:

. . . the chief of an area would always be called in in a consultative capacity if any matter concerning such an area had to be dealt with together with the local headmen. Lists of areas were tentatively prepared but they will need to be amended before they can be deemed official documents or put forward for sanction as such. Above all a better map of the Division will have to be available to illustrate further sub-division of Native Court Areas which later now take place of sub-departments or 'Ridings' of an English Shire, if we take a Division to be the equivalent of a County.[30]

By the Roads and Rivers Proclamation of 1903, chiefs were empowered to compel men to work on the roads and railways, to serve as carriers, and to build government rest houses and courthouses. Anyone who disobeyed the chief as he exercised his executive duties was liable for prosecution in court. Often this resulted in the person or even families being fined or imprisoned or both. Warrant chiefs by and large exploited the opportunities offered by the proclamation to ingratiate themselves. There were instances, for example, of chiefs diverting laborers to work in their own farms. There were complaints too that chiefs deprived laborers of their meager wages for the formers' enrichment. Besides, those "who refuse to turn out to work" often attempted to circumvent the law by offering the chiefs varying sums of money hoping thereby "to escape a sentence of imprisonment in the Courts." Litigants also generally offered bribes to the chiefs to have the latter decide cases in their favor. Such practices were of course known by the government officials. "The people have been warned by me for a whole year," reported the DO, "to complain at once if blackmailed" by the chiefs. When they ultimately brought complaints, he regretted, "the wrong is always alleged to have been committed months or even years ago, a fairly sure sign that the complainant himself agreed to pay up for some unlawful consideration" by the chief. While deploring the exploitative practices of the chiefs, the DO, however, regretted that chiefs seemed to succumb to bribery because of their not being paid regular salaries. "It is a misfortune," he pointed out, "that the chiefs have no legalized income. As matters stand they serve the community and the Government for nothing and can only make a living by taking illegal fees of some kind apart from their share in communal land and produce."[31] The warrant chiefs did not, of course, work for nothing; they were actually paid for the period of time during which they tried cases at the native courts. During the sitting of the court each warrant chief member received five shillings per day. Chiefs who had to walk great distances to court were also paid some special fees for any one session of the court.

That chiefs were notoriously corrupt was never in dispute. Commenting on the corruption of the chiefs in the Owerri court area, one district officer stated, "It is well known that the Owerri Native Courts have stunk to high heaven for years, and Administrative Officers have reported *ad nauseam* on their thoroughly unsatisfactory state." In yet another report of 1922 Secretary of Native Affairs S. M. Grier pointed out that if an officer devoted much of his time "to the investigation of charges of bribery and corruption, 90% of the present warrant chiefs would be imprisoned." Each year, he added with evident concern, "brings an increase of the injustice and oppression arising from the chiefs' abuse of the power given them." Referring specifically to the native court system, he complained, "If we cannot evolve any other system than the present one, if we are to continue to destroy the last vestiges of tribal organisation, then the Government should admit it had failed abysmally in its political objective." According to the DO at Owerri, chiefs at the Nguru and Ngor native courts appeared to have been the most notoriously corrupt chiefs in the division. Because Owerri Native Court was located at the headquarters and under the constant supervision of the district officer, he explained, "corruption is not so pronounced."[32]

But whether it was in the Owerri Division or elsewhere, corruption and self-aggrandizement seemed indeed to have been the way of life of the warrant chiefs. Consider this indictment of the chiefs in the Okigwe Division by the resident in 1917. "The majority of the chiefs in Okigwi [*sic*] have a keener sense of their opportunities of personal gain than of their duties to the people and this does not help matters to advance." Because of the selfishness and corruption of the chiefs, he contended, coupled with "the influence of the Aros, who are inveterate slave dealers, and of uneducated and turbulent mission boys from Uburu, the division has not much chance of making progress." With respect to the political state of the division, he remarked that

this district is still backward and likely to remain so, the East and North being the most troublesome areas. Friction and fighting took place between the people of Lengwi and Mbowo in Okigwi [*sic*] and the adjoining and allied people of Amakor in Udi and fines had to be imposed on both under the Collective Punishment Ordinance. A number of the other towns in the same area gradually got out of hand and this culminated at the end of the half-year in a rather serious state of unrest for which a patrol was required.[33]

THE SCRAMBLE FOR WARRANTS

After 1914 anyone designated as chief or headman of an area desperately sought to acquire a warrant, possession of which enabled the recipient to become a member of the native court. Court membership, as already noted, was generally regarded as a rich prize, a quick avenue to wealth and power. This was largely the reason for the extraordinary demand for warrants in the Owerri Division and elsewhere. "The warrant of a member of a Native Court is much coveted," reported J. M. Pollen. "Applications come in steadily from all parts of the Division; the same argument is invariably used,—that applicant's authority over his people is insufficient without a warrant. At Nguru the applications are laughably numerous." The peculiar political problem at Nguru, he remarked, was that "no one knows where one compound begins and another ends," with the result that "anyone who has charge of a few huts lays claim to a warrant." With respect to the political fragmentation in the Nguru court area, Pollen stated that "the towns are scattered in compounds over miles of country and the compounds again in clusters of two, three or a dozen houses, and the allegiance owed by the compounds to the head of the compound is always shadowy and constantly disputed while the authority of the head of the town is barely recognised."[34]

In the Owerri court area, the struggle for warrants was no less intense. In fact, the deaths of Chief Njemanze and Chief Njoku Nwansi of Akabo in 1920 resulted in acute succession struggles which assumed the appearance of a contest between educated young men and the old generation. The educated young men challenged the assumption of political authority by the so-called illiterate and decrepit old men. Commenting on this new phenomenon, the DO, A. F. M. White, observed that "the rapid development of the country during the last few years combined with the spread of education has produced a young generation whose ideas are out of sympathy with the outlook of the older men. The inevitable effect is that the authority of the elders over the young people had diminished."[35]

The challenge of the warrant chiefs by the younger generation, according to one opinion, was due to the fact that the government had not made its selection of chiefs on the basis of Igbo democratic tradition. Had this been done years ago, remarked the DO, John Ross, confusion and difficulties would have been minimized. At least, he said, "one would not have been faced by the problem of the semi-educated young man, blessed or cursed with education in a greater or less degree, who has to a great extent lost his respect for the Elders."[36] In the case of Chief Njemanze, the expectation was that his son J. O. Njemanze, who was then an inspector of police at Port Harcourt, would succeed him. But he refused. So a struggle for succession ensued, and each of the five villages presented candidates for the succession. Ihenmeje Njemanze (d. 1932) was ultimately issued a court warrant, but he did not wield executive authority as his father did in Owerri Town. Given the tendency toward political decentralization, the new chief became for all practical purposes the chief of his village of Amawom. Indeed, as the DO pointed out then, there was no more head of the whole town.[37]

At Akabo in 1920 the death of Chief Nwansi, who had dominated the political scene, also provoked prolonged succession disputes. Chief Nwansi's oldest son John was challenged for the succession. The challenge was mounted by one Mr. Nnorom, said to have had "no claim to a position of authority by native custom." Nnorom was the leader of the young elements who wanted to wrest control of the town from the Nwansi family. The struggle for succession here tended to split the town of Akabo into factions. John Nwansi was supported by one group whereas Nnorom was supported by another. Town meetings were held in attempts to resolve the problem of succession. John Nwansi, however, was supported by the Isu chiefs and eventually issued a warrant even though, as the DO put it, "his acts, so far, have not been above suspicion." To make sure he did not abuse the power conferred upon him, the government decided that "a very strict watch will have to be kept on him for the next few months."[38]

It would appear indeed that the twenties brought an era of political struggles. Chief Onukogu of Ngwoma, for example, was accused of corruption and abuse of power, the intention being to remove him from the Ngor court. His warrant was temporarily suspended. Upon being proven innocent, however, the warrant was restored. But then a political struggle for the headship of the Ngor court ensued. Onukogu, Akujobi, and Ihejirika led the opposition against Chief Oparaocha Ekwe. At Uratta, Chief Odu Obi of Owalla forced himself into prominence. And at Nguru the bitter struggle between Nwachukwu Daku and Anyamele dominated the political scene for quite some time.[39]

Political ambition thus encouraged sectional conflict; it also promoted vicious accusations against chiefs. The case of Chief Onwunali of Amuzi Obowo is another case in point. Chief Onwunali Obasi was accused by his opponents of exercising far more power "than was his due by native law and custom." Consequently, his warrant was not only removed, but he was sentenced to a long term of imprisonment for alleged abuse of power. Thereupon one "Wokonkwo" (probably Nwaokonkwo) of Umulogho was appointed as the new chief. Not long after, wrote the local DO "it was then discovered that the charges against Onwunali were fabricated, so he was given a free pardon and released from prison." As might be expected, a bitter dispute followed between Onwunali and Nwaokonkwo, the result of which remains uncertain for lack of further evidence.[40]

Perhaps as a result of the succession disputes, chiefs wanted to exert their influence in matters relating to the appointment of new chiefs. Thus when the acting lieutenant-governor visited Owerri in 1925, a petition to this effect was presented to him. The chiefs demanded, among other things, "that when the appointment of a new Court Member is brought up the Chiefs of the Court Area in question should be consulted" for their approval. Given the fact that the death of a chief often led to succession struggles, the chiefs called upon the government to adopt a policy which, in effect, would mean that whenever a chief died his oldest son would succeed him. The chiefs also pleaded that the sitting fees paid to warrant chiefs should be increased and that salaries of court messengers should also be raised. Above all, His Excellency was made to understand that no paramount chiefs had yet been recognized in the whole division, and so the lieutenant-governor was asked to ensure that such appointments were made. To these, His Excellency replied: "There is no PARAMOUNT CHIEF at present, and none will be recognised at present since the chiefs are divided one from another upon the subject of who should be the paramount chief." With regard to the appointment of chiefs' sons to replace their fathers, he stated, "This procedure is not in accordance with Native Custom. When a chief dies another man is appointed who is by no means of necessity the son of the deceased man but his son may not be a good man. The only people who can be appointed as chiefs are really good men and the right men according to Native Custom. It is essential that they should be persons capable of ruling." His Excellency also rejected the suggestion that chiefs should be consulted before appointments of new court members were made. This, he argued, was contrary to accepted practice, and he insisted that only those who were selected by the townspeople and acceptable to the government would be appointed as native court chiefs. On the request for increase of sitting fees and court messengers' salaries, the reply was equally negative. "At present," he told the petitioners, "it is not possible either to increase the SITTING FEES of the chiefs or to augment the pay of Court Messengers." All in all, none of the chiefs' demands were given favorable consideration. In conclusion, the acting lieutenant-governor told them: "I am very glad to have seen you and I hope that you will all return to your homes safely."[41]

As had happened in other places, the death of the chief, Chief Nkwazema in 1928, accentuated the "home rule movement" in Nekede. Chief Nkwazema's son Oke was strongly opposed by claimants from the different Nekede quarters. Oke is said to have been very unpopular with the people, and according to official reports he was generally blamed "for all troubles anyone in Nekede has suffered" over the years. Given the clamor for decentralization of power, each of the compounds in Nekede fielded a candidate for the chieftaincy. Each of the compounds wanted to provide the new chief. For reasons that are not exactly clear, Oke was ultimately confirmed as the successor to his father and issued a warrant. But it must be emphasized that Chief Oke Nkwazema did not wield the same extensive powers as his father did. This was because by the 1930s Chief Oke was only one among the many chiefs that sat at the Oja court. In other words, many more warrants were issued to heads of families who now represented their own villages or compounds at the newly reorganized native courts. The DO at Owerri must have had Nekede in mind when he reported in 1928 that "in 75% or more of the towns, compound clamour gives the Chief (whether Head Chief, Warrant Chief or Town Council) little or no support or obedience, and *fights for its own ends.*" (emphasis added). "This present lack of central authority in the majority of towns," he stated, "is a tremendous handicap" in providing effective administration.[42]

The decentralization scheme resulted in the appointment of too many chiefs. At the Oja court the presence of so many chiefs drew some sharp criticism from some Nekede patriots, especially servicemen in Southeast Asia. To these men, who learned about the political changes in their hometown from newsletters in Owerri, and who were evidently patriotic, having too many chiefs from Nekede seemed detrimental to progress and unity— hence the petition to the district officer at Owerri for reform. Pointing to the unwieldy nature of the Oja court the servicemen protested: "we in Nekede ask for a good change in Oja Court to have a few Chiefs but of good understanding and wisdom of average education and experience and God-fearing and lover of their people and town, who are unanimously elected and approved by you that we no more be a mock to others of Yoruba, Hausa and the coast. For when the ungodly and uncivilized are exalted the nation shall depreciate." The DO was quite impressed by the soldiers' expression of concern for their town and hoped that when they eventually returned home they would be able to contribute their quota to the development of their town. "If they are handled in the right way, and not allowed to become 'bolshie,' the broadening influence of the returned soldiers from overseas may give a filip to those who have not left the boundaries of the Division."[43] (The term "bolshie" was in reference to the Bolshevik revolutionaries of Russia who seized power in November 1917 and introduced socialism in Russia.)

Servicemen from the Owerri Division in the Middle East and Southeast Asia were informed regularly of events at home by means of a newsletter. This newsletter was started officially in 1944 and was produced by J. K. Nzerem, then the headmaster of Our Lady's School, Emekuku. According to Nzerem, communication with the soldiers started in the form of private letters from wives to their husbands overseas. Because of the interest which the letters generated, being spiced with accounts of local events, a systematic newsletter was devised. This was then circulated among the more than ten thousand soldiers from the Owerri Division, especially those in India and Burma. The newsletter came to be known as the *Owerri Bulletin*. It proved very popular indeed. "Its popularity was far greater than had been anticipated," the DO confirmed in 1945. Because of its great appeal, reported the DO, "the Headquarters of a number of Units asked for copies so that they might arrange for the Bulletin to be roneoed [cyclostyled] and circulated within those units." Even the general officer commanding the Middle East forces is said to have written to the district officer at Owerri to applaud the effort that had been made to keep the soldiers informed of what was happening in their division. He also requested that copies of the *Bulletin* be sent to him as regularly as possible. As a testimony to the *Owerri Bulletin*'s popularity, reported the DO, "soldiers returning from service overseas have made a point of calling at the Office to express their appreciation." The district officer, H. F. P. Wetherell, for whom one of the streets at Owerri Township is named, was equally appreciative of Nzerem's selfless service. Indeed, said Wetherell, "the Soldiers owe him a heavy debt of gratitude, and I wish to pay tribute to his public services" as well.[44] In recognition of his educational and unselfish public services, Nzerem was awarded the M.B.E. (that is, Member of the British Empire) in 1950, a title he apparently no longer wears. Instead, he now prefers the Nigerian title of Order of the Niger (OON), awarded to him in 1983.

TAXATION AND REVOLUTION

Throughout the eastern provinces, the warrant chief system was condemned because it caused serious social and political disruption. But it continued to exist until 1929. Thereafter a new system of local government was introduced which by and large heralded the collapse of the old Lugardian system. The new pattern of local government approximated the democratic traditions of the Igbo people because the method adopted for choosing local representatives conformed in large measure to traditional systems. More will be said on this later. We should emphasize here that the collapse of the old native court and warrant chief system was hastened by the Women's Revolt of 1929. This war (*Ogu Umunwanyi*), popularly but inaccurately known as the Aba or "women's riot," was the result of the introduction of direct taxation in the eastern provinces of Nigeria in 1928. Much has already been written about the taxation issue and the revolt itself,[45] so we do not intend to repeat the whole story here. Instead we shall summarize the salient aspects of the crisis to provide a clear background for the reorganization scheme of the 1930s.

In his letter to the British Colonial Office shortly after the outbreak of the First World War in 1914, Sir Frederick Lugard, then governor-general of Nigeria, proposed the introduction of direct taxation in the southern provinces similar to what had been done in Northern Nigeria. "Recent events in Europe," he wrote, "have completley altered the outlook [of the economy] and it may be that the institution of direct taxation will be necessary . . . to enforce revenue." He went on, "I anticipate a very serious shortage of imports and exports for some time to come which will decrease the revenue both from customs and railway freights. In the circumstances it may be imperative to augment the revenue by direct taxes." The suggestion hit the Colonial Office like a thunderbolt. Considering that the British government was already at war and also the fact that previous experience in Sierra Leone in 1898 was "not encouraging," the Colonial Office therefore demurred. Said one official angrily, "Only Sir F. Lugard would raise a question like this at the outset of a European war and demand an answer immediately." The secretary of state was even more pointed in his remark on the proposal. "This is a ridiculous suggestion in such a crisis as this." Lugard, who was then in England on leave, the secretary said, "had better get back to Nigeria and deal with actualities." Fear of provoking local revolt at a time when government resources and energies were committed to the prosecution of the war led to the rejection of the proposition. Lugard was accordingly informed that "the general question of taxation in the Southern Provinces . . . should stand over for the present."[46] Although Lugard persisted in asking for permission to introduce direct taxation in Southern Nigeria, no such taxation was imposed in Eastern Nigeria until April of 1928.

The imposition of direct taxation was not simply a matter of raising revenue; it also touched on the fundamental question of authority and control. As one administrator put it, "Its successful collection [was] not only a proof of authority, but a most useful means of asserting and augmenting that authority [over the people]. Where it is absent the people have that much more excuse for attempting to flout the Government." In the eyes of the Africans, continued the official, "to pay tax is to admit the overlordship of the person to whom it is paid." In England, he said, "each [tax]payer, even the unwilling and slippery one, regards himself as merely a contributor to his country's finance. This is not so in Africa." And even though he conceded that for the African to pay tax to the colonial government implied his admission of "inferiority and the payee's authority," he argued that "once it is successfully imposed, a great step forward [would have] been made in the firm foundation of administration, and in the political education of the people."[47]

The imposition of taxation was preceded by the compilation of nominal rolls of taxable adults. In the Owerri Division suspicion grew as to what the exact intentions of the government were. Although the people generally submitted to the counting, they were increasingly restive as to what lurked behind the detailed enquiries about their state of well-being. "Enquiries, except in a few isolated cases, into economic conditions and family earnings have invariably caused restiveness," reported F. Ingles, the DO at Owerri in 1928. Because of the deep suspicion that lurked in the people's minds, he stated, the answers that were given to the enquiries were "palpably false." However, he expressed the view that it would be a mistake to pressure the people unduly at this juncture: "To stampede the population would be disastrous, and in view of local susceptibilities I have considered it unwise to attempt the introduction of disturbing factors." In Ingles's view the wisest thing to do was to approach the matter slowly. For as he pointed out, "Although very excitable when their land is involved, the people are, as a whole, intelligent, and once the idea of taxation has sunk in as a necessary evil, it would be possible to prosecute enquiries in detail into individual and communal assets." Here are the figures of taxable males from the six court areas in the Owerri Division (1928): Owerri, 41,595; Nguru, 28,322; Okpala, 11,339; Ngor, 11,451; Umuapu 5,422; Oguta, 2,000 (not completed); total, 100,129. At the time the figures were compiled, counting in the Oguta area had just started. The DO had this to say of Oguta:

> Oguta town is giving trouble. The people have given lists of names, but these are obviously well under the correct figure. This town cannot be counted in the ordinary way. So many people live in the "Farms" and only appear in Oguta from time to time. In times of distress the population departs in canoes to their farms where they can be hidden comfortably. I have told the elders that unless the correct names were given they will have to pay a lump sum on the census figure of 3044.[48]

The tax rate in the first year (1928) was seven shillings per head. Its collection went on rather smoothly in most areas, although there was some complaining in other areas. "Owerri gave considerable trouble over assessment," reported Ingles, "and the collection of taxes was, I think I am right, faced with some misgivings as to result." Despite such misgivings no serious incidents were reported. In fact, admitted Major U. F. H. Ruxton, the lieutenant-governor in charge of taxation in the five eastern provinces, "The result far surpasses my expectation." He attributed the remarkable success to the efficient work done by the residents, divisional officers, junior officers, and cadets. For the lieutenant-governor, the collection of over £100,000 from the Owerri Province alone in the first year of taxation was indeed "unique in the History of Nigeria."[49]

Major Ruxton should have mentioned also that the warrant chiefs, headmen (*Eze Amala*), and others actually bore the brunt of tax collection from their people. Admittedly, warrant chiefs were suspected. There was a general feeling that because of their corrupt practices they would likely pocket the money paid to them for their own private ends. This lack of confidence in the chiefs led to the clamor that in fact chiefs should not serve as tax collectors. But since tax receipts were issued, the government was not overly worried that chiefs would embezzle the money paid to them. As a matter of fact special effort was made to ensure that the chiefs' good names were protected. Said E. Falk, now resident at Calabar, "We have to protect the chiefs against charges made *after* the tax has been paid in that they failed to hand over the whole collection to the Government, or that they extorted more than the total assessment for personal gain."[50]

As in the case of warrants, there was equally clamor to serve as tax collectors. Humphrey A. Nwansi of Akabo, for example, petitioned the district officer at Owerri in 1931 requesting permission to serve as a tax collector.

I have the honour to apply through you for the post of a tax collector under the native administration. Many headmen in this area have asked me to assist them in collecting the taxes from their Compounds; and I have done so unknown to you. Even Chief John Nwansi would recommend me for the work.

I understand that another tax will be collected by June of this year; and I hope you will employ me for the work which I promise to carry to perfection with the aid of some helpers: if only a uniform of distinction will be given to us. I have been doing works for the Government . . . such as arresting culprits and finding out absconding criminals, etc. Fearing how such works could be paid the usual ten P.C. [percent] given to town heads may be deducted and half of it paid to the Collectors. Anticipating a favourable reply from you.

The application was referred to the resident and the reply was terse: "No such position exists."[51]

An atmosphere of euphoria prevailed among administrative officers following the successful collection of taxes in 1928 and preparations for the 1929 collection began with optimistic predictions. However, as new nominal rolls were being collected from the various areas, the rumor spread that women were about to be taxed along with the men. Since the previous count meant taxation, this present renumeration which included women sparked hostile reaction from them. Given the disturbing fall in the price of palm produce and the general rise in the cost of living, women angrily asked how, if included, they could reasonably afford the money to pay tax. The situation came to a climax in November 1929 when Chief Okugo of Oloko in the Aba Division sent a schoolteacher, Mark Emeruwa , as his agent to compile the list of men, women, livestock, and all in the various Oloko compounds. When Emeruwa confronted Mrs. Nwanyeruwa Ojim, who was preparing palm oil, passions flared. Their altercation led to physical assault which triggered off the Women's Revolt of 1929. "Nwanyeruwa ran to inform other women who were holding an already scheduled meeting.

. . . They at once proceeded to 'sit on' Emeruwa and Okugo and sent messengers with palm leaves to neighboring villages, which in turn sent the message to other villages."[52] The revolt spread from the Aba area into the Owerri, Bende, Okigwe, and Degema divisions. It was characterized by physical attacks on warrant chiefs and destruction of courthouses and European factories. In many areas several courts were burnt down, European factories looted, and chiefs beaten. At Ngor, Obike, Okpala, and Nguru in the Owerri Division, chiefs' houses and farms were besieged and looted.

The government, as might be expected, sent in soldiers and police to quell the disturbance. At Okpala, it is told, the women were "thoroughly overawed by the presence of the soldiers in the neighbourhood." The women demanded that the caps of the warrant chiefs should all be seized from them. These tyrannical chiefs, they also insisted, should be punished. And unless the demands were met they were going to continue their demonstrations. To some of the officials, acceptance of the demands, especially the confiscation of the chiefs' caps, seemed reasonable as this might quickly bring the whole insurrection to an end. Reporting on the situation of events in the division, the resident of Owerri pointed out that as a matter of fact "the women's movement or Ohandom, as it is called in Ibo, has lost its kick as far as this part of the country is concerned and if an order were issued calling in all Chiefs' caps it would subside altogether." The secretary of the southern provinces, however, dismissed the suggestion outright: "I cannot consider the question of 'calling in all the Chiefs' caps' at once so as to stop the meetings, this would be weakness in the extreme as I have already said that none of the demands will be listened to until the women give up these meetings and return to their homes. I have no doubt that many of the old Court Members will lose their position after the enquiry but I cannot be dictated to by disorderly mobs of women." By the time the revolt was over, about fifty-five women had been killed and scores of them wounded. "It was a brutal charge," some women still recollect; "the soldiers beat us with clubs and gun butts." The Commission of Inquiry Report of 1930 confirmed this as well.[53]

THE SEARCH FOR STABILITY

The Women's Revolt of 1929 marked a turning point in the political history of Eastern Nigeria. If the ultimate goal of the revolt was to ensure that "all white men . . . go to their country so that the land in this area might remain as it was many years before the advent of the white man,"[54] it clearly failed. Yet it succeeded in bringing to an end the warrant chief system and led to the introduction of far-reaching reforms. After almost thirty years of administrative bungling and insensitivity to indigenous political systems, the government was now forced to admit that the warrant chief system was a failure. A frantic search for a new social order resulted in the return to traditional patterns of local government. Thus the political and judicial reforms of the 1930s tended to be more amenable to the local people than the previous forms of administration.

The reforms started in 1930 following the conclusion of the women's uprising. Under Sir Donald Cameron, who was then governor of Nigeria (1931–35), a new system of local government evolved. Prior to the reforms, however, the government had at last made some sincere and sustained effort to understand better the nature of indigenous political organization in Eastern Nigeria. This search for stability therefore led to intensive investigations into the modus vivendi of the different Igbo communities, as well as others in southeastern Nigeria. The primary objective of course was to find out how best to adapt British rule to indigenous systems of government. The reports of the investigations furnished by anthropologists such as Dr. C. K. Meek and others as well as by administrative officers provided valuable information not only about the patterns of traditional political organization but also on the precolonial history of most of the communities. These "Intelligence Reports," as they are generally referred to in official documents, contain the first recorded versions of the oral traditions of most communities in the former Eastern Nigeria.

These traditions, however, are not very reliable sources for the study of the precolonial history of the people involved. There are many reasons for this. First and foremost is the problem of the validity of the evidence. Much of the tradition, as the colonial collectors themselves acknowledged, was simply invented for the purpose of serving the immediate social and political interests of the people. Consider this report by N. A. Mackenzie, the DO at Okigwe, for example: "Great difficulties have been encountered when attempting to trace the early history of these clans. Different men of the same town will give vastly different accounts of the history of the clan, and on a subsequent visit to the town the information previously given may be denied. It does appear that much is invented merely to appease or occupy the investigator." Secondly, the general suspicion surrounding the intentions of the colonial administration militated against the collection of authentic traditions of the local people: "There have been two principal difficulties in obtaining accurate information [about the people's early history]. The people are extremely distrustful of the objects [*sic*] of Government, and are reluctant to tell their ancient customs lest these be thought either illegal or foolish; and there are many self-seekers, hoping for recognition by Government, who distort information for their claims."[55] Indeed, confessed another official, "however much tact is exercised in the framing of questions, the men's replies are influenced by a suspicion that our inquiries may be connected with some proposal, if not of reshuffling the court Membership, at least of modifying the basis of taxation."[56] Thus the deliberate distortions and falsifications in the recorded traditions render them quite unreliable as sources for the study of the traditional history of the various social groups. Yet in spite of the weaknesses in recorded traditions, historians and social scientists still find them very useful in the study of many aspects of the people's culture and social organization.

Utilizing the information thus collected, the administrative officials began the process of judicial and administrative reforms. Since the native courts had been the source of social and political unrest, they were the first targets of the reorganization scheme. Attempts were made to restructure the whole native court system to make them more amenable to the wishes and aspirations of the local people. Hence, instead of the few territorial courts, which had forced previously autonomous and unrelated communities into uneasy political units, several group courts were established. By this action, judicial power was decentralized as the rule of the few was replaced by the rule of the many. Furthermore, the system of representation at the courts had to be changed to reflect the Igbo principle of equal representation. "To build a Native Administration on a sound foundation," said G. L. Stockley, the assistant district officer at Owerri in 1935, "representation must be accorded to each extended family."[57] In other words, representation at the new courts was based on the extended-family system.

Each extended family or kindred (*Ọnamara*) was represented by the head of the family, that is, the holder of Ọfọ Ukwu. Even though emphasis was placed on the rule of the elders in accordance with "native ideas" of government, some officials felt that young men should not be totally excluded from the proposed new courts or councils. To obviate the risk of creating a new oligarchy or even autocracy, it was considered politically prudent to include "younger men of intelligence and personality [in] the councils of their elders." For, said J. G. C. Allen, "a system which places power [solely] in the hands of the elders to the exclusion of the progressive element among the young men may justifiably be regarded as retrogressive, and in these days of progress can only be of temporary advantage." It was therefore necessary, he added, that the best qualities of both elements should be harnessed. The selection procedure is as follows:

A family freely and democratically selects a man to represent them; he may or may not be the senior man in the family. The selected man or his family then reports to an Administrative Officer who arranges to meet the whole family *coram publico* [i.e., publicly] in the Native Court. This meeting is for the sole purpose of verifying that the man put forward is the unanimous choice of the whole of the adult males in the family, and unless virtual unanimity is shown the family is informed that they must remain unrepresented. If unanimity is shown the man is informed that as he has been selected by his people to represent them, he may do so.[58]

Two observations may be made with respect to this representation system. First, the method of selection tended to conform with the traditional decision-making process in most areas of Igboland—decision by consensus. This is the hallmark of Igbo democracy. And since the representative is the unanimous choice of the people and not arbitrarily selected by an outsider, it would be assumed that he would enjoy the respect and support of his people. Secondly, it would appear that because the family representative was put in a position of power by his people, the latter could remove the former if he became oppressive. The people in the Owerri area certainly believed "in their heart of hearts" that they could in fact get rid of a bad and an objectionable court representative. In some areas this was actually done, as at Ovoro, where we learn that "the entire adult population of one family requested the removal of their representative on the grounds that he had been oppressing them and cheating them over tax. Detailed enquiry proved that the charge was a true one and that there had been some chicanery over his original selection. He was therefore told that he no longer represented that family and a fresh representative was chosen by the family."[59]

If the people could remove their representative at the court, then the new system was diametrically opposed to the warrant chief system. For in the latter system, only the government could remove a warrant chief. Furthermore, the jurisdictional power or authority of the chief was now radically curtailed. For all practical purposes, the new chief's influence was strictly limited to his kindred since several chiefs were appointed within each village. By and large most of the new chiefs were simply tax collectors, although many of them also adjudicated cases at the native court. My father, Ekechi Egekeze of Umuorii Uratta, was one such chief at the Uratta court until his death in 1950. That the extensive power of the pre-1930 chiefs had dwindled and almost become a thing of the past may be appreciated from this statement by a discredited former warrant chief from Okigwe Division. "Those who became Court members after the Women's Riot," he told an interviewer, "were chiefs in name only. Some of them could not even earn enough from the court to maintain their families. By then everything had been spoilt, people had got 'wise.' "[60]

The drive toward political decentralization and family representation invariably led to the establishment of many more courts with correspondingly enlarged membership. In the Owerri Division, for instance, some twenty-two courts were established, and the court membership was two thousand. This means an average of ninety chiefs per court area. Indeed, the decentralization policy set in motion a new scramble for court warrants. In some places this new scramble for court membership tended to create social and political disharmony. "The question of Court membership," reported the resident of Owerri Province in 1937, "has been much in evidence and in parts, particularly in the Owerri Division, it has loomed large on the political horizon. The somewhat nebulous terms of membership such as 'all family heads,' 'all members of the village council,' are in some degree responsible. . . . There is no doubt that in the Owerri Division 'families' are constantly splitting into smaller units, adopting a new 'family' name and claiming membership for one of their members."[61]

By the late 1930s the administration had in fact recognized that the family system of representation had serious drawbacks. For one thing, it led to the fantastic increase in court membership, and the unwieldy character of the court tended to promote irresponsibility. Furthermore, there was the general apprehension that the court members might become permanent and thus likely to develop into Lilliputian warrant chiefs. To prevent this from happening, practical safeguards were initiated. "A file for each Native Court is kept at Owerri and in it are recorded details of any outstandingly bad judgments given in the Court, together with the names of the sitting members who gave it, and the remarks of the reviewing officer." Because this file was scrutinized periodically, "if it is found that the same set of members have given a series of really bad judgments they will be suspended or dismissed." And "whenever I have expanded this system," noted the DO gleefully, "the public has acclaimed it with gusto."[62]

As a further solution to the "unwieldy Benches," it was proposed that village rather than family representation should be adopted. Not only would this reduce the number of chiefs but it would prove less disruptive. "It is an established fact," reasoned one administrative officer, "that the higher the point in the social organization at which Government takes official cognisance the less likelihood there is of disruption of native life and institutions below." In essence, a shift from family to village or even village-group representation was viewed as promoting a higher level of political consciousness. Progressive as this seemed, colonial administrators cautioned against undue haste: "Let our policy be gradually to educate the people to think beyond the restricted sphere of the family, but it should be a very long-time policy. Let us meantime be thankful that the Owerri Ibo does possess in a marked degree a strong sense of family and base our administration on that until the people are ready for the next step."[63]

THE REORGANIZATION OF THE OWERRI NATIVE COURT

The Owerri Native Court area prior to the reorganization covered approximately 270 square miles and had an estimated population of about 137,500 people. Two major groups occupied this area, the Oratta and the Isu. The Oratta group (pop. 35,000) consisted of about thirty towns, namely Uratta, Owerri, Egbu, Awaka, Ihitte, Naze, Emekuku, Emii, Agbala, Ulakwo, Ngwoma, Egbelu (Obube), Emeke-Obibi, Amaeze, Amorie, Ogbeke, Nekede, Ihiagwa, Obinze, Eziobo, Okolochi, Amakohia Ubi, Irette, Ndegwu, Orogwe, Ohi, Oforola, Okuku, Avu, and Umuguma. The Isu group (pop. 96,000) on the other hand, consisted of twenty-two towns. The Isu group may be divided into two groups, the Ikeduru Isu and the Mbieri Isu. The Ikeduru Isu comprised the following towns: Inyishi, Ikembara, Ata, Avuvu, Ugiri, Okwu (Okwunkikereagba), Amaimo, Amakohia, Eziama, Ngugo, Ihuo, Uzoagba, Amata, and Akabo. The Mbieri group consisted of Mbieri, Ubomiri, Orodo, Ifakola, Afara, Ogbaku, Eziama, Umunoha, and Ogwa.[64]

Evidently, the Owerri court was too large. Besides, some of the towns and villages included in the court area were too far from Owerri. Many people, in fact, travelled between four and twenty miles to attend court sessions at Owerri. As was the case at the Oguta court, the people living at a considerable distance tended to show "marked disinterest in the Court." Given the trend toward decentralization and because of the increasing demand by many towns to have a court of their own, the Owerri Native Court had to be demerged. For if the reorganization program was to be a success and full representation accorded to each extended family as the government policy stated, it was politically essential that the existing Owerri Native Court should be discontinued. It was therefore recommended that group courts should be set up "on the lines of those established in other parts of the Owerri Division."[65] Therefore, in keeping with the decentralization policy the Owerri Native Court was broken up in 1935 into seven separate group courts—two for the Isu group and five for the Oratta.

By 1932 the Isu group had actually demanded independence from the Owerri court. Apart from the distance involved, they argued that they were culturally different from the Oratta and should therefore have their own court. Dr. C. K. Meek, the government anthropologist who investigated the social and political organization of the Owerri Division, conceded that there were in fact some minor cultural differences between the two groups.

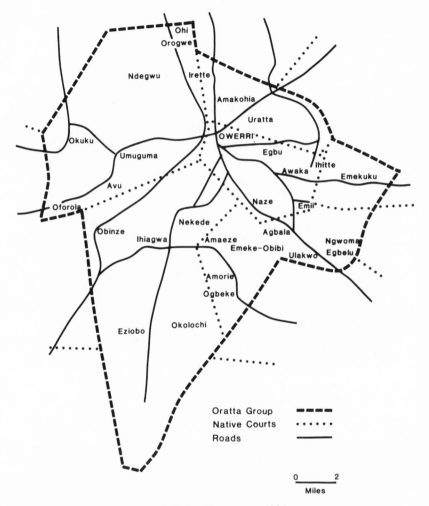

The Oratta Group of the Owerri Native Court area, 1934.

The Isu group, for example, eat *Ọna (dioscorea dumetoreum),* a species of yam. Also, while the Oratta use spoons in eating, the Isu, on the other hand, use their fingers. It would appear indeed that deep-seated cultural prejudice had induced the Isu to demand separation from the Owerri court. According to Meek, "The Isu and Oratta have long regarded each other with ill-will. The Oratta scorned the Isu for their trading propensities and prided themselves on their own more warlike qualities. They married the daugh-

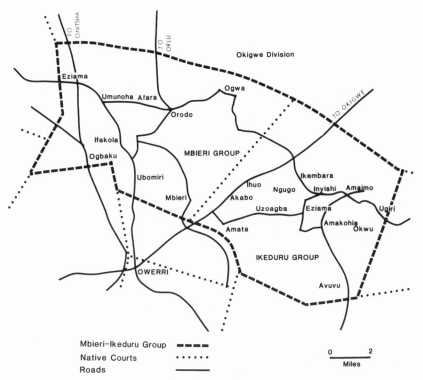

The Mbieri-Ikeduru Group of the Owerri Native Court area, 1932.

ters of Isu, but refused to give their daughters in return. To an Oratta the term Isu still bears the connotation of 'bush-people.' "[66]

In accordance with the policy of political decentralization, two separate courts were created for the Isu, one at Nwaorie Ubi (Orie Ubi) for the Mbieri group and another at Eziama for the Ikeduru group. Because Inyishi was regarded as the senior town among the Ikeduru group, there was some agitation that the court should have been located there. Eziama, however, was considered more central than Inyishi. Besides, said Meek, "if it were placed at Inyishi, which is generally admitted to be the senior Ikeduru town, it would be too far away from the southern towns such as Atta, Akabo, and Uzoagba. Moreover, the towns of Ugiri and Oko [Okwu], which are at present permitted to attend the Obohia Court, would probably refuse to join in with the rest of the Ikeduru, owing to jealousy of Inyishi." With regard to the whole question of reorganization, Meek had this word of caution: " . . . in view of the extra-ordinary density of population in the Owerri Division it is necessary to proceed slowly, and to avoid thrusting on the people a greater measure of self-government than they are prepared to accept."[67]

Because of the demand for wider representation by the Oratta group, five group courts were also carved out of what remained of the old Owerri Native Court. G. L. Stockley writes,

> The Oratta people have asked that . . . judicial and administrative changes be made. They wish for the separate Courts as proposed, realising that these reorganized Courts are more likely to give better judgments than are always given at present, and judgments [would be] more strictly in accordance with native law. The Oratta people are, however, anxious that their clan-sense shall in no way be weakened and for this reason wish to contribute to one Native Treasury. . . . I am in agreement with the people on this point and recommend that the Oratta Native Treasury be established [at Owerri] to serve the Oratta Native Administration.

Table 3 shows the group courts, the number of towns involved, and the estimated adult male population.[68]

The native court reorganization in the Owerri Division was completed by the end of 1935, although several adjustments continued to be made until 1938. At least for the Oratta clan, 1938 was a year of intense political activity. Scramble for court and council membership, as the DO affirmed, was "by far the biggest feature of Owerri politics in 1938."[69] In Nguru and elsewhere too there were strong demands for native courts. Demand for a separate native court at Nguru was purely a matter of pride, since a native court had been there earlier but was destroyed during the 1929 uprising. Each of the group courts, known also as group councils, was constituted as a native authority. In other words, each native court was by itself a native authority. Since there were twenty-two group courts in the Owerri Division, there were therefore twenty-two native authority councils. In an attempt to harmonize group interests the native authorities were grouped under six clans or federal councils, each with its own treasury.

The clan, which then formed the basic administrative unit, consisted essentially of village-groups or towns grouped together on the basis of cultural and language similarities and on their closeness to one another. It was an ingenious political organization or integration. The 1925 government definition of a clan as consisting of "one or more Village Groups descended from one historical ancestor, speaking the same language and dialect, having the same customs, observing one common 'shrine' and actively recognizing one Clan Chief or Council, through whom the taxes are paid," is almost synonymous with a town or village-group. But this concept of a clan

TABLE 3
Population and Coverage of Group Courts

Group courts	Towns	Estimated population
Owerri Native Court	Owerri	1,750
	Ihitte	380
	Awaka	500
	Egbu	1,400
	Naze	1,575
	Total	5,605
Emekuku Native Court	Emekuku	3,000
	Azaraegbelu	1,100
	Emii	3,500
	Agbala	800
	Ulakwo	3,500
	Amaeze	900
	Amorie	800
	Ogbeke	800
	Emeke Obibi	670
	Total	15,070
Uratta Native Court	Amakohia	175
	Akwakuma	190
	Orji	1,400
	Owelu	420
	Owalla	770
	Okwu	500
	Umualum	225
	Umunahu	800
	Umuoba	1,100
	Umuorii	630
	Total	6,210
Ihiagwa Native Court	Ihiagwa	2,800
	Nekede	3,500
	Obinze	2,100
	Eziobo	1,850
	Okolochi	190
	Total	10,440

TABLE 3
Population and Coverage of Group Courts (continued)

Group courts	Towns	Estimated population
Ara-Umunwoha Native Court	Amakohia Ubi	2,160
	Irette	1,900
	Ndegwu	1,050
	Orogwe	1,050
	Ohi	1,190
	Oforola	1,800
	Okuku	2,660
	Avu	1,150
	Umuguma	1,330
	Total	14,290

differs substantially from that of the 1930s, in view of the fact that the towns (*mba, obodo*) which make up the political unit may not necessarily share the common features enumerated. In fact, not all members of the clan trace their origin to a common ancestor, nor do they all share a common shrine. Thus, it is better to view the clan in territorial rather than in socio-logical terms. Of course, some members of this large territorial grouping may have "some consciousness of unity and kinship between the constitu-ent elements based on the similarity of culture-pattern." Mbaise is perhaps a classic example. Table 4 shows the new structure of local government as of 1945.[70]

In some of the native court areas, there was considerable resistance to the political decentralization policy. Oguta, for example, disputed the division of the existing Oguta court area into separate parts. But many of the people who lived at a considerable distance from Oguta had shown marked disin-terest in the court and had found it simpler and cheaper to settle their cases in their own towns. Because of the general demand for reorganization in-volving the establishment of more courts to serve the various groups of towns which did not admit having any close connections with Oguta and its immediate neighbors, the Oguta protest was dismissed as being politically motivated. Said V. H. Moult (DO), "These objections are based upon a desire to maintain the importance of Oguta itself as a judicial centre, and should not, I suggest, be allowed to weigh against the expressed wishes of the other groups."[71]

The Oguta court was formerly attended by fourteen towns (Oguta,

TABLE 4
Owerri Local Government Organization, 1945

Group councils or group courts	Number of villages	Federal councils or clans
Ezinihitte	16	Mba Ise
Agbaja	7	
Oke-Ovoro	4	
Ekwereazu	6	
Ahiara	11	
Oru	7	Oguta
Izombe	6	
Owerri	5	Oratta
Uratta	10	
Ara-Umunwoha	9	
Agbala	11	
Nekede-Ihiagwa	6	
Obudi	1	
Ohoba	6	Ohoba
Awarra	4	
Umuapu	11	
Isu Mbieri	9	Mbieri Ikeduru (Note:
Ikeduru	15	Approval was sought to change the federal name to Qgu Mbano)
Etche	6	Ngor-Okpala
Okwe	6	
Umuaro-Imerienwe	7	
Obike	5	
Total	168	

Nkwesi, Orsu-Obodo, Orsu-Obahu, Nebuku, Izombe, Ejemekwuru, Akabor, Awa, Abiaziem, Mbelle, Ebu, Egwe, and Obudi Agwa). The first five towns, known collectively as Oru towns, are said to be made up of immigrants into the area. They differed somewhat from the other groups in customs and economic ways of life. The 1934 report on these towns states that "the peoples comprising the Oru group are traditionally riverside dwellers, and migrated in olden times to what is now the Owerri division. . . . They do not climb palm trees, in which they differ from the peoples of the other . . . groups, all of whom derive incomes from the gathering and manufacture of palm produce. The Orus on the other hand, are experienced traders, and act as middle-men between the producers of palm oil and the Europeans." With respect to court membership, Ebu and Egwe, said to have migrated from Orlu, wanted to join with the Oru group instead of the Izombe group for reasons of politics rather than of cultural connection. The strong objections raised by Ebu and Egwe to joining their relations in the Orlu court at Ibi, said Moult, "are probably not due to a mere conservative distaste for change. Both towns have long-standing feuds with Uli, a related town over the Orlu boundary, and it was with Uli—a militant and aggressive people—which drove them to migrate to the land on which they now live. This feud is not merely traditional but has lasted right up to the present, and though the establishment of Government has prevented anything like open hostilities, the feeling of Ebu and Egwe for Uli and others of its close neighbours is far from friendly." In view of this mutual hostility, said Moult, "it would be a mistaken policy to endeavour to force these two towns against their wishes to join a Clan Court of their relatives under Orlu."[72] For this reason Ebu and Egwe were allowed to attend Oru court at Oguta whereas the rest of the towns, with the exception of Obudi-Agwa, were grouped under Izombe Native Court. The grouping of the towns under two separate courts was largely based on geographical proximity and close affinity of customs and interests rather than on any claims of common ancestry. For, as a matter of fact, no two towns in the area claim descent from a common ancestor; hence Obudi-Agwa was transferred to the Oratta clan. During the recent local government reorganization in Imo State (1977), however, it opted out of Oratta and joined the Ohaji-Egbema-Oguta group.

The 1935 reorganization had certainly reduced if not eliminated undue concentration of power in the hands of a few chiefs. To some extent the new government structure reflected the demands and interests of the local people. To the administration, too, the reorganization heralded a new era in modern Igbo political history. The new native court system, said one official, "may well be an important milestone on the road of progress of the Owerri Ibo." Yet the new courts were "by no means all they should be." For example, corruption persisted although, according to official opinion, this was not as bad as it used to be during the days of the warrant chiefs. Nor was the quality of justice significantly improved despite claims to the contrary. The steady rise in appeals and reviews, a feature which caused annoyance and frustration to the administrative officers, meant that court decisions were not popular. "The hearing of reviews and appeals," complained A. E. Cook in 1939, "occupies something like 50% of the time of all Administrative Officers. This is a high price to pay for justice when there is so much else of importance to be done." Because of the "meagre salaries" paid to the chiefs (that is, ten shillings per session), many of them are said to have encouraged or even "fomented" litigations with the hope of collecting extra fees from litigants. To some degree, the government's low-wage policy certainly tended to encourage corruption. The chiefs at any particular court served in rotation. Those on duty sat on the bench for an average of one month in three years. As a matter of fact, the members sat for about twenty-four days per month for which they received ten shillings each as remuneration. It seemed rather unrewarding to serve as a sitting member for such a paltry sitting fee—hence the charge of one pound (£1) by some chiefs as tips before a case was called up for trial. Nonsitting members also devised strategies designed to yield some high dividends. This is how the DO described the situation:

> An interesting but somewhat disquieting feature of the fall in the number of cases heard is that 50% of it is accounted for on the criminal side. This is due to no startling reformation in the habits of the people but to the activities of societies known as "Ezeji" whose members specialise in the settlement of criminal matters out of Court, a not unlucrative practice. The members consist for the most part of Court Members who are not sitting on the Court for that particular month, and thus profitably fill in their "off-duty" periods.[73]

By the 1940s the enthusiasm with which the reforms had been received had faded away. It had become obvious once more that the existing system of selecting court members in itself was no panacea to the political question. Instead of ensuring political stability, the system had in fact proved socially and politically disruptive. Besides, it multiplied the number of court members and, given the fact that administrative officers had to supervise the process of selection and listen to myriads of challenges and counterclaims, it imposed extreme strain on the administrative officers. In 1944 it was therefore agreed at the District Officers' Conference at Port Harcourt (December 15-17) that the new native court system needed drastic reforms. Labelled "the best-man policy," the proposed reforms included: (1) the selection of the best man from every village in the court area irrespective of age; (2) the reduction of the number of court members; (3) the reduction of the number of courts; (4) an increase in the salary of court members—ranging from £2 to £3 a month per court member. In the Owerri Division, the reform program started with the Mbaise clan because, as the district officer explained, "the people had expressed more forcibly than elsewhere their dissatisfaction with their own Courts." Besides, he added, "the Courts were without doubt the most unsatisfactory." The five Mbaise courts are said to have handled on the average almost forty-one hundred cases a year—they were "the busiest in the Division." Thus by 1945 the membership of the courts was reduced to twenty-one, and only five members sat at one time for a given period. Each member was paid a salary of two pounds (£2) per month. Although the government viewed the process of representation as democratic, given that each village selected its own representative, yet the administrative officials had the final say in the matter. Not only was each nominee interviewed by the DO to determine his character and suitability, but also inquiries were made about each and every nominee "and the names of the best put forward for His Honour's [that is, the resident's] approval." Reflecting on the whole reform exercise the DO remarked, "The steps leading to the reform have taken up a vast amount of time and much other work had to be left. It was felt, however, that any other work lost its value and could not be of permanent worth . . . while justice as we know it was denied to over half a million people."[74]

THE ORATTA CLAN COUNCIL

The native court reform of the 1930s was accompanied by the introduction of the clan council system of local government. Each clan council was defined as a "native authority" (NA) with its own treasury generally known as Native Administration Treasury. The Oratta Federal or Clan Council was inaugurated in 1935 but it was not until 1938 that the council met. As elsewhere, membership of the council was based on village representation. Each of the six group councils, for example, provided a number of delegates from the village council. The members served for a term of six months and meetings were held monthly. By 1945 Godwin K. Njemanze "worked loyally and well" here as the NA staff. By the 1950s he had become head of the NA. While the courts handled judicial matters, the council was entrusted with administrative responsibilities. The Owerri Native Administration, for instance, was responsible for the day to day administrative affairs in the Oratta clan. It provided money for the maintenance of the Owerri Government School, gave scholarships to students to study at higher institutions, and supervised the sinking of wells for the clan. The establishment of dispensaries, agricultural stations, and the like, as well as the running of the Owerri hospital, fell under the purview of the NA. Its Finance Committee generally prepared the monthly financial estimates. It would appear that the finance committees were powerful; for as H. F. P. Wetherell remarked, "The Committees meet regularly once a month when all vouchers are subjected to close scrutiny, and woe betide the District

Officer if he has signed away money the expenditure of which they do not approve."[75]

The Oratta Clan Council, as we learn from the DO, was also helpful in the area of tax collection. Without the help of the council, said the DO in 1939, "the story of the 1938–39 tax collection in this Division might well have been a different one" indeed. The DO was referring to the role played by the council during the women's uprising of August 1938, precipitated by the intrusion of men "in the sphere of women's crops, especially cassava." The protest movement spread from the Oratta clan to the other clans.[76]

Cassava was introduced as a food crop among the Igbo only recently, certainly after the 1914 war.[77] Because it was looked upon as an inferior crop to yam—the prestige staple crop and generally regarded as a man's crop—cassava thus became virtually women's crop. In Africa, of course, there is the division of labor on sex lines. Thus sex segregation in this context implied autonomy, meaning that the cultivation of cassava, its preparation for food (in the forms of *akpu, gari,* and *eberebe* or *jigbo,* etc.), and marketing devolved essentially on women.[78] In fact, the adoption of cassava as a food crop tended to enhance the economic position of women in society. Wrote Phoebe Ottenberg, "Women's acceptance of cassava meant not only the alleviation of the traditional famine period preceding the yam harvest but also a profound alteration in the economic and social relations between husbands and wives. In pre-contact [i.e., precolonial] days if a woman's husband did not give her food, she was in a sorry plight; now it is possible for her to subsist without her husband." Besides, cassava offered a potential for capital accumulation and ultimately the assertion of some degree of independence. An Afikpo woman reportedly told an interviewer in 1952 that "if a woman has any money she buys land and plants cassava. The year after she does this she can have a crop for cassava meal, which she can [also] sell and have her own money. Then she can say, 'What is man? I have my own money!' "[79]

Seen against this backdrop, it is not surprising that women strongly resented any attempts to challenge their dominance in the cassava cultivation and trade. Thus in 1938 women complained vehemently "against unfair male competition in the sphere of women's crops, especially cassava." In addition, women are said to have been agitated by the fall in the prices of palm produce (palm oil and palm kernel), as well as the new proposals for taxation in that year. Said the DO, "It is probable that [the fall in] produce prices and tax rates were more in their minds" than perhaps the cassava question. A local councillor concurred: "When our women say one thing they [really] mean twenty."[80]

Whatever the causes of the women's discontent, there is no question that women did not simply complain; they in fact organized a collective inter-

community protest movement in August 1938. That this women's movement made the administration somewhat jittery is clear from official specu-
lation that it was probably the revival of the 1929 women's revolt.[81] Thus,
memories of the recent women's war of 1929 influenced official attitude
toward the 1938 movement. Therefore, instead of using force to suppress
the movement, the colonial officials resorted to a diplomatic resolution of
the crisis. The principal concern, of course, was the probable effect the
women's movement would have on tax collection if it were not handled
immediately. It was for this reason that the district officer appealed to the
Oratta Clan Council to investigate the causes of the women's movement
and to make recommendations. The council obliged and in September
1938 began investigating the problem of the women's protest. Writing ap-
preciatively of the council's cooperation, the DO informed the resident that
"the Council members chartered a lorry at their [own] expense and made
an extensive tour—some of it outside the area of their own Clan."[82]

Upon conclusion of the investigation, the council submitted its report,
written in "true 'Commission of Enquiry' style." Regrettably, this report,
which contained the council's findings and recommendations, has not yet
surfaced at the Nigerian archives. However, references to the report appear
in the annual reports, although these are not very precise. From these
fragmentary pieces of information, the following inferences have been
drawn. First, the councillors invariably recognized the seriousness of the
women's grievances, especially alleged male participation in the cassava
business, as well as the fluctuations in the prices of palm produce. Accordingly, the councillors very likely sought to diffuse the crisis by assuring
women that the government had their best interest at heart and that it
would do whatever was necessary to safeguard their economic well-being.
Secondly, to dissuade women from resorting to violence, assurances were
probably given them that the "fantastic rumours" about the government
imposing taxes on them were totally false. Finally, the women were promised that produce prices would improve and that the colonial officials were
ready to listen to their concerns, whether collectively or individually.[83] In
fact the DO seems to have endorsed this latter assurance; he informed the
resident that easy access to the administrative officials had become the new
policy of his administration: "The privilege of easy access to a European
Officer for the individual has been maintained, and although a large proportion of these interviews are frivolous, it is highly important that this
privilege be not denied for many years to come. Particularly is it important
that the women, who in many ways are the backbone of the community,
should know that they will find a sympathetic ear for any reasonable complaints." It does not appear in available evidence that the women's protest
movement achieved any concrete results. What both the council and the

administration offered seem to have been mere palliatives rather than specific solutions. Nowhere could we find evidence of any specific measures being taken with regard to the women's complaints about men's unfair competition in the cassava question. What seems clear is that not only did men intrude into this sphere of women's economic activity, but also they ultimately dominated it, especially its long-distance trade sector. Several factors seem to have made this possible. First, the infrastructural developments (roads and railways) as well as the introduction of bicycles and motor lorries had facilitated the expansion of trade. Thus, while women still dominated the cassava trade at the local markets, men had very likely ventured into long-distance trading using bicycles and motor lorries as modes of hauling cassava. And since these new modes of transport afforded increased opportunities for bulk trading as compared to the traditional headloading, they invariably helped to promote higher profits.[84] It is therefore reasonable to assume that prospects of a lucrative trade must have provided the impulse for men to engage in the cassava trade. Accordingly, it was probably the use of bicycles and motor lorries for transporting cassava that constituted the alleged unfair competition against women.

Secondly, the commercialization of the market, which implied greater emphasis on a money economy, colonial exactions (such as taxation), and the drive toward self-improvement may have all combined to induce men to intrude into the sphere of women's business. Equally important are cultural factors which also may have given men a decisive commercial advantage over women. For example, by the 1930s and 1940s few women if any ventured into long-distance trading involving the use of bicycles and motor lorries. These were actually monopolized by men. Besides, long-distance trading entailed being away from home. In fact, social and cultural (sexual?) constraints tended to prohibit women from engaging in long-distance trade. For women who habitually returned home late from even the local markets invariably incurred the displeasure of the elders as well as reprimands from their husbands. Furthermore, such "latecomers" generally became the objects of family and village gossip because lateness was associated with moral laxity. Besides, was it really practical for women to leave their homes for long periods of time, as the men did, when domestic responsibilities and social expectations demanded their presence at home? Furthermore, until recently there were few women indeed who could afford to transport cassava by bicycles or motor lorries as these were virtually monopolized by men. Thus from the 1940s the marketing of fermented cassava (*akpu*) in far-away markets seems to have devolved largely on men, especially those who were able to utilize the new modes of transportation. In fact by the 1950s, when this writer was a headmaster in Mbieri parish, men dominated the long-distance trade in cassava. It was a common spectacle on Sunday mornings to see male cassava traders unloading cassava from motor lorries which had arrived from parts of the present Rivers State of Nigeria. The cassava was sold in bulk to women who then retailed it in the local markets. In essence then, while men were engaged in wholesale trade, women by and large became the ubiquitous petty traders who sold unprocessed (uncooked) cassava in the markets as well as cooked cassava in the makeshift "restaurants."

Without a doubt, colonialism altered the economic and political position of women. Dr. Nina E. Mba summed it up nicely when she wrote,

The position of women in Southern Nigerian society was both diminished and enhanced under colonialism. In government and administration, there was almost total loss of their traditional areas of responsibility and participation because they were excluded from all levels of administration. In the economic realm, while colonialism provided increased opportunities for some women in trade, it also led to a takeover by men of many areas formerly reserved for women and to a gross underutilization of women in their traditional roles in agriculture.[85]

The council's intervention appears to have helped in diffusing the crisis and thus facilitated the tax collection for the year. "Looking back on the events of the past four months," the DO acknowledged, "it seems more than likely that had this [women's] movement not been nipped in the bud, the story of the 1938–39 tax collection in this Division might well have been a different one." Gloating on his so-called spectacular achievement, the DO further stated,

The collection of the bulk of the tax [£13,566] during the month of November [1938] is possibly the most noteworthy achievement of the year. This would not call for special comment in any ordinary year, but the combination of the September crisis, low produce prices and a whole series of fantastic rumours had so unsettled the people that it was obvious from the outset that we were in for a difficult collection. This being so it was decided to insist, as far as possible, on a quick collection. Strong opposition was encountered during the early part of November and intensive touring coupled with sharp measures against recalcitrant Family Heads became necessary. These measures eventually proved successful and by the middle of November the tax was coming in at a good pace.

Even though taxes had been collected without any serious outbreak of violence, the DO was far from being complacent. In fact, he warned that unless the economic hardship in the country was alleviated, women particularly might still make things pretty difficult for the administration. "If only some means could be devised of stabilizing produce prices at a reasonable level," reminisced the DO, "it would make the task of the Administrative Officer a much happier one." He was also concerned that Africans, particularly women, hardly differentiated between the government and the companies. This was in reference to the price-fixing policy of the United African Company (UAC) which had resulted to some extent in the sharp decline in the prices of palm produce. Indeed, regretted the DO, "despite assurances to the contrary, he [the African] still thinks that Government and the Firms are more or less hand-in-glove over the question of price control," adding that "the severe dropping" of the prices of produce "has been an unhappy setback to the prosperity which conditions at the end of 1936 had promised." And he continued apologetically, "The violent fluctuations in the produce market are quite unintelligible to the native, especially when they are not accompanied by any like fluctuations in the price of imported goods [which remained high]. The best one can do is to encourage him to the production of a better quality grade of oil."[86]

Clearly, 1937–38 were bad years. In contrast to 1935–36, for example, when the economic conditions were reported to have been "the chief factor in contributing to the contentment of the people," the 1937–38 period proved to be the years of "gloom" and general discontent. In his annual report for 1937, for example, E. R. Chadwick, DO said, "The year has been remarkable for the pronounced fluctuations in trading conditions, and owing to the continued fall in palm prices during the last six months the year closes on a note of gloom." The year 1938 was even worse, at least as we gather from the report of the senior manager of the UAC: "Produce prices show[ed] approximately a decrease of 65 % oil and 42% kernels compared to the year ending 1937."[87]

All in all, the district officer seemed satisfied with the state of affairs after the tax collection of 1938. Hence in his annual report for 1939 he informed his superiors that "despite low produce prices and the unsettling effects of events in Europe the people of the Division remain[ed] on the whole contented. They have seen a good return for their tax in the way of Native Administration works in the past years and in the year under review, and politically the Administration has done all in its power to meet their wishes, particularly in the matter of Court Memberships." But he conceded that if not for the containment of the women's movement, thanks to the Oratta Clan Council, the situation could have been much different. Thus in recognition of the council's crucial role, the DO enthusiastically supported the reelection of the council members, whom he described as among "the best material in the Clan." In his words, the Oratta Clan Council "has shown real promise. Meetings are held monthly and minutes are recorded which are later circulated to the Group Councils, together with a statement of revenue and expenditure for the month." However, the possibility of reelecting all the council members for another term seemed quite remote, given Igbo aversion for political monopoly. Not surprisingly, the DO felt compelled to modify his stand, arguing instead that "it is probably not a bad thing" should there be a total reshuffling of the council. After all, "a fair number of people should be given the experience of Council membership at this stage of the development of the Clan." And he went on, "It is my firm belief, and I realise that this is a large statement, that the bulk of the people in the Owerri Division . . . can get rid of a representative who oppresses them. That is the crux of the matter. To keep alive this knowledge without encouraging the jealous rival with his ready gold and smooth words, is perhaps the main task confronting the administration in this Division. To keep burning the lamp of self-determination, without turning up the wick that extra fraction which causes smoke."[88]

In the election of 1939 only two members of the original Oratta council were reelected, one of them being Mallam Sule, the representative of the Hausas in Owerri. The election itself gave rise to a good deal of bickering and intravillage squabbles. Local jealousies in Owerri Town, for instance, prevented the people from selecting their quota of representatives. "It will do Owerri town no harm to be unrepresented on the present Council," said the district officer rather cynically, adding that perhaps "they will come to their senses by the time the next election takes place." Indeed, said the DO, "the petty rivalries and jealousies which are such a great bar to progress in every direction, are as strong and persistent as ever" here. The new council is said to have been dominated by Sydney Akalonu of Ulakwo, perhaps because of his education and force of personality. As for the members of the new council generally, the DO's assessment was that "they have not as a whole the personality of the old Council" even though "they adopted a reasonable attitude over tax rates and their suggestions for the next year's Estimates were on the whole sound." He went on to comment that "although the present Council lacks the virility of the old one, it is by no means a failure, and useful development is taking place under its regime. I consider it would be a great mistake to condemn the six-month monthly term of office system on the evidence of the first re-election. The people must learn for themselves that it is in their interest to send their best people to the Council and that a complete change of personnel every six months is bound to retard development."[89]

From all indications, it appears the people found the political reorganization somewhat baffling and confusing. The constant changes of policy tended to allow the people little or no initiatives whatsoever. In handing over his notes to A. E. Cook, DO, in 1938, W. F. H. Newington, ADO wrote,

> The people are as yet unaccustomed to the idea of making decisions even on
> minor matters for themselves, and when consulted about a change in policy

merely put forward the view, which they are under the impression the officer wishes to hear, and consider any subsequent innovation as another government experiment which they do not understand but are prepared to accept as government knows best. Reorganization commenced in 1931, and since that date the people have been whisked from Warrant Chiefs to kindred representation and are now completely at sea with family representation, which under the present system of appointment varies little from the old method of appointing warrant chiefs, and results in enormous benches and nebulous councils with many of the members totally unfitted for the position which they hold.[90]

The new council elections, however, provoked strong protests from the *Osu* social group ("cult" or "ritual" slaves), who complained that they were "shut out and excluded from Native Court and Clan Council affairs." As in most societies, democratic Igbo society has its own peculiar social contradictions. For the Igbo make a clear distinction between the status of a freeborn (*Diala*) and that of the slave (*Ohu/Osu*). Thus this "structural principle of duality embedded in the Diala–non-Diala distinctions, divides Igbo society into two clearly defined social strata." In practical terms, the Ohu/Osu group was not expected to assume a status equal with the Diala. In Professor Victor C. Uchendu's apt characterization, "The Osu system of slavery constitutes the greatest contradiction to Igbo [equalitarian] ideology."[91]

In a petition submitted to the district officer at Owerri in 1936 and signed by representatives of the Osu group from the different towns in the division, the petitioners vehemently protested the alleged "unanimous conspiracy" of the Diala to deny them their civil and political rights. They argued that their exclusion from the councils was based on the "tragic theory of Osu (human living sacrifice)," adding, the Diala are "determined to keep us and our children under everlasting serfdom, while and whereas the liberation of slaves under British Flag has been pronounced. They have thus deprived us of our birthright and liberty." Arguing purely on moral grounds, the petitioners rightly contended that "sacrificing human beings alive to idols is quite inhuman, brutal, tyrannical and oppressive," and that "it is shameful and desgraceful [*sic*], and needs stern resistance." For this reason, "we collectively cry unto your mercy for British Government intervention." Because the Diala "have refused us every advantage in the Native Council . . . contrary to Native Custom and usage," it was then the responsibility of the colonial government to abolish this "evil" Osu system so that "we may be brought to have equal advantage with the freemen [Diala]." In conclusion, the petition called upon the government

(a) To stab the act of buying, selling, and sacrificing a human being to idols, while cows, goats, sheep, dogs, fowls and eggs can serve the same purpose.

(b) To grant us and our children freedom and liberty as freemen, so long as we all are under the British Flag.
(c) To make us represent our various families interest in Native Councils and in Judicial Clan Courts.
(d) To grant us the advantage of collecting tax from our own men by those our family Heads.

Unless these demands were granted, the petitioners threatened, "we shall be obliged to refuse the payment of . . . taxation which appears of no use to us." There is no evidence of a tax boycott, however; nor is it clear what specific action the government took, if any. Nevertheless, the Osu system was ultimately abolished in Eastern Nigeria in 1956 thus making it possible for all Nigerian citizens to participate fully in both local and national political affairs. In his speech at the Eastern House of Assembly on March 20, 1956 Premier Nnamdi Azikiwe (Zik), not only supported the abolition of the Osu system but also denounced the "evil" institution in no uncertain terms:

> Mr. Speaker, I call upon all nationalists on both sides of this House to dissociate themselves from a satanic practice which sentences our kith and kin to social degradation. Mr. Speaker, I appeal to all patriots of this country to join this Government in its noble crusade against a vicious social system. Let us recognize a person for what he is and not who he is. . . . Mr. Speaker, this Bill offers a challenge to the morality of the Easterners. I submit that it is not morally consistent to condone the Osu or Oru or Ohu system. I submit that it is devilish and most uncharitable to brand any human being with a label of inferiority, due to the accidents of history. I submit that human beings are entitled to the right of social equality. Because of my personal convictions, I am seconding this motion. . . .[92]

This legal abolition did not mean that Osu is no longer a social reality. In Imo State, to be sure, the political and social repercussions of this liberalization are still being felt in many communities.

THE DEVELOPMENT OF SOCIAL SERVICES

Earlier we discussed the role of the missions and the colonial administration in the field of education. Indeed, the provision of social services was by no means limited to the establishment of schools, but included the opening of hospitals, clinics, maternity and child welfare centers, as well as dispensaries. Furthermore, the sinking of wells and the promotion of sanitation and other related health measures contributed in no small measure to the social and material progress of the people in the division. A brief examination of some of these developments will help us to understand the patterns of social change in the Owerri Division.

First, let us look at the evolution of hospitals and their impact on society. The earliest hospital in the Owerri area was the Owerri Government Hospital (now General Hospital), which was opened in 1903. It was initially intended for the colonial soldiers, police, and other government officials. In time, of course, services were extended to the local population. When the governor visited the institution in 1905, he discovered among other things that the hospital was in fact underutilized insofar as African patronage was conspicuously absent. And because the stock of medicine there might become useless with age, he suggested that the unusued stock be sent to Calabar or, better still, be sold. Although the hospital had an African ("native") wing, it hardly attracted a large number of the local inhabitants. Thus official after official commented on the African reluctance to attend the hospital. As late as 1923 the DO, A. F. M. White, reported that "the native hospital does not appear to be patronized to any great extent by the people. The number of in-patients varies from 5–15." Even by the 1930s and 1940s when Western medicine was steadily gaining ground, the Owerri Government Hospital continued to be shunned by Africans. Why? Several factors combined to render the hospital unattractive to the people. First and foremost, we must recognize the intrinsic fear in the minds of the local people that admission to the hospital was a sure road toward one's death, a notion that has not yet been completely eliminated. Moreover, there seems to have been a general lack of faith in the efficacy of the white man's medicine. Indeed, here as elsewhere, Nigerians preferred African to Western medicine, an innovation they did not quite understand. In addition, the lack of patronage for the Owerri hospital appears to be related to the general dislike of the government, its personnel, and its institutions. Here as elsewhere in Africa, "only a small fraction of the total population received modern medical attention." The women were perhaps more suspicious of Western medicine, and so "clung to traditional remedies."[93]

In time, of course, rejection turned to grudging acceptance. Even then the Owerri hospital remained generally unpopular. By 1937, for instance, when the Roman Catholic hospital at Emekuku had become fully operational, it attracted far more patients than the Owerri Government Hospital. The Catholic Holy Rosary Hospital at Emekuku, known at its inception as St. Brigid's Hospital, was reportedly established in 1934. It was not until 1935, however, that the first doctor, a woman named Dr. Kutsie from Germany, arrived.

The proposal for the hospital actually started in 1932 when the Catholic bishop raised the alarm of Protestant domination in the provision of medical services. To the Propaganda Fide therefore, Bishop Heerey wrote, "The Protestant missionaries are much more in advance of us with regard to hospitals. They have a number of these, staffed with European doctors and nurses and they are, apparently, having considerable influence in the districts in which they are located."[94] Thus arose the proposal to build at least two hospitals in the vicariate, certainly to promote missionary evangelism but also to contain the Protestants. The proposed hospitals, explained the bishop, would be under the management of Catholic nuns.

> Our sisters who, thank God, are rapidly increasing in numbers, open schools for native girls [and operate] small dispensaries where the poor people are treated by the Fathers at the mission's expense. . . . During the coming year, we shall have to build a hospital or, perhaps, two in our Vicariate. The government will give us a small grant for the building but the remainder must be provided from the mission funds. . . . These hospitals, which have always been a great need will, it is hoped, be the means of ransoming many, especially poor women, from the slavery of paganism and Satan.[95]

Between 1933 and 1936, three Roman Catholic hospitals were built in Eastern Nigeria: St. Luke's Hospital at Annua, Calabar (1933), the Holy Rosary Hospital in Emekuku (1934), and the Holy Rosary Maternity Hospital in Onitsha (1936). Interestingly enough, even though the hospitals were managed by Catholic nuns, they were not officially permitted to pursue studies in the medical profession until 1936. It was perhaps demand for nuns in this field, especially in Africa, that ultimately prompted the Roman Catholic liberalization policy which allowed religious missionary sisters to become medical doctors and nurses. According to a 1936 Catholic document:

> In certain parts of Africa, some tribes are daily decreasing and will soon become extinct unless the lives of the mothers and children are provided with more efficacious assistance. In other places too, where the elementary rules of health are neglected, children are dying in very large numbers. . . . It is indeed desirable that new societies of sisters should be formed for the care of mothers and children. . . . This new employment demands both adequate medical knowledge and special discipline of the soul. It is, therefore, necessary for the sisters to obtain either a degree in medicine or a diploma in nursing.[96]

The lifting of the ban on Catholic nuns therefore promoted the deployment of Holy Rosary Sisters and others as doctors and nurses. As for the Holy Rosary Hospital at Emekuku, it was not until the late 1940s that Holy Rosary Sisters became doctors at the hospital, the first nun to serve as a doctor there being Sister Macartan (1949–66). In contrast to what took place within the Church, Africanization or indigenization of the hospital began almost at its very inception. The pioneer Igbo nurse at the hospital was Priscilla Obua (later Mrs. Nwadialo) from Oguta, who worked from about 1935 until 1937. To workers and patients alike, Obua was the embodiment of what a nurse ought to be, compassionate and efficient. Hence she was popularly known as the "Santa Philomena." Thus on the occasion of her departure from the hospital in 1937, this statement appeared in the local newspaper: "May she have the full benefit of our never ending prayers and the prayers and the best wishes and fond regards of those patients who will always think of and pray for our popular 'Miss Priscilla' the 'Santa Philomena' of the Emekuku Hospital."[97]

Significantly, the deployment of Holy Rosary Sisters as nurses contributed to the popularity of the hospital as well as to the expansion of medical services to the hinterland, oddly referred to as "bush" stations. These outstations were visited frequently, and women and children were provided with medical care. In time, maternities were established in several of these stations, notably at Ogbor Nguru, Umuokirika, Nekede, Ogbaku, Ngugo, Inyishi, Orlu, Oguta, Obowo, Mbieri, and elsewhere. In 1940 the hospital opened the School of Nursing which became one of the famous centers for the training of midwives in Nigeria. Indeed, from about 1937 medical work had become a major preoccupation for Catholic nuns—hence the establishment of Catholic hospitals and maternities throughout Eastern Nigeria. The Holy Rosary Hospital at Emekuku in particular gained extraordinary fame and popularity largely because of its efficiency and, as we shall soon see, because of the role played by the Holy Rosary Sisters.

Let us now return to the comparison between the Government Hospital at Owerri and the Holy Rosary Hospital at Emekuku. In 1937, as already indicated, it was reported that while only a few patients were admitted to the Owerri hospital, the RCM hospital, on the other hand, was said to be "usually full and sometimes overfull," an indication obviously of its popularity vis-à-vis the government hospital. Available figures for 1939 are even more striking. At the Owerri hospital, some 830 patients are said to have been admitted, while a total of 17,760 were treated as outpatients. In contrast, over 3,000 are said to have had admission at the Catholic hospital, while about 43,000 were treated as outpatients. These "astonishingly high figures,"[98] in the words of the DO, give a true reflection of the popularity of the RCM hospital. Why was this so? In other words, why were more Africans attracted to the Catholic than the government hospital? Without question, the popularity of the Catholic hospital was directly related to its organization and the confidence it apparently infused on the local population, especially since it had no connection with the government.

For comparative purposes, it might be useful to look at the operation of the two institutions. For much of its lifetime the Owerri hospital operated under serious handicaps. It was plagued by dire shortage of trained medical staff and lack of adequate space and equipment. By as late as 1937 there were one medical officer, three African health staff, and nine other African employees at the hospital. And even though its full capacity was for eighty-two beds and six cots, it could hardly accommodate half that number in relative comfort. Perhaps more seriously, the medical staff could not, it seems, inspire confidence in the minds of potential patrons. On the other hand, the Catholic hospital with its imposing structure and adequate facilities tended to inspire greater confidence in the African patrons. A government report on medical services for 1938 confirmed this observation. "The RCM Hospital," commented the DO, "with superior equipment, European Nursing Sisters, and African staff both male and female, undoubtedly affects adversely attendance at the Government hospital." Again comparing the two hospitals in terms of their infrastructure, H. F. P. Wetherell (DO) said of the Catholic hospital: "The buildings at this Hospital put those at the Owerri Government Hospital to shame." Judging from contemporary opinion it would indeed appear that this chronically under-staffed and underequipped hospital was clearly no match for the apparently well-organized Catholic hospital. A recent opinion on the disparity between the two institutions states that the superiority of the Catholic hospital derived from the humanitarian objectives of the Catholic missionaries. As for the government, we are told, "they came to exploit," not to extend British largesse.[99]

Indeed, when in 1940 the chief commissioner of the eastern provinces visited the two hospitals, there was no doubt in his mind of the superiority of the Catholic hospital vis-à-vis the government hospital at Owerri. Not only did he view the Catholic hospital as "a magnificent institution, worthy of all the help we can give," but he also was very favorably impressed by its organization. He was particularly impressed with the work of the two German doctors there, Noeth and Diedrich, who were granted permission to remain in Nigeria at the outbreak of the war in 1939 to continue their medical work at Emekuku. "If I had any apprehension as to the advisability of retaining these experts and devoted German doctors in the service of the hospital," the commissioner remarked, "I should have been completely reassured and the patients clearly have complete confidence in their doctors and the staff."[100] In fact, both oral and contemporary documents confirm that the great acclaim of the hospital throughout Nigeria derived largely from the work of these German doctors who incidentally are still very fondly remembered.

Nowhere else perhaps was the weakness of the government hospital more pronounced than in the area of child welfare. Its maternity section in fact was probably the most neglected in terms of staffing. While the Catholic hospital's maternity ward and the CMS maternity center at Egbu flourished principally because of their being well staffed with trained female nurses, the government hospital's maternity section actually languished for lack of them. Trained female nurses were not employed at the government hospital until 1941. At the urging of the Oratta Clan Council, the native administration rather belatedly took steps in 1939 to remedy the critical shortage of trained female nurses at the government hospital. In that year, a girl was sent to the government hospital at Port Harcourt for training, with the hope that she would take charge of the female ward at the hospital at Owerri. Even though the council applauded the action as a move in the right direction, it felt, however, this was rather too late and too little— hence the increased agitation for the employment of female nurses at the hospital. This demand was fully articulated in the petition the council submitted to G. G. Shutte, the chief commissioner, during his visit to Owerri on January 5–8, 1940. The council demanded among other things improvements on the hospital and the appointment of several female nurses to cater to the needs of expectant mothers. The commissioner, it appeared, was in no mood to oblige. Insofar as a girl was already being trained "at government expense," he told the petitioners, the government would not in the meantime consider any additional staff at the hospital. But, he added, "the position would be reviewed when she [the girl in training] had taken up her duties, but not before." The reaction of the council is unclear, but the commissioner assumed the members were satisfied. "The Council heard me out with patience and restraint. Their attitude confirmed my impression that the Oratta Clan Council is a responsible body competent to deal sanely and soberly with the problems of the day." Recently, a former member of the Oratta Clan Council remarked in a somewhat different context, "The problem with our people is that we are easily satisfied. If we took our guns and matchetes and confronted the Government, many of our demands would have been met." With respect to the question of female nurses, three were finally posted at the Owerri hospital in 1941 and according to one official this long-awaited appointment resulted in "good work in the ante natal ward."[101]

The opening of maternity centers and dispensaries in the various parts of the division also widened the frontiers of Western cultural penetration. During the 1930s and 1940s these centers actually proliferated. Some of the major centers were located at Egbu, Mbieri, Atta, Ihiagwa, Oguta, Obohia, Umuneke Ngor, Ife, and Ogwa. The Egbu center was of course the premier institution and appears to have been subsidized by the government. Its infant welfare section, for example, was subsidized by the native administration. It also paid the full salary of the woman doctor there and all transportation expenses connected with the infant welfare center. Thus treatment at the center was free except for those under confinement who paid a charge of five shillings. Yet all was not well with the dispensary. "Dr. M. P. Roseveare, who has been at Egbu during the later part of the year," wrote E. N. Mylius (DO) in 1937, "reports that the work is not yet satisfactory. The large number of attendances renders much of the work inadequate, and the sum of £156 per annum which is all that can be spent on drugs, has proved insufficient."[102]

Although many details of the operation of these health centers are obscure due largely to the lack of data, available statistics suggest that the facilities were becoming increasingly popular from the late 1930s. At the Egbu center, for example, about 15,800 women are reported to have received prenatal care in 1938, while about 404 babies are said to have been born there in that year. And by 1945 some 1,622 babies are said to have been born at the eight CMS maternity centers.[103] Figures for the Roman Catholic hospital are unavailable, but there is little doubt that the numbers would be close to the above figures, if not higher, given the influence of the Catholic sisters at the hospital. Regardless of the growing popularity of these medical centers, however, they never supplanted African practices of child delivery nor in fact did Western medicine totally eclipse African health care delivery systems. The fact that only a tiny proportion of the African population patronized the hospitals and maternity centers is a clear indication of the strong hold of tradition in this region undergoing radical social change.

To the innovations already indicated we should perhaps add the establishment of government dispensaries, known more popularly as NA dispensaries. These were located in the different court areas and staffed with African paramedics. Like other medical institutions, they were avoided at first. In time they became one of the centers of health care, especially for schoolchildren. The figures in table 5 give some indication of the growing acceptance of Western medicine although, as the figures also reveal, the impact on the society was as yet not quite revolutionary. One factor that seems to have affected the spread of dispensaries was the influence of clan councils and local improvement unions. As in the case of schools, the location of dispensaries and maternity centers at strategic areas became symbols of social development and cultural progress. Thus various clan councils and improvement unions pressured the local administration to establish dispensaries in the different court areas. By the fifties several of these were opened at various places. The influence of improvement unions in this regard and in the promotion of general societal progress remains to be carefully studied. The Owerri Divisional Union, with branches in various

TABLE 5
Attendance at Owerri Dispensaries

Location	1943	1944	1945
Amakohia	9,048	3,926	30,897
Ife	13,369	12,321	13,292
Ngor	17,904	20,349	20,081
Obohia	11,914	10,785	10,945
Obudi Agwa	10,390	14,968	7,352
Oguta	68,354	35,410	11,621
Ogwa	17,524	20,457	18,383
Ohuba	8,881	9,073	11,438
Total	157,384	127,289	124,009

parts of Nigeria, however, played a vital role in advancing self-help projects, opening schools, and fostering a sense of community in the different areas where union branches were established. Inasmuch as the activities of these unions seemed to advance the cause of Western civilization, colonial officials were quick to applaud their progressive influence. According to a report of 1938,

> This . . . report would be incomplete without some reference to the various Unions and Societies. Chief among these is the Owerri Union, with branches all over the country, of which the Owerri Mother Union, which has recently changed its name to the Owerri Home Union, is the local branch. These Unions, which represent generally the progressive and more enlightened element, are beginning to take a lively interest in the problems confronting the local Administration and can be of real assistance if properly handled.[104]

Not only did administrative officials endorse many of the programs of the "progressive educated elite," they also in fact attended their annual meetings, especially at Christmas when development programs were discussed. Upon attending the Mbieri Children Association meeting in 1938, A. E. Cook seemed pleasantly "astonished" at the large number of educated Africans present and the sense of order and social purpose that governed their deliberations. "This particular society," he remarked, "has built its own Hall, a very creditable effort," in the drive toward local development. Other officials spoke equally approvingly of the work of improvement unions. "This writer," stated Wetherell in his 1945 report, "wishes to record his deep appreciation of the way in which . . .the Owerri Divisional Union [has] worked hard and in harmony for the progress of their country."[105]

There were yet other areas of improvement or change relating to health. Of significant interest was the deployment of sanitary inspectors who enforced health rules in the townships as well as in the villages. Not surprisingly, their enforcement of official sanitary ordinances provoked widespread resistance, especially as the inspectors insisted on cutting down cash crops like orange trees, bananas, coconut trees, and others which were considered health hazards. Moreover, bushes surrounding homesteads were ordered cleared, some of course being the repositories of ancestral spirits. Whatever the case, there were furious protests from various quarters against the "meddlesome" sanitary inspectors. This petition from Obudi Agwa is perhaps typical:

> We the undersigned Court Members of Obudi Native Court hereby unanimously submit our petition to inform Your Worship that we do not like the Sanitary Inspector to come and inspect our town Obudi Agwa. The reasons being that we are naturally bush-men. We drink from ponds and wells. We usually have bad waters, rubbishes, bushes and all sorts of nuisance near our surroundings. Therefore we wish you to inform the Sanitary Inspector in charge of Oratta Clan not to come.

Despite protests of course the inspection of villages and the enforcement of modern health regulations continued. There is no doubt that the work of the health inspectors had beneficial effects. Who knows how many lives would have been lost without the work of these men? Although some of them were corrupt like most public officials of their time,[106] they nevertheless performed wholesome service. Certainly their efforts at disease control through immunization (vaccination), the inspection of water containers (*udu mmiri*), the enforcement of general cleanliness, and a variety of other functions helped in advancing the standard of living of the people and perhaps reduction of the mortality rate. As such these health officials deserve a place in the annals of Nigerian social history.

8. EPILOGUE AND CONCLUSION

This study has sought to examine carefully and systematically the patterns of social and political change in the former Owerri Division. The discussion and analysis of evidence clearly indicate that Owerri and its hinterland underwent a fundamental sociopolitical transformation under British colonial rule. In the political sphere, as shown here, the democratic character of Igbo society was subverted by the imposition of the warrant chief system, which inaugurated the painful era of political and social disharmony, political corruption, authoritarianism, and various forms of colonial oppression and exploitation. But, as we have also seen, the Igbo and their neighbors totally rejected the warrant chief system and thus forced the British administration "to go back, to begin again, to find some remnant of traditional organisation which would be recognised by the people." Thus was born the native authority system of local administration of the 1930s.[1] But the native authority system proved inadequate. In other words, it failed as the panacea for the political problems arising from the indirect rule policy. Consequently, a new political experiment was initiated in the 1950s, that is, the introduction of the local government system in the whole of the Eastern Region of Nigeria.

THE INTRODUCTION OF LOCAL GOVERNMENT

Strictly speaking, the 1950s, marking the introduction of the local government system in Eastern Nigeria, falls outside the limits of this study. However, because its conception began well before the close of our period, it might be useful to at least provide a brief background to its evolution, especially as a way of further illustrating the almost endless process of political innovation in colonial Nigeria.

As might be expected, the impulse for the new experiment derived from the need to adapt local administration to the changing political environment, implying a departure from the Lugardian policy of indirect rule. For to many colonial officials, especially those in the eastern provinces, the philosophical basis of indirect rule crippled the reforms of the 1930s. Consequently, if a new approach is to be successful, there must be a total departure from the concept of indirect rule. In the words of a contemporary, "In planning the new approach [local government], we must be quite sure about the past, in what respects the old approach was inadequate and the shortcomings of the present position. Unless judgment on these points is sound, the likelihood that the new approach will be sound is greatly reduced." Indirect rule, argued advocates of the new approach, was an undemocratic system, precisely because the native authorities were essentially creatures of the government. For despite the fact that families or villages chose their representatives to the councils, the district officer or resident had the power to reject the nominee or even to dissolve the native authority. Thus the councils could aptly say, "Government has made us, and made us the depositories of traditional authority; it is for government to unmake us or change us if it wants to."²

Besides, the native authority system by and large excluded the "growing literate youthful minority . . . separated from tradition by its education and desiring change and progress." Thus it was that the educated elite reportedly perceived the native authorities as "collections of ignorant [and illiterate] stick-in-the-mud bushmen . . . to be swept away." Indeed, some administrative officials agreed. Brigadier E. J. Gibbons, whose "Report on Local Government Reform in Eastern Nigeria" formed the basis of the local government system of the 1950s, perceived the native authorities or clan councils as being "strongly conservative in outlook" and "naturally unable to appreciate the need for reformation." Their conservative attitude, he noted, was often reflected in their opposition to "progressive measures proposed by Government," and they regarded such opposition as even "estimable and patriotic."³ To Gibbons, therefore, the indirect rule system which gave rise to the creation of native authorities had outlived its usefulness and had to be replaced with the electoral system, thus making the local government system more democratic.

It would seem therefore that the composition and parochial outlook of the native authorities had rendered them "quite out of place now that Nigeria is becoming a modern nation with Africans predominating in its legislatures." Furthermore, because the native authority system did not offer "the really enlightened African educated gentleman" the scope or the prestige to serve in the councils, it seemed reasonable to discard the whole policy of indirect rule upon which the native authority system was based. Indeed, continued Gibbons, it seemed "idle to expect an educated African gentleman, eager to work for self-government of Nigeria, to fritter away his efforts in argument with yokels round the parish pump." And he added, "It has become clear . . . that nowhere in the Eastern Provinces (with some exceptions . . .) is there any future in the policy of waiting for the people, as advised by their District Officers, to realise the need for reform and to evolve satisfactory institutions by trial and error."[4] In more specific terms, Gibbons's view was that the formal recognition of traditional elders should be abandoned, and the introduction of local government based on elections would be the preparatory ground for eventual self-government in Nigeria. For the new system to work, therefore, it had to be democratic, effective, and progressive.

Gibbons's criticism of the native authorities drew a negative response from a contemporary, R. A. Stevens, formerly DO and one of the officials directly involved in the political drama. In the opening section of his long "Memorandum on the Future of Local Government in Eastern Nigeria" (1949), Stevens wrote,

> I write as (a) an officer of nine years' experience, most of which has been in the Calabar Province, (b) who has now, in the Devonshire Second Course, had opportunity and time to read and think about local government, (c) at a time when the future of local government in the Eastern Provinces is receiving much attention, and, following the report on Local Government Reform by Mr. E. J. Gibbons, C.B.E., Senior Resident, discussion is likely to be translated in the near future into action.

From his standpoint, Gibbons's view of local government per se seemed curious and misleading. Thus while Gibbons saw the introduction of local government as the laboratory for ultimate self-government—that is, preparation for national politics—Stevens perceived it as essentially a parochial affair. In essence, local government is meant to instill in the Africans (as elsewhere) a sense of commitment *to the community* rather than concern for national politics. Disputing Gibbons's interpretation of "parochial outlook" as being "out of place in modern Nigeria," Stevens argued that a parochial attitude was in fact the very essence of local government. "I do not regard this parochial attitude as a bad thing, for without it there would not be *local* government. . . . In England, prestige of being a councillor is more a factor with the worthy [*sic*] of parochial outlook than with the gentleman of wide experience."[5]

If, as Gibbons has suggested, the educated elite "are unwilling to attempt to control the parish pump, how do they expect to be regarded as sufficiently responsible to attempt to control Nigeria?" Surely "it is by mastering the parish pump and other affairs of local government that they will learn the job of self-government." It is by harnessing the services of the educated elite and their illiterate counterparts that "a democratic effective progressive government" in Eastern Nigeria can be assured. Of course, Stevens went on, "the best machinery we can devise for local government" should be created "whereby educated African gentlemen can become members of local government bodies more easily than at present." Unless the opportunity existed for the educated elite to provide "excellent services to the community" as members of the local government, "then we have failed" in the quest for a democratic and progressive local government.[6]

Equally important, Stevens emphasized, is the fact that British tutelage ought to be considered crucial, for Nigerians "must be taught the job."

> Certainly we cannot leave them to work out their own salvation. It took the people of Britain centuries to evolve their present local government institutions, which are not altogether satisfactory although as good as any in the world. It has taken 115 years from the introduction of the elective principle in the Boroughs to reach the present position. It is the curse of the colonies that in all matters, including local government, we cannot wait for natural growth, but must always be trying to telescope centuries of experience in other countries into a few years. It is Government's responsibility to work out the new approach to provide the best institutions possible for democratic effective and progressive local government. In discharging this responsibility, we must take full advantage of the lessons of our own past. We may also take advantage of any lessons of English experience which are applicable to conditions in the Eastern Provinces.

But Stevens cautioned against creating a carbon copy of the British system. "We must . . . be careful to adopt with discretion and adapt with wisdom." Furthermore, local government bodies must be allowed to make their own mistakes and to learn from them, "for without it there would not be democratic local government." After all, "democracy is incompatible with perfection in anything, most of all with perfect efficiency." Thus, "what we are seeking is a working compromise, a system which will enable the people to do what they want for themselves as and when they wish and with reasonable efficiency." Consequently government should avoid unnecessary or arbitrary interference in the affairs of local government bodies, for it was government's virtual control of native authorities that robbed them of initiative and efficiency. And should the government once more dominate the local councils, the same inefficiency and unprogressiveness "might happen again."[7]

Stevens was quite emphatic on this matter and hence objected strongly to Gibbons's recommendation that the central government should exercise the right to remove members of any local government of whose actions it did not approve. Said Stevens,

> Mr. Gibbons now proposes that any local government council which misbehaves should be removed, and replaced by a nominated council. But we have introduced the elective principle. We have transferred the responsibility for choosing the council from government to the people. We have given up the right to object to the man the people choose, unless that man disqualifies himself; and the only possible grounds for disqualification are exactly the same grounds as in the case of Legislative Council members or House of Assembly members. We have also given the people the right, in periodical elections, to throw out the men they chose first if they wish to do so.

Arguably, the government could dissolve the local government bodies or even remove members of councils for whatever reasons, but this would invariably amount to an undemocratic approach to local government. Hence, wrote Stevens,

> I would submit that it must be accepted that "Off with his head" may be good pantomime but it is not practical politics. If I am wrong in this, then the whole argument of this memorandum falls to the ground. If we are aiming at democratic effective local government, we must have it democratic from the start, and all the way. We must trust the people. We must make the best arrangements we can to ensure that it will be effective, that is, we must have the best organisation. In action and execution we can advise, we can guide, we can prod, we can point out what we think are mistakes and what we think the consequences will be. But having done that, we must trust the people.[8]

The establishment of local government in Eastern Nigeria began effectively in 1950 with the promulgation of the Eastern Region Local Government Ordinance of 1950, "the first of its kind in Nigeria." It was largely based on the Gibbons's "Report," but the demand by the Eastern House of Assembly in 1948 for local government reform seems to have quickened the passage of the ordinance. In keeping with Stevens's recommendation, however, the elected local councils were given a relatively free hand in the management of their affairs, but the local government structure followed the British three-tier system and imitated the British pattern even in name. "Thus came into existence the county, district and local councils in Eastern Nigeria." The Eastern Regional Local Government Law of 1955 defined the structure and functions of the new local government system. From all accounts, the local government ordinance of 1950 marked a point of departure in modern local government administration in Eastern Nigeria. "Unlike the native authority system one council is never made subordinate to another. No local government council is dependent in the exercise of its functions on the consent of another council." Furthermore, unlike the native authority, the local government law evolved from the people and not in accordance with British officials' "assessment of the needs and possibilities of the political situation." In Philip James Harris's words, "The local government law of both [the Eastern and Western] Regions is being applied in accordance with the policy of Regional Ministers of State. In both Regions local government has been made to conform to the present constitutional position."[9] In essence, the result of the local government reform, especially in Eastern Nigeria, was the assumption of political power by the younger and more progressive (educated) men, while the elders and more traditional people were elected to the courts.

In conclusion, it might be necessary to reiterate that colonial rule was essentially rule by coercion, thus changes and innovations were largely imposed. But the colonial government was not, of course, the only agent of change and transformation; the Church was an important factor to the equation. Much has lately been written about the impact of missionary propaganda on African traditional religion and way of life. In many instances the effect was pernicious, and Professor Beidelman has put it succinctly by saying,

> The *raison d'être* of mission work is the undermining of a traditional way of life. In this the missionary represents the most extreme, thoroughgoing, and self-conscious protagonist of cultural innovation and change. . . . The missionary, at least in the past, was unashamedly ethnocentric, though he saw the struggle to impose his values as loving and altruistic. He was cruel to be kind. His ethnocentrism and proselytization represent a blend of exclusion and inclusion, domination and brotherhood, and exploitation and sacrifice. Most curious of all, he exalted modern Western life but loathed many of its features; he felt a parallel fascination and contempt for simpler societies.[10]

That the missionaries contributed significantly both in the transformation and undermining of traditional Igbo society is further illustrated in Chinua Achebe's famous book *Things Fall Apart* and other studies.[11] Yet there is the interesting perspective that the missionaries were not only destroyers but also builders, indeed progenitors of sociocultural change. For instance, missionary intervention at Egbu in 1907 ultimately resulted in the stopping of the ancient custom of throwing slaves into the Otamiri River. Also, it was missionary activity that contributed to the ending of the various forms of infanticide, especially the throwing away of twins. Thus a positive image of the foreign missionaries often emerges, and this was clearly and forcefully projected at the Workshop on Igbo Culture held at the University of Nigeria at Nsukka in 1977. In responding to this writer's paper on "Christianity and Igbo Culture," a distinguished Igbo scholar pointed out the many "positive contributions" of the missionaries, especially in abolishing the killing of twins and human sacrifice. "Aren't we better off today as a result of these changes?" he asked pointedly. Had it not been for the missionaries, he went on, "the obnoxious customs and practices in our society might not have come to an end."[12] This is false, of course, but this rejoinder by another commentator is more clearly to the point: "Who invited the missionaries to come? They were intruders." Nonetheless, "had they not come, the Igbo certainly would have, in time, modified their customs and practices as other peoples elsewhere have done. We did not need foreigners to force us to abandon our way of life" After all, he asked peremptorily, "was there no infanticide in Europe in the nineteenth century?" And were there no obnoxious customs and practices in European society? Who forced them to give them up?[13]

Clearly, as the foregoing discussion suggests, perceptions of the missionaries vary. What is equally sobering, at least as my fieldwork reveals, is that a good number of the Igbo people, literate and illiterate, tend to share the view that, "yes, the missionaries undermined our culture"; they were indeed iconoclasts. Yet they "brought us development," especially in the provision of social services, particularly education. In so doing, the argument goes, they invariably enabled the Igbo to make unprecedented progress in modern Nigeria. "In less than a quarter of a century" after the arrival of the missionaries, wrote a patriotic Igbo man, "[the Igbo] have, as it were, wakened up from their deep slumber and in the race for progress they have completely outstripped most of the other tribes." Thus Western education "brought by the missionaries" has been hailed as the critical factor that catapulted the Igbo to positions of influence and power in pre–civil war Nigeria. The Dike Commission report of 1962 mirrored this viewpoint very succinctly.

Everywhere the opening of a missionary outpost was accompanied by the erection of a school. During the first fifty years of their existence and over, the Voluntary Agencies (as the educational Missionaries came to be called) depended almost entirely on funds from overseas for their pioneering work in education. As has been indicated elsewhere systematic and sustained Government support by way of grants-in-aid emerged a decade ago. Throughout the century of their existence the Voluntary Agencies have dominated the educational scene in this Region; and, as a result, all Eastern Nigerian leaders in Church and State, in business and education, owe their training in whole, or in part to missionary enterprise. The Committee found everywhere evidence of the widespread and wholesome influence which the missionaries have exerted throughout the Region. Everywhere their unrivalled contribution to the moral educational and material progress of the East is acknowledged.[14]

Yet Western education also sounded the death knell of traditional Igbo religion and way of life and led to the cultural disorientation of the educated elite. Hence the role of the Christian missionary should not be viewed simply in terms of the "balance sheet" of imperialism, for to do so is to fall victim to the rationalizations of the missionary who perceives himself as a self-sacrificing humanitarian. Indeed, "the missionary always gave the colonial set-up an aura of humanitarianism" and glamorized and glorified Western culture in the name of "Christian" civilization. Thus, as Geofrey Z. Kapenzi has pointed out, the missionary not only "annoited the European as the superior custodian of values, morals and ethics and as the sole measurer of culture, civilization and history," but also he sought to make imperialism and colonization "look like humanitarian responsibilities."[15]

TOWARD CULTURAL REVIVAL

The revisionist trend in African studies, to be sure, has resulted in the reexamination of accepted notions of European imperialism in Africa and elsewhere. Thus Professor C. S. Whitaker has argued that in fact elements of African traditional institutions and practices, rather than having been completely smothered by European colonial rule, continued to coexist with colonial innovations and modern Western influences. Consequently, the notion that "confrontation societies" were "inevitably racked with strain, conflict or instability" as they absorbed aspects of Western culture seemed exaggerated. With particular reference to Northern Nigeria, Whitaker writes, "In sum, the political policy-makers in Northern Nigeria [in the colonial era] neither clung to a strict pattern of traditional government nor accepted modern elements indiscriminately." Thus "the marked *internal* political stability of Northern Nigeria [today], stemmed from the persistance of authoritarian relationship of traditional rulers to subjects in the emirates." In essence, "Hausa society continued to accord the highest degree of respect and prestige to persons whose social position most closely approximated that occupied by members of their family in past generations." Consequently, "many Western educated commoners who aspired to political leadership deduced that their own aspirations were apt to be more

nearly and quickly fulfilled by achieving an accommodation and association with the established ruling class than through directly making a bid for
recognition from the society at large."[16]

In contrast to Hausa society, personal achievement more or less determined the social status and prestige of the individual in Igbo society. Thus,
unlike in Hausaland, in Igbo society Western education significantly altered the patterns of authority; for literary education "with special emphasis upon the English language bestowed prestige and status" and thus
enabled the newly educated elite to control and dominate modern political
affairs. This revolutionary impact of Western education on Igbo society has
been described in this manner by H. C. Swaisland, formerly senior district
officer and principal of Institute of Administration at Enugu: "The traditional form [of government] is the pyramid based on age. Ideas went up and
authority came down. . . . By taking the youngest and lowest part of the
pyramid and educating it, so that it alone is capable of operating the new
government form and economic processes, we have sown the seeds of decay
in the traditional power structure." But while Swaisland recognized the
negative impact of colonialism on Igbo traditional power structure, he nevertheless acknowledged the remarkable resilience of traditional culture.
Yet "despite the present apparent continued strength" of tradition, it was
clear, he said, that social and economic forces were causing the "rapid
break-up" of traditional institutions. Swaisland, however, spoke approvingly of the emergent rugged individualism of the educated elite which, he
admitted, was clearly inimical to the traditional concept of "each for all and
all for each" that characterized the African extended-family system. In specific terms, the new social and economic order had fostered selfishness and
the decay of traditional systems and values. Quite typically, Swaisland perceived extreme individualism as one of the wholesome legacies of European colonialism.

Assuming that all else we have done to the blackman is bad, the one glorious
service the whiteman has done is to put the nettle danger in his hand. We have
shown that choice is a reality; nay, more than that, we have shown him that it
exists. In traditional society there was scarcely any scope for individual initiative.
"No" was merely an affirmative of a negative fact (evidenced by the fact that
where we would say "No" a Nigerian, logically, says "Yes"); it was not a statement
of intention of will. Where was there to go if you said "No" when society said
"Yes"? More than that, I believe it probably never occurred to a Nigerian in
traditional society that alternatives existed; why should it have done, because
they didn't. Fish don't know that there is anything else but water.[17]

Certainly, the painful recognition of the collapse of traditional authority, the disappearance of traditional systems and values, and in fact, the passing away of traditional culture, stemming from colonialism, has galvanized the movement toward cultural revival throughout Igboland and beyond. Speaking at the Workshop on Igbo Culture held at the University of Nigeria at Nsukka in 1977, an eminent Nigerian statesman and former governor of Eastern Nigeria (1960–66), Eze Akanu Ibiam, called upon his Igbo compatriots to do their utmost to rediscover Igbo culture, especially "at a time when [peoples] the world over . . . are deeply conscious of their own particular lifestyles, their peculiar identities, dignity," and so on. "It is my avid hope," he went on, "that this Workshop will grow to be the right platform to bring to the forefront . . . the variety of ways of living which marked our forefathers as men and women of sagacity, great intelligence and foresight, men and women of outstanding courage, and who were serious and deeply rooted to a religion which vividly recognised the existence of a Supreme Being who is Omnipresent, Omnipotent and Omniscient." In proudly extolling Igbo culture and philosophy of life, Eze Akanu Ibiam reminded his listeners of the high moral code of conduct and sense of justice that animated "the lives of our forefathers." "And what is happening today to the community of the people?" he asked. In evident rejection of the selfishness or individualistic orientation of the new generation, he remarked, "We have lost a good deal of the wonderful heritage which our fathers built up and left behind for us. We are now a mixed group of Christians and non-Christians. We are composed of literates and illiterates. There are the very rich and the very poor. Our beautiful and praiseworthy extended family system is crashing and might finally become a thing of the past if we do not wake up to our blessed responsibilities." In short, it is incumbent upon all Igbo men and women to reclaim their heritage, to work toward the revival of Igbo culture.[18]

Yet, like most concerned Igbo men and women, Eze Akanu Ibiam was fully aware that "no generation can ever succeed in reviving any culture in its entirety." Consequently, the movement toward the revival of Omenala must be both selective and practical. As with cultures of the rest of the world, Igbo culture is not static, but prone to change "and changing fast." And just as the world "has contracted considerably, so also [have] customs and cultures." He added, "We, the Igbos in particular, and Nigerians in general, should look closely to our customs and cultures" and determine which aspects should be revived and which should be discarded. As a matter of preference, he went on, it would be better to retain or revive only the customs and cultures "which give us dignity and prestige," and reject those which are "retrogressive." Also, "there is no reason not to borrow from other cultures which are progressive and Christian." It was against this background that this former president of the World Council of Churches predictably upheld the superiority of the Christian religion over African traditional religion. "To our forefathers Chukwu was an enigma. They did now know where to find him. . . . We find him through Jesus Christ."[19]

But while accepting the foreign Christian religion, Eze Akanu Ibiam warned against copying foreign cultures blindly, especially those that demean the personality of the African man and woman. In his own words, "It behooves us to throw overboard lock, stock, and barrel all those foreign ways of life which are inimical to our dignity and personality as a people." As examples of foreign ways, he cited the prevailing attitude of disloyalty to constituted authority, the lack of pride in things African, and the "self-centredness" that characterizes the actions of the present generation of Igbo men and women.[20] In essence, cultural revival implies pride in one's cultural heritage.

For the cultural revival to be successful, according to Professor A. E. Afigbo, the school and all educational institutions must play a vital role because it was through the school that things fell apart. To achieve this search for cultural identity "the school curriculum has to be indigenised more and more with a view to making our children realise that they are not English men or Romans but Africans." The irony is that while great stress is being placed on indigenization, some elements tend to equate this with the "Christianization" of Igbo culture. Let me illustrate this with what I consider to be a bizarre event that occurred in 1977. In that year the people of Emekuku celebrated Ugu Emeke festival "in the Christian way."[21] Traditionally, the festival is celebrated with pomp and pageantry, the sharing of kolanuts, dancing at Achara Ubo, and other rituals. But, alas! Indigenous Roman Catholic priests opted to say Mass at Achara Ubo, the traditional locale for Ugu Emeke rituals. To the Christians, it seemed, the Catholic Mass represented the "modernization" of traditional culture, and thus the Mass served as the Christianization of the Ugu Emeke "pagan" custom! In this instance, it would appear that Ugu Emeke festival had been made acceptable to the Christian adherents through the Christianizing process. This clearly illustrates the ambiguities or problems inherent in the drive toward achieving African "authenticity" in cultural revival.

APPENDIX A
NATIVE CLERGY

Ordinations of native clergy since the beginning of Owerri Diocese in 1950 have been as follows:

1954: A. Aghaizu

1959: C. C. Ibe

1961: I. Onyewuenyi

1962: T. Okere

1963: (Msgr.) C. Chigbu, (Msgr.) J. Ibekwe, (Msgr.) I. Okoroanyanwu, M. Onyema, J. Opara, A. Uwakwe

1964: M. Ibe, S. Nworgu, R. Onwuanaibe

1965: B. Nwachukwu, T. Nwalor, L. Nwigwe

1966: B. Agumanu, V. Chikwe, L. Etoh, B. Maduike, Don Okoro

1967: C. Ogu, P. Onyeachu, T. Osondu

1969: J. T. Ezeji, Des Okoro

1970: M. Ngirika

1971: D. Igwe

1972: K. Akagha, P. C. Amakiri, B. Chima, C. Egege, I. Emechete, B. Nwokeleme, A. Obinna

1973: D. Amadi, J. Anaele, J. Mmegwa, P. Ndugbu, S. Nwachukwu, B. Obiukwu, E. Ogu

1974: A. Amanze, G. Anyanwu, L. Asiegbu, C. Ebii, A. Eke, A. Ekechukwu, M. Iwuji, P. Njoku, R. Nwachukwu, N. Okere, A. Onyeocha

1975: J. Azu

1977: J. Ejimofor, E. Emetoh, A. Iheonunekwu, S. Nwachukwu, A. Nwokeji

1978: L. Abara, C. Mbanu, J. Mbonu, M. Ndulaka, B. Osigwe, L. Ugbor, T. Uwakwe

1979: A. Anukam, L. Egbuchulem, C. Ogbonna, J. Ononiwu, C. Osuji, S. Ugochukwu

1980: E. Akpaka, E. Azorji, M. Elekwachi, A. Ihenacho, C. Ojiaku, J. Onuoha, O. Onwubiko, P. P. Ugwokaegbe, J. Uwalaka

1981: C. Akalonu, C. Chimeziri, P. Ibele, S. Igbokwe, A. Ihedinma, C. Nwosu, R. Okorigbo, J. Onyegbule, H. Osuagwu, V. Ozokpor

1982: W. Akaegu, F. Ekwugha, S. Ikea, S. Iroegbu, C. Maduike, M. Njoku, T. K. Nwachukwu, E. Nworu, I. Olekamma, E. Uwadoka

There are 101 indigenous diocesan priests working in Owerri diocese today.

Religious priests working in Owerri Town now are as follows: D. Ononuju C.S.Sp., B. Chilaka, C.S.Sp., M. Ojobo C.S.Sp., C. Ihedoro C.M.F., J. Rabb C.M.F., G. Nze C.M.F., P. Opara C.M.F., A. Ibeawuchi C.M.F., G. Okoye C.M.F.

Source: *Centenary History of the Catholic Church in Owerri Diocese* (1983), 183–87.

APPENDIX B
PORTRAIT OF AN IGBO
CATECHIST/TEACHER:
ARCHDEACON FELIX E.
CHUKWUEZI

Place of birth: Umudim, Ikeduru

Date of birth: Unknown (c.60 years in 1979)

Education: Primary education at CMS School at Umudim and Atta. Passed standard six (std.6) at Atta in 1933. Baptized 1925.

Career: Appointed a schoolteacher from 1934 to 1949, he taught in several schools and towns, including Elele, Bonny, Emii, Mbieri, Aba, Awka, and Umuahia. In 1949 he entered Awka Training College to be trained as a catechist, a course that he completed in 1951. From 1952–53 he served as catechist, and from 1954–56 he was at Trinity College, Umuahia, where he received further training for the priesthood. On December 22, 1956 he was ordained deacon, and on December 23, 1957 he was ordained pastor (priest). For a brief period after the ordination, Reverend Chukwuezi was tutor at St. Paul's College, Awka, and later assigned pastor of St. Michael's Church in Aba, where he served from 1958 to 1962. In 1962 he proceeded to St. Augustine's College, Canterbury, England where he studied theology. Upon his return in 1963, Reverend Chukwuezi was located to Holy Trinity Church, Calabar, where he remained until the outbreak of the Nigerian Civil War in 1967. Thereafter he was posted at Egbu where on December 16, 1968 he was appointed the archdeacon of Owerri; from there he was transferred to Nkwerre in 1972 as the archdeacon of Okigwe and Orlu. With the division of Okigwe-Orlu into two archdeaconries in 1978, Archdeacon Chukwuezi was then appointed archdeacon of Orlu with residence at Nkwerre. There he remained until 1984, when he was appointed archdeacon of Mbaitoli/Ikeduru. He died in 1986.

Personal Reminiscences: Archdeacon Chukwuezi recounted to me some of his life experiences, including his visions (dreams). According to him, he saw a vision at a young age which instilled in him a love and desire for the ministry. "If you want to be prosperous in life," the spirit(s) allegedly said to him, "be baptized and take the name Felix" (Happiness). Accordingly, "I dropped the name Vincent, which I had earlier chosen, [when] I was baptized in 1931 at St. Barnabas Church, Umudim." Also, in 1951, recalled the archdeacon, "I had another dream in which I was assured that I would be among those selected to be trained as pastors." Thus, "God has been with me all these days," even during times of crisis and temptation, which included the long illness of his wife (1952–71) and the death of his elder brother Paul (1968) "who trained me." As a result of Paul's death, "I was then left as the only son of my mother. It appeared the world had come to an end [*Ọdim ka chi jiri*]." In addition, the Nigerian Civil War brought with it feelings of despair and hopelessness as evidenced by the return home of his son Barnabas from the University of Lagos and daughter Georgina from the University of Nigeria, Nsukka as a result of the war. Once again, "It seemed to me all was lost [*Ọdi ka ihe dum emebichana*]. I was frustrated; my children were frustrated. I then asked my son to marry but he refused."

Yet there was another source of pain and anxiety, "my almost penniless situation in 1957. I had four children but was not paid a salary. I only received an allowance of about £1:5/- per month. My wife came to Awka for training at the Women's Home," which compounded the financial difficulties. At one time, recounted the archdeacon, "There was no money in the house. I took the only money in the house from my wife, which was one shilling and six pence, to fix my bicycle tire. At Umuahia, the bicycle had a flat tire again! There was no help from anybody." But in 1969 his daughter Georgina got married and a year later the son also got married. The end of the war soon "brought good life again, and God has been with us ever since." Of course, the financial situation improved considerably; for as deacon he was paid about £170 per annum. Also, as pastor his salary rose to about £240 per annum, and while he was archdeacon it increased to £750 per annum plus an entertainment allowance of £120. Overall, "God has been with us" despite moments of trial. Being a teacher or catechist in those days, recalled the archdeacon, required a great deal of commitment, moreso for the catechist. For the pay was meager. "As catechist I was paid £5:3:4d, whereas my colleagues in the teaching profession received £12:13:4d." Though it was not enough, yet "we accepted it as part of the service of God." In Igbo parlance, *"Owu oru Chineke ka anyi n'aru."*

Source: Interview at St. Paul's Church, Nkwerre, September 20, 1979.

NOTES

ABBREVIATIONS USED IN NOTES

CMS	Church Missionary Society, London
CO	Colonial Office, London
HGFA	Holy Ghost Fathers Archives, Paris
JAH	Journal of African History
JAS	Journal of African Studies
NNAE	Nigerian National Archives, Enugu
NNAI	Nigerian National Archives, Ibadan
PRO	Public Records Office, London
RHL	Rhodes House Library (Oxford)
SMA	Society of African Missions, Rome

CHAPTER 1

1. Interview with Nze Okereke (about eighty-five years old), Sept. 19, 1975 (interviews hereafter are preceded by "Owerri Field Notes"); information from Owerri Council of Elders (*Oha Owere Nchi Ise*).

2. "Owerri Field Notes," interviews with Osigwe Mere (about ninety-five years old), Sept. 16, 1975, Ezem Oparalika (about ninety-eight years), Sept. 17, 1975, Nze Okereke, Sept. 19, 1975; Austine A. Oparanozie, "A Short and Unbiased History of Owerre (Owerri)," an unpublished document submitted to the Jones Commission on the position and status of chiefs in Eastern Nigeria, 1956. I am indebted to G. I. Jones (Cambridge, England) for making this document available to me (1974).

3. There seem to be two different traditions here, obviously suggesting the telescoping of two separate events.

4. "Owerri Field Notes," interview with Owerri Council of Elders, Sept. 28, 1979. The tradition was read by Francis M. Manuwuba. Although the elders concurred basically with the narrative, some expressed reservations about the details. The debate that later arose prompted the secretary to warn: "Anyone who wants to speak should think well before speaking to avoid error."

5. Based on interviews at Owerri with Osigwe Mere, Sept. 16, 1975, Ezem Oparalika, Sept. 17, 1975, Nze Okereke, Sept. 19, 1975, and George Anam (Umuorii Uratta), Sept. 17, 1975.

6. Geoffrey E. Emenako, *Oru Owerre and the Week of Weeks* (Owerri: Imo Newspapers Ltd., 1980), 1. Emenako contends that Oru Owerre stands for "orugh[i] Owerre," meaning "it is not Owerre's fault" to have fled from Uratta (8).

7. Ibid., 8, 11–12.

8. Oparanozie, "History."

9. Jan Vansina, *Oral Tradition* (Chicago: Aldine Publishing Company, 1965), 73–74; "Owerri Field Notes," interviews at Uratta, Aug. 16, 1979 and Sept. 5, 1979. Arugo is said to have been born at Owalla Uratta.

10. Cf. Patrick D. Okoroh, *A Short History of Uratta* (Owerri: The Express Printing Press, 1963), 2 ed.; "Owerri Field Notes," interview with Lawrence Anowe, Aug. 26, 1977.

11. Fage quoted in Elizabeth Tonkin, "Investigating Oral Tradition," *Journal of African History* 27 (1986): 203; Vansina, *Oral Tradition*, 79.

12. "Owerri Field Notes," interviews with George Anam, Sept. 17, 1979 and Okanyirinwa of Umuoba Uratta, Dec. 21, 1983.

13. Jan Vansina, *Oral Tradition As History* (Madison: Univ. of Wisconsin Press, 1985), 192.

14. Cf. John N. Oriji, "History of Ngwa People: A Study of Social and Economic Developments in Igboland from the Precolonial Period to the 20th Century" (Ph.D. diss., Rutgers University, 1981); Elizabeth Isichei, *A History of the Igbo People* (New York: St. Martin's Press, 1976), esp. chapter 1; J. C. C. Allen, "Intelligence Report on the Ngwa Clan, Aba Division" (1934), NNAI, CSO 26/29033/11.

15. "Owerri Field Notes," interviews with Osigwe Mere, Sept. 16, 1975, Nze Okereke, Sept. 19, 1975; Vansina, *Oral Tradition*, 74; Tonkin, "Investigating Oral Tradition," 209.

16. "Owerri Field Notes," interview with George Anam, Sept. 17, 1979.

17. Cf. D. H. Jones, "Problems of African Chronology," *JAH*, 11 (1970): 161–76; David Henige, *The Chronology of Oral Tradition: The Quest for a Chimera* (Oxford: Oxford Univ. Press, 1974).

18. H. F. Matthews, "Second Report on the Aro. Supplementing the 'Discussion on Aro Origins etc.,' " 5–8, RHL, Mss. Afr. S. 783; P. A. Talbot, *The Peoples of Southern Nigeria* (London: Frank Cass, 1969), 1: 184, 248–49; also personal communication from G. I. Jones, Dec. 28, 1974.

19. Talbot, *Peoples of Southern Nigeria*, 184. Cf. G. I. Jones, "Who are the Aro?" *Nigerian Field* 8 (1939): 102.

20. Cf. K. O. Dike who warned that "the African historian . . . must outgrow the conventional outlook of the [Western] historians" and thus treat oral traditions in their African context; "The Importance of African Studies," in Lalager Bown and M. Crowder, eds., *The Proceedings of the First International Congress of Africanists* (Evanston, Ill.: Northwestern Univ. Press, 1964), 64. Also, cf. Jan Vansina, "Once Upon a Time: Oral Tradition as History in Africa," *Daedalus* 100 (1971): 442–68; G. I. Jones, "Time and Oral Tradition . . . Eastern Nigeria," *JAH*, 6 (1965): 153.

21. A. E. Afigbo, "Oral Tradition and the History of Segmentary Societies," *History in Africa* 12 (1985): 4; Ifemesia, personal communication, May 1983. Professor Ifemesia's comment was in reaction to my paper, "Some Problems and Prospects in Writing Local History," presented at the History Department Post-graduate Seminar, University of Nigeria, Nsukka, May 1983.

22. Chinweizu et al., *Toward the Decolonization of African Literature* (Washington, D.C.: Howard Univ. Press, 1983), 1: 6, 1.

23. "Owerri Field Notes," interviews with Osigwe Mere, Sept. 16, 1975, Nze Okereke, Sept. 19, 1975.

24. The Oratta group then comprised the towns which make up the present Owerri Local Government Area, including Ngor and Okpala, which are no longer in that region.

25. F. M. Hensley, *Niger Dawn* (North Devon: Arthur H. Stockwell, n.d.), 163.

26. I am indebted to my brother William D. Ekechi, formerly headmaster at Umunoha and supervisor of schools in Owerri, for this information. See also "Owerri Field Notes," interviews at Umunoha, Sept. 30, 1975.

27. A. E. Afigbo, *The Warrant Chiefs: Indirect Rule in Southeastern Nigeria, 1891–1929* (New York: Humanities Press, 1972), 64.

28. CO 520/14, Moor to CO, No. 183, Apr. 17, 1902.

29. "Owerri Field Notes," interviews with Osigwe Mere, Sept. 16, 1975, Nze Okereke, Sept. 19, 1975, Ezem Oparalika, Sept. 17, 1975, and Oha Owerri Nchi Ise (Owerri Council of Elders), Sept. 28, 1979.

30. "Owerri Field Notes," interview with Ezem Oparalika, Sept. 17, 1975. Cf. interview with John Egejuru Onugha of Owelu Uratta (about one-hundred years old), Oct. 2, 1975. At the time of the interview, Egejuru was the oldest man in all of Uratta and Owerri. The social impact of the Nigeria-Biafra war is yet to be seriously studied. But as this song clearly dramatizes, the war imposed striking dietary changes in the Biafran enclave:

> Ihe Awusa mere umu Igbo eh eh eh
> Ihe Awusa mere umu Igbo eh eh eh
> Ihe Awasa mere umu Igbo eh eh eh
> Achogalam ihem eri rie okoriko.
> Ihe Awusa mere umu Igbo eh eh eh
> Ihe Awusa mere umu Igbo owuu ihe ekwu ekwu.

In literal translation: What the Hausas (i.e., Nigerians) did to the Igbo is absolutely unforgettable. For it was because of extraordinary hunger that I was forced to eat *okoriko* (a detestable form of wild coco yam). "Owerri Field Notes," recorded at Umuorii Uratta, Oct. 1, 1975.

31. "Owerri Field Notes," interviews with Osigwe Mere, Sept. 16, 1975, Ezem Oparalika, Sept. 17, 1975, Nze Okereke, Sept. 19, 1975.

32. G. Adams Papers, "A Resurrection of the Long Juju" (n.d.), RHL, Mss. Afr. s. 375 (3), 6; "Owerri Field Notes," interview with Osigwe Mere, Sept. 16, 1975.

33. See F. N. Uka, "A Note on the 'Abam' Warriors of Igboland," *Ikenga* (*Journal of African Studies*, University of Nigeria, Nsukka), 1 (July 1972): 76–82. Dr. Uka writes that the Abam warriors "were motivated . . . by the strong desire and the compelling need to bring home the head of a victim. In so doing the individual would win the 'Ufiem Title,' a socially, highly desirable status of the time" (76).

34. Isaac M. Okonjo, *British Administration in Nigeria, 1900–1950: A Nigerian View* (New York: Nok Publishers, 1974), 57; submission by the Mbaise Clan Council to the Jones Commission, Apr. 14, 1956.

35. Cf. Afigbo, *The Warrant Chiefs,* 70, and note 31.

36. C. K. Meek, *Report on Social and Political Organization in the Owerri Division* (Lagos, Nigeria: Government Printer, 1933), para. 72. Emphasis added.

37. Robert L. Tignor, "Colonial Chiefs in Chiefless Societies," *Journal of Modern African Studies* 9 (Oct. 1971): 346; CO 520/18, Moor to CO No. 16, Jan. 7, 1903.

38. CO 520/14, Moor to CO No. 203, May 17, 1902; CO to Moor, (Draft) No. 526, Nov. 7, 1902, NNAI: CSO 26/3/27937, "Intelligence Report on the Ezinihitte Clan, Owerri Division" (1932), by E. H. Dickinson, 13, para. 32.

39. For the delimitation of boundaries see CO 591/1, *Nigeria Gazette,* July 31, 1902; CO 591/2, *Gazette Supplement,* June 9, 1905; ibid., *Gazette,* Oct. 27, 1905; CO 592/3, *Annual*

Report, Eastern Provinces, 1906, 219; NNAE: OWDIST 10/1/3, "Annual Report 1938," by E. R. Chadwick.

40. NNAE: OW 5709 OWDIST 7/1/7, "Owerri Division. Annual Report 1945," by H. F. P. Wetherell, para. 2.

CHAPTER 2

1. A. W. H. Haywood and F. A. S. Clarke, *The History of the Royal West African Frontier Force* (Aldershot: Gale and Polden, 1964), 68.

2. For Douglas's brief biography see *The Colonial Office List,* 1921 and *Southern Nigerian Civil List,* 1910, PRO.

3. CO 520/14, "Report in Connection with the Aro Field Force Operations, 1902," by Lt. Colonel Montanaro.

4. See F. K. Ekechi, "Portrait of a Colonizer: H. M. Douglas in Colonial Nigeria, 1897–1920," *African Studies Review* 26 (Mar. 1983), 26–35.

5. CMS Archives (London), G3/A3/0, Bishop Tugwell to Douglas, Dec. 18, 1905.

6. CO 583/30, Douglas to Lt. Governor (Confidential), Jan. 17, 1915; ibid., Governor to Douglas (Conf. No. C287/14), Dec. 28, 1914, enclosure in Lugard to Harcourt (Conf. A), Jan. 29, 1915.

7. CO 583/30, *The Times* newspaper clippings attached to correspondence; ibid., Douglas to Lt. Governor (Conf.), Jan. 17, 1915; ibid., Governor to Douglas, Dec. 28, 1914.

8. CO 520/31, Extract of Report on the Owerri District for the quarter ending 30th June, 1905.

9. CO 520/31, Report of the Norie Operation by Lieutenant Half-penny, 1905; NNAI: Calprof. 10/3, Report by Captain P. K. Carre, July 10, 1905, encl. in Carre to Divisional Commissioner, July 30, 1905.

10. CO 520/31, Extract of Report on the Owerri District for the quarter ending 30th June, 1905.

11. See F. K. Ekechi, "The Igbo Response to British Imperialism: The Episode of Dr. Stewart and the Ahiara Expedition, 1905–1916," *Journal of African Studies (JAS),* 1 (Summer 1974): 145–57.

12. CO 520/31, "Overland Journey Lagos to Calabar via Ibadan 1905," 29. There were 235 prisoners at Owerri prison.

13. "Owerri Field Notes," information from Ahiara and Onicha (Ezinihitte), Mar. 3, 1973. I am particularly indebted to Okeahialam Elem of Onicha (about ninety years old) for most of the information on Dr. Stewart and the Ahiara incident.

14. *Times,* Mar. 1906, cited in S. N. Nwabara, *Iboland: A Century of Contact with Britian, 1860–1960* (Atlantic Highlands, N.J.: Humanities Press, 1978), 124.

15. CO 520/22, Telegram from Douglas to Colonial Secretary (Calabar), Nov. 21, 1905.

16. Haywood, *History,* 80.

17. See note 13.

18. CO 520/32, Thorburn to CO (Conf.), Dec. 9, 1905.

19. CO 520/35, Report by Trenchard, Dec. 22, 1905; CO 520/36, Report by H. C. Moorhouse, encl. in Egerton to CO, June 9, 1906; ibid., Thorburn to Elgin, Jan. 5, 1906.

20. CO 520/35, Report by Trenchard, Dec. 22, 1905. Trenchard indicated that the skull was taken to and buried at Calabar on Feb. 20, 1906. Other personal effects recovered included the amount of thirty-one shillings. The alleged skull must have been that of someone else. Cf. note 21.

21. NNAI: CSO 26/3/27937, "Intelligence Report on the Ezinihitte Clan, Owerri Di-

vision" (1932), by E. H. C. Dickinson, p. 12, para. 27; communication from Professor Afigbo, 1974. See also T. Uzodinma Nwala, *Mbaise in Contemporary Nigeria* (New York: Gold & Maestro, 1978), 26. Nwala writes, "The fate of the skull of Dr. Stewart has remained a mystery to all 'strangers' to this day."

22. CO 520/32, Enclosure in Memo of Instruction, Dec. 9, 1905.

23. CO 520/81, Egerton to Crewe (Conf.), Sept. 22, 1909; see Ekechi, "Igbo Response," 155.

24. CO 583/58, F. P. Lynch (DO) to Resident, June 1, 1917, encl. in Lugard to CO, June 11, 1917; NNAE: OWDIST 9/6/3, Report on Owerri Division for half-year January-June 1920. For colonial agitation in the 1950s see *Eastern Nigeria Guardian,* Apr. 19 and May 8, 1950. Cf. NNAE: OWDIST 7/1/8, No. OW7732, Powell to Resident, Apr. 1, 1949.

25. Afigbo, *The Warrant Chiefs,* 176–77; G. Adams Papers, "A Resurrection of the Long Juju," RHL, Mss. Afr. s. 375 (3), 4–5.

26. CO 520/93, Tew to Governor, No. 204, Apr. 14, 1910; CO 583/58, F. P. Lynch to Resident, June 1, 1917. Also NNAE: OW 346/17 RIVPROF 8/5/353, "Report on the Owerri Division for the Half Year ending 30th June, 1917."

27. NNAE: OWDIST 24/1/2, Tew to Provincial Commissioner (PC), Eastern Provinces, Oct. 10, 1910.

28. Boniface I. Obichere, "Oracles and Politics in West Africa: A Precolonial Legacy for Contemporary Nation States and Republics," unpublished paper presented at the African Studies Association, Baltimore, Maryland, Nov. 1978, 3.

29. Cf. G. T. Basden, *Among the Ibos of Nigeria* (London: Frank Cass, 1966), 203.

30. See CO 520/18, Heneker to High Commissioner (HC), Dec. 26, 1902. During the 1901–2 operations in the Bende Division, Umuajata and Ibeku in Umuahia were reported to have sworn a sacred oath and made medicine "to oppose the whiteman, kill all his messengers and drive him out of the country." What "saved us," reported Heneker, was surprise attack of enemy positions and the use of the Maxim gun. "A heavy fire was poured in and before the enemy recovered from their surprise the leading Company dashed across and extended out in the open yam fields beyond, driving the enemy before them. . . . [But] the enemy contested *every inch of the way* and attacked both flanks and rear continuously" (emphasis added).

31. Frank Hives, *Juju and Justice in Nigeria* (London: John Lane, 1930), 106.

32. C. K. Meek, *Law and Authority in a Nigerian Tribe* (New York: Barnes & Noble, 1937), 44, 48.

33. NNAE: OWDIST 24/1/2, Tew to Capt. Ambrose, Sept. 20, 1910; Tew to PC, Oct. 10, 1910; Capt. Ambrose to Tew, Sept. 23, 1910.

34. "Owerri Field Notes," interviews at Ezumoha in Osu (Mbano), Aug. 4, 1984. I am particularly indebted to Opara Onugo of Okohia (about seventy-five years old) for the information about the activities of Ogbunorie. Cf. F. K. Ekechi, "The War to End All Wars: Perspectives on the British Assault on a Nigerian Oracle," *Nigeria Magazine* 53 (Jan.-Mar. 1985): 61.

35. Ekechi, "The War to End All Wars," 61.

36. NNAE: OWDIST 24/1/2, Tew to PC, Oct. 10, 1910; Givens to PC, Mar. 22, 1911; Tew to PC, Dec. 18, 1910; John M. Buing to PC, Apr. 17, 1911; OWDIST 5/2/3, Mair to PC, June 14, 1910; OWDIST 24/1/2, Tew to PC, Oct. 10, 1910.

37. See F. K. Ekechi, "The British Assault on the Ogbunorie Oracle," *JAS* 14 (Summer 1987):73.

38. NNAE: OWDIST 24/1/2, Givens to PC, Mar. 22, 1911; "Owerri Field Notes," interviews at Ezumoha, Aug. 4, 1984.

39. G. Adams Papers, "A Resurrection of the Long Juju," 14–15, 11.

40. Ibid., 12, 13, 16.

CHAPTER 3

1. NNAE: OWDIST 24/1/1, "Owerri District Office Letter Book, 1909–11," 261.

2. NNAE: OWDIST 9/5/10, "Annual Report on the Owerri Division for the year ending 31st December 1919."

3. Joyce Cary, *Britain and West Africa* (London: Longmans, Green & Co., 1946), 51; CO 520/48, Thorburn to Elgin, Sept. 7, 1907. Cf. Rex Stevens's view that in precolonial Nigeria "you are born in a village, there you stayed and had your being. There was no question of travel; wandering a mere two miles from your village square might easily result in death. . . . Today [1949] . . . there has for many years been freedom unknown ever before in the history of travel from one end of the land to the other." R. A. Stevens Papers, "Preface," RHL, Mss. Afr. s. 1068 (1), 6.

4. C. S. Whitaker, Jr., *The Politics of Tradition: Continuity and Change in Northern Nigeria, 1946–1966* (Princeton, N.J.: Princeton Univ. Press, 1970), 3.

5. It has also been suggested that Chief Njemanze was exiled because of his slave-dealing activities in addition to his opposition to forced labor.

6. "Owerri Field Notes," interview with Ezem Oparalika, Sept. 17, 1975.

7. CO 520/92, Egerton to CO (Confidential), Mar. 17, 1910; CO 520/26, Egerton to CO (Conf.), Nov. 5, 1904.

8. CO 520/24, Report on the Operations in the Akwette and Owerri Districts, 1904.

9. Report by Douglas, July 4, 1904, cited in Cletus E. Emezi, "British Administration in Owerri, 1900–1930" (Ph.D. diss., University of Nigeria, Nsukka, 1978), 81(a)–81(b).

10. Ibid.

11. CMS: ACC/89/F1, Dennis to Mother, Apr. 11, 1905; CO 520/31, "Overland Journey . . . 1905," 33.

12. "Overland Journey . . . 1905," 31–32.

13. Ibid., 27.

14. Hensley, *Niger Dawn,* 141.

15. CO 591/2, *Nigeria Gazette,* Sept. 22, 1904, 287–88; *Supplement,* June 9, 1905, 336.

16. "Owerri Field Notes," information from John Egejuru, Oct. 2, 1975.

17. CO 520/92, Egerton to Crewe, Mar. 17, 1910; encl. in ibid., by F. S. James, Acting Colonial Secretary (Eastern Provinces); ibid., Report by Fosbery, encl.

18. CO 520/24, Report on the Operations in the Akwette and Owerri Districts, 1904.

19. CO 520/82, Egerton to Crewe, Oct. 8, 1909.

20. CO 520/28, Probyn to Under-Secretary of State, Jan. 1, 1904.

21. Ibid.

22. CO 520/28, CO to Egerton (Draft), Apr. 13, 1904. See also Minutes by J. Antrobus and others, Mar. 30, 1904.

23. CO 520/25, Report by Fosbery, May 27, 1904.

24. Ibid.

25. Ibid.

26. Ibid., Egerton to Lyttleton, No. 278, June 16, 1904.

27. CO 520/25, CO Minutes on Egerton to Crewe, June 6, 1909; Arthur N. Cook, *British Enterprise in Nigeria* (London: Frank Cass, 1964), 220; Lugard quoted in Innocent Uzoechi, "The Social and Political Impact of the Eastern Nigerian Railway on Udi Division 1913–1945" (Ph.D. diss., Kent State University, 1985), 73.

28. CO 520/106, Egerton to Harcourt, Oct. 18, 1911; Elgin quoted in Uzoechi, "Eastern Nigerian Railway," 80.

29. NNAE: OWDIST 9/5/10, "Annual Report on the Owerri Division for the year ending

31st December 1919." See also OW 5709 OWDIST 7/1/7, "Annual Report on the Owerri Division, 1945." In the words of H. F. P. Wetherell, "Administrative Officers are compelled to sit and watch golden opportunities of real progress disappear . . . because no real attempt has ever been made to achieve continuity or because their time is fully occupied with matters which the average underpaid girl in [a] London office would take in her stride."

30. NNAE: 60/1925 OWDIST 9/11/54, "Owerri Township 1925," Report by the Local Town Planning Sub-Committee, Feb. 5, 1925.

31. NNAE: OW 34/1925 OWDIST 6/8/1, "Visit of His Excellency the Officer Administering the Government . . . to Owerri, 28th–29th August, 1925."

32. NNAE: OWDIST 7/1/3 File No. 2518, "Petition From Owerri Chiefs for Extension of Railway to Owerri," 1934, Sid O. Quenoy.

33. NNAE: OWDIST 7/1/3 File No. 2518, G. C. Whiteley (for Chief Secretary to the Government) to the Owerri Chiefs, Aug. 3, 1934.

34. "Owerri Field Notes," interview with J. K. Nzerem, Aug. 24, 1977.

35. See Ekechi, "Portrait of a Colonizer," 33–35. Also, F. K. Ekechi, "The Colonial Rebel: H. M. Douglas and the Nigerian Administration," *Nigeria Magazine* (forthcoming).

36. Ekechi, "Colonial Rebel"; Bushe quoted in John Flint, "Planned Decolonization and Its Failure in British West Africa," *African Affairs* 82 (July 1983): 395.

37. See NNAE: CSE 5/14/2, No. C11/1919, Douglas to Colonial Secretary, Dec. 28, 1918; CO 583/73, CO Minutes, May 21, 1918.

38. According to Petro Grigorenko, the Russian dissident, "whomever wanted to struggle against tyranny had to destroy within himself the fear of tyranny." Quoted in M. D. Henry, "Confronting the Big Lie," *The Collegiate Review* 20 (Spring/Summer 1984): 57.

39. Cf. I. F. Nicolson, *The Administration of Nigeria, 1900–1960* (London: Clarendon Press, 1969), chaps. 7–8; Afigbo, *The Warrant Chiefs,* chaps. 4–5.

40. NNAE: CSE 5/14/2, No. C 11/1919, in Douglas to Colonial Secretary, Dec. 28, 1918. Cf. Sir Alan Burns, *Colonial Civil Servant* (London: George Allen & Unwin, 1949), 61, 300; L. H. Gann and Peter Duignan, *The Rulers of British Africa, 1870–1914* (Stanford: Stanford Univ. Press, 1978), 217, 219, for comparative salaries.

41. Ibid.

42. Ibid.

43. Ibid.

44. Ibid.

45. Ibid.

46. Cf. Burns, *Colonial Civil Servant,* 164, 166. Burns, formerly governor in the Gold Coast (Ghana) and Nigeria, shared Douglas's opinion that the promotion policy required "immediate change" and that "there should be a rule of the Service that officers will retire on pension if within a certain period they do not get promotion."

47. CO 583/30, Lt.-Governor to Douglas, Jan. 28, 1915; CO 583/73, Language Examination Report, encl.; Nigerian *Daily Times,* Nov. 15, 1929, emphasis added. Ruxton wrote under the pseudonym "Rexal." Cf. Burns, *Colonial Civil Servant,* 164. In Burns's words, the promotion system depended "too much on fortuitous vacancies and too little on the merits of the officers."

48. NNAE: CSE 5/14/2, Douglas to Secretary of State, Dec. 28, 1918.

49. Nicolson, *Administration of Nigeria,* 231, 232.

50. Cf. Wordworth to Geoffrey, Feb. 6, 1904, RHL, Mss. Afr. s. 1373. On the issue of "bush allowances" Burns writes, "The provision of free furnished quarters was formerly part of the emoluments of European officers in West Africa. Where no quarters were available and the officer had to live in a 'bush house' . . . an allowance in lieu of quarters was paid"; *Colonial*

Civil Servant, 60. To this day, the house allowance continues to be paid by the government to Nigerian workers—including teachers.

51. Quoted in Nicolson, *Administration of Nigeria,* 225.

52. NNAE: OWDIST 9/5/10, "Annual Report on the Owerri Division for the year ending 31st December, 1919"; Nicolson, *Administration of Nigeria,* 218.

53. NNAE: CSE 5/14/2, Douglas to Secretary of State, Dec. 28, 1918.

54. See Nicolson, *Administration of Nigeria,* 221.

55. NNAE: CSE 5/14/2, Douglas to Secretary of State, Dec. 28, 1918.

56. Ibid.

57. Ibid. Cf. Burns, *Colonial Civil Servant,* 61, 300. "I consider the policy of a levy on officials' salaries at times of depression as a most unfair breach of faith with public servants" (300).

58. Ibid.

59. Ibid.

60. Ibid.

61. Ibid.

62. CO 520/80, Minutes on Clifford to Milner, Dec. 3, 1919.

63. NNAE: CSE 5/14/2, Moorhouse to Milner, Jan. 24, 1919.

64. Ibid.

65. Ibid.

66. Ibid. Burns agrees with Moorhouse on the housing question: "I should certainly prefer to live in a well-built 'bush house' than in some bungalows I have known. The government bungalows are, as a rule, badly designed, and compare unfavourably with the bungalows provided by most of the European firms for their employees"; *Colonial Civil Servant,* 60.

67. NNAE: CSE 5/14/2, Moorhouse to Milner, Jan. 24, 1919.

68. CO 583/73, Minutes, May 21, 1918. See also minutes by G. J. Evans and J. C. Maxwell, Aug. 14, 1918.

69. CO 583/73, Minutes on Moorhouse to Milner, Jan. 24, 1919. The officials viewed Douglas's letter as being not only "scandalous" but "irritating." Wrote one angry official, "[It] is to my mind conclusive evidence of the fact that he is not fitted to hold the post of Resident in Nigeria."

70. CO 583/73, Milner to Officer Administering the Government of Nigeria, Mar. 26, 1919.

71. CO 583/73, Douglas to Boyle, May 5, 1919. See Boyle to Douglas, Apr. 24, 1919; NNAE: CSE 5/14/2, No. C11/1919, Douglas to Secretary of State, Dec. 28, 1918.

72. Quoted in *West Africa,* Mar. 29, 1919, 173.

73. Ibid., 177.

74. Quoted in ibid., 180.

75. See Afigbo, *The Warrant Chiefs,*161.

CHAPTER 4

1. CMS: ACC/89/F1, Dennis to Mother, Apr. 11 and 12, 1905.

2. Ibid.

3. Hensley, *Niger Dawn,* 134; CMS: G3/A3/0, Tugwell, "Journey to Owerri," No. 173, 1905; Tugwell to Baylis, Nov. 20, 1905.

4. CMS: G3/A3/0, Tugwell to Baylis, Nov. 20, 1905.

5. Hensley, *Niger Dawn,* 136–37. The tropical rains also posed some problems. "When the . . . rain came it was preceded by tornadoes that paralyzed," and "there were no protection from the rain . . . and it was as wet inside the house as out" (138, 142). Cf. HGFA, 191/A/111, General Report on the Catholic Mission Prefecture Apostolic on the Lower Niger (1914).

6. Hensley, *Niger Dawn,* 140.

7. Basden, *Among the Ibos of Nigeria,* 97.

8. See F. K. Ekechi, "African Polygamy and Western Christian Ethnocentrism," *JAS* 3 (Fall 1976): 329–49; Edmund Ilogu, *Christianity and Igbo Culture* (New York: Nok Publishers, 1974), 223. Professor Ilogu placed emphasis on "those who become converted whilst having more than one wife."

9. Hensley, *Niger Dawn,* 153.

10. Ibid., 170.

11. CMS: G3/A3/0, "Report of the Southern District (Egbu)," Jan.-July 1913, by Fred G. Payne. See also ibid., "District Reports" in Appendix to Executive Committee Minutes, Aug. 1910; "The Niger Mission," 1910 by G. T. Basden.

12. S. Smith, "The Progress of the Forward Movement in the Ibo Country," *CMS: Niger and Yoruba Notes* (Feb. 1902), 66. See also "Un Apôtre Indigène au Niger," *L'Echo des Missions Africaines* (Jan.-Feb. 1905), 21-29.

13. For the debates see Robin Horton, "African Conversion," *Africa* 41 (1972): 85-108; Caroline Ifeka-Moller, "White Power: Social-Structural Factors in Conversion to Christianity, Eastern Nigeria, 1921–1966," *Canadian Journal of African Studies* (*CJAS*), 8 (1974): 55–72; Robin Horton and J. D. Y. Peel, "Conversion and Confusion: A Rejoinder on Christianity in Eastern Nigeria," *CJAS* 10 (1976): 481–98; Robert M. Baum, "Rational Conversion and the Diola-Esulalu (Senegal) Religious Experience," paper presented at the African Studies Association (Boston), Nov. 1976.

14. Chinua Achebe, *Things Fall Apart* (Greenwich, Conn.: Fawcett Publications, 1959); Ekechi, *Missionary Enterprise,* chap. 1.

15. See *CMS: Niger and Yoruba Notes* (Sept. 1897), 24. Though said about Onitsha this certainly applied to almost all of the Igbo communities.

16. Hensley, *Niger Dawn,* 144–45.

17. T. O. Beidelman, *Colonial Evangelism: A Socio-Historical Study of an East African Mission at the Grassroots* (Bloomington: Indiana Univ. Press, 1982); James Ngugi, *The River Between* (London: Heinemann, 1965), 162–63.

18. Cf. E. A. Ayandele, *The Missionary Impact on Modern Nigeria, 1842–1914: A Political and Social Analysis* (London: Longman, 1966).

19. CMS: G3/A3/L6, Durrant and Baylis to Smith, Mar. 5, 1908; Hensley, *Niger Dawn,* 91.

20. Quoted in Austine O. Okwu, "The Mission of the Irish Holy Ghost Fathers Among the Igbo of Southern Nigeria, 1905-1956" (Ph.D. diss., Columbia University, 1977), 368. I am grateful to Dr. Okwu for sending me a copy of his dissertation.

21. Ibid., 387–88.

22. Hensley, *Niger Dawn,* 167; R. A. Ozigboh, "A Christian Mission in the Era of Colonialism: A Study of the Catholic Missionary Enterprise in South-Eastern Nigeria, 1885–1939" (Ph.D. diss., Birmingham University, 1980), 169. I am grateful to Dr. Ozigboh for making this work available to me in 1983.   •

23. Hensley, *Niger Dawn,* 168, 141.

24. G. C. Onyeche, "The Seed," unpublished manuscript, n.d., 1. I am indebted to the Venerable Archdeacon F. E. Chukwuezi of St. Paul's Church, Nkwerre for this reference.

25. Hensley, *Niger Dawn,* 139, 140.

26. Ibid. With respect to Igbo belief in afterlife, Hensley writes, "This belief was very strong and it weakened our Message considerably, because they thought they would get further chances of salvation in other lives if they were not saved in this." Ibid., 141. She was probably referring to the Igbo belief in reincarnation.

27. See Isaac D. E. Anyabuike, "Christian Missionary Enterprise in Isu-Ama Igbo, 1900–1948: A Historical Survey" (Ph.D. diss., Ibadan University, 1981), 140. I am very grateful to Dr. Anyabuike for providing me with a copy of his thesis.

28. Onyeabo was accused in a sex scandal by an Onitsha girl, but after a thorough investigation was found innocent of all charges. See CMS: G3/A3/0, Minutes of E.C., Jan. 1913.

29. London *Times*, Feb. 19, 1954, cited in Hensley, *Niger Dawn*, 10.

30. Emezi, "British Administration," 170.

31. Quoted in Ozigboh, "Christian Mission," 240. Cf. J. P. Jordan, *Bishop Shanahan of Southern Nigeria* (Dublin: Clonmore & Reynolds, 1949), 102.

32. HGFA, 191/A/111, "Nigeria: Journal of Father Feral, March-April 1912" (hereafter cited as Father Feral's journal). See also CMS: G3/A3/0, Minutes of E.C., July 15 and Sept. 7, 1914.

33. Ibid.

34. CMS: G3/A3/0, Cecil Brown, District Reports, Report on Owerri District, July 1912. See also F.K. Ekechi, *Missionary Enterprise and Rivalry in Igboland, 1857–1914* (London: Frank Cass, 1972), 217.

35. Ozigboh, "Christian Mission," 240; Father Feral's journal, 1912. The English translation is from Elizabeth Isichei, *Igbo Worlds: An Anthology of Oral Histories and Historical Descriptions* (Philadelphia: Institute for the Study of Human Issues, 1978), 223.

36. See the accounts of early Roman Catholic activities in the Owerri area in Rose A. Njoku, *The Advent of the Catholic Church in Nigeria: Its Growth in Owerri Diocese* (Owerri: Assumpta Press, 1980), 42–52; Uche A. Ogike, ed., *Centenary History of the Catholic Church in Owerri Diocese* (Owerri: Assumpta Press, 1983).

37. "Owerri Field Notes," interview with Chief Amadi Obi and others, Nov. 17, 1975.

38. Ogike, *Centenary History*, 52.

39. Jordan, *Bishop Shanahan*, 112–13; "Owerri Field Notes," interview with Chief Amadi Obi and others, Nov. 17, 1975. See Nina Emma Mba, *Nigerian Women Mobilized: Women's Political Activity in Southern Nigeria, 1900–1965* (Berkeley: Univ. of California Press, 1982), 59.

40. Quoted in Ozigboh, "Christian Mission," 347.

41. For a full treatment of Catholic and Protestant rivalry see Ekechi, *Missionary Enterprise.*

42. CMS: G3/A3/0, Report on the Owerri District in "District Reports," July 1912; G. T. Manley, "C.M.S. Policy in Pagan Africa," *Church Missionary Intelligencer* (1917), 75; HGFA, 192/A/11, Shanahan to Directors, Sept. 21, 1917.

43. Jordan, *Bishop Shanahan,* 110; CMS: G3/A3/0, Basden to Manley, Aug. 2, 1915.

44. Jordan, *Bishop Shanahan,* 35; Okwu, "Holy Ghost Fathers," 221, 229.

45. Adrian Hastings, *A History of African Christianity 1950–1975* (Cambridge: Cambridge Univ. Press, 1979), 114; Jordan, *Bishop Shanahan,* 155.

46. Cf. Njoku, *Advent of the Catholic Church,* 53.

47. Okwu "Holy Ghost Fathers," 355–56; Njoku, *Advent of the Catholic Church,* 103–5.

48. HGFA, B192/A/VII, Shanahan to His Eminence, Sept. 5, 1920, cited in Ozigboh, "Christian Mission," 342.

49. CMS: G3/A3/0, "Sub-committee Recommendation on Rearrangement of Districts," 1913. Also ibid., Minutes of E.C. Meeting, Jan. 1913; "Annual Letter," by Julius Spencer, Nov. 24, 1911.

50. CMS: G3/A3/0, Minutes of E.C. Meeting, Sept. 7, 1914; Minutes of E.C. Meeting, July 15, 1914; Manley, "C.M.S. Policy in Pagan Africa," 75; Jordan, *Bishop Shanahan,* 100.

51. Anyabuike, "Missionary Enterprise," 179. Also pp. 174–78.

52. Ibid., 180.

53. CMS: G3/A3/0, Report of the Southern District, July-Dec. 1913; "Owerri Field Notes,"information collected at Obinze, Oct. 10, 1979. I am indebted to Dr. Lawrence Amadi for the information about the Baptist mission at Obinze.

54. NNAE: OWDIST 9/5/6, No. 42/9, "Half Yearly Report on the Owerri Division, January 1st to June 30th, 1919."

55. NNAE: PHLANDS 2/1/5, No. C116, "Memorandum: Hostility Between Members of the Roman Catholic Mission and C.M.S.—Owerri Division, Nov. 21, 1933" (hereafter "Memorandum"). See DO to Resident, Nov. 21, 1933.

56. NNAE: PHLANDS 2/1/5, No. C116, "Memorandum."

57. Foreman quoted in ibid.; see also Father Foreman to Dickenson, Nov. 12, 1933 in ibid.

58. Ibid. Father Foreman to Dickenson, Nov. 12, 1933.

59. NNAE: PHLANDS 2/1/5, No. C116, "Memorandum."

60. Ibid., "Memorandum," DO to Resident, Nov. 21, 1933.

61. Ibid., Foreman to Dickenson, Nov. 12, 1933.

62. Ibid., "Memorandum."

63. D. Ibe Nwoga, "Culture and Religion in Contemporary Mbaise: A Comment," in Nwala, *Mbaise,* 32. I am deeply grateful to G. E. S. Njoku (National Archives Enugu) for a copy of this book.

64. Emezi, "British Administration," 170.

65. NNAE: PHLANDS 2/1/5, No. C116, "Memorandum."

66. Ibid. Transportation difficulties precluded fieldwork in the Ikeduru area in both 1975 and 1979.

67. Ibid.

68. Father A. Aghaizu, "Second Conversion," *Annals* (July 1956): 4–5. See Okwu, "Holy Ghost Fathers," 523; Hastings, *African Christianity,* 115. As Hastings points out, "The earliest membership of most Christian churches in Africa had been predominantly male." By the 1950s, however, "the majority of active members of a congregation might well be women, and there is a growing sense that Christianity and the church belong to them."

69. HGFA, 191/A/1, "Circular No. 10," Aug. 1924. See also Shanahan to Bubendorf, Oct. 14, 1924.

70. HGFA, 191/A/1, "Circular."

71. John Vernon Taylor, *Christianity and Politics in Africa* (New York: Greenwood Press, 1957).

72. Quoted in Nwabara, *Iboland,* 73.

73. J. P. Jordan, "Catholic Education and Catholicism in Nigeria," *African Ecclesiastical Review* 1–2 (1959–60): 60–61. For discussions on the church-state conflict see A. E. Afigbo, "The Missions, the State and Education in South-Eastern Nigeria, 1956–71," 176–92, and Colman M. Cooke, "Church, State, and Education: The Eastern Nigeria Experience 1950–1967," 193–206, in Edward Fashole-Luke et al., eds., *Christianity in Independent Africa* (Bloomington: Indiana Univ. Press, 1978); E. Amucheazi, "The Background to the East Central State Public Education Edict, 1970," *Ikenga* 2 (July 1973): 72–82.

CHAPTER 5

1. "Owerri Field Notes,"interviews with John Egejuru, Oct. 2, 1975; Obinze elders, Oct. 10,

1979. I am particularly grateful to Oparanozie Enyinna of Obinze for the information provided and for his generous entertainment.

2. Information from interview with the Director of Education (July 1979).

3. See Ekechi, *Missionary Enterprise,* 178.

4. CO 520/31, "Overland Journey . . . 1905."

5. See A. M. Kirk-Greene, ed., *The Principles of Native Administration: Selected Documents, 1900–1947* (London: Oxford Univ. Press, 1965), 109.

6. NNAE: OW261/16 RIVPROF 8/4/224, B. Hooges to Commissioner, Apr. 25, 1916; ibid., Walker to Inspector-General of Police, Mar. 17, 1915; "Owerri Field Notes," interview with Chief Amadi Obi, Nov. 17, 1975.

7. PRO: *Colonial Annual Reports* (1906).

8. NNAE: OWDIST 9/5/10, "Annual Report on Owerri Division for the year ending 31st December 1919." "Chiefs like schools as it seems to them a mark of authority and doubtless the teacher is useful to them. Most of the head-chiefs are . . . equally desirous of having schools as of having warrants," para. 13.

9. "Owerri Field Notes," interviews with Owerri Council of Elders, Sept. 16 and 17, 1975. Cf. particularly interview with John Egejuru, Oct. 2, 1975.

10. Jordan, *Bishop Shanahan,* 97. My uncle Ibeawuchi Egekeze strongly encouraged me to "study clerk" when I was in the secondary school, perhaps because of his encounter with court clerks.

11. Eke Kalu, "An Ibo Autobiography," *Nigerian Field* 7(1938): 164–65. See also G. D. Johnston, "Ohafia 1911–40: A Study in Church Developments in Eastern Nigeria," *Bulletin of the Society for African Church History* 2 (1966): 139–41.

12. NNAE: OWDIST 6/8/1, No. OW 34/1925, "Visit of His Excellency," Aug. 28–29, 1925.

13. Ibid.

14. H. C. Swaisland to Dr. Don Nylen, Apr. 7, 1961, RHL, Mss. Afr. s. 862, No. 13.

15. NNAE: OWDIST 10/1/2, "Annual Report on the Owerri Division, 1937."

16. NNAE: OWDIST 10/1/3, "Annual Report on the Owerri Division, 1939," by A. E. Cook; NNAE: OWDIST 10/1/4, "Annual Report 1939," by J. E. White, Dec. 16, 1939.

17. "Owerri Field Notes," interview with Oparanozie Enyinna of Obinze, Oct. 10, 1979.

18. Elizabeth Isichei, *A History of the Igbo People* (New York: St. Martin's Press, 1976), 195.

19. Rev. Hope M. Waddell, *Twenty-nine Years in the West Indies and Central Africa: A Review of Missionary Work and Adventure 1829–1858* (London: Frank Cass, 1970), 346; *World Missionary Conference, 1910, Report of Commission III: Education in Relation to the Christianisation of National Life* (London: Oliphant, Anderson & Ferrier, 1910), 3:377; S. A. Hammond, "Pagan Schools: The Training of Teachers" (1927), RHL, Mss. Afr. s. 1325; CMS: G3/A3/0, Minutes of Niger Council, Aug. 1894; CMS, *Western Equatorial Diocesan Magazine* (Jan.-Dec. 1917): 211. See also Ian Linden, *Church and Revolution in Rwanda* (New York: Africana Publishing Company, 1977), 172.

20. "Owerri Field Notes," interviews with Oparanozie Enyinna, Oct. 10, 1979; Ezem Oparalika, Sept. 17, 1975; Achebe, *Things Fall Apart,* 133.

21. HGFA, 192/A/V, Shanahan's Report for 1909.

22. CMS: G3/A3/0, "Supplementary Report," in Minutes of Women's Informal Conference 1913; ibid., "Annual Letter," by C. Brown, Nov. 1912.

23. NNAE: OWDIST 10/1/4, "Education Returns: Annual Report and Statistics 1923"; OWDIST 9/12/14, "Annual Report: Owerri Division 1926"; OWDIST 10/1/2, "Annual Report 1937." See submissions from Father P. P. Cloonan to DO, Dec. 22, 1937; Father Whelan to DO, Dec. 22, 1937; Rev. H. O. Nweje to DO, Dec. 23, 1937. None of these missionaries

could vouch for the accuracy of the statistics. Of course, juggling with numbers was a yearly routine largely for purposes of looking good before the government.

24. Society of African Missions, Rome (SMA): 15794/148/0404, "Le Vicariat Apostolique de la Nigeria Occidentale Depuis sa fondation jusqu'à nos jours," part 3; NNAE: CSO 26/03928, Hives to Resident, Mar. 15, 1922.

25. See Ekechi, *Missionary Enterprise,* chap. 8; also Ekechi, "Colonialism and Christianity in West Africa: The Igbo Case, 1900–1915," *JAH* 12 (1971), 103–15; Isichei, *A History of the Igbo People,* 167.

26. NNAE: OWDIST 9/12/9, No. 49/1926, Fr. O'Connor to DO, May 19, 1926; ibid., DO to Rev. Father in charge, May 27, 1926.

27. C.O. Onuoha, Submission to Jones Commission, 14.4.56 (April 14, 1956).

28. CMS: *Report of the Proceedings of the First Session of the First Synod of the Diocese on the Niger, held at Onitsha, March 24th to 27th, 1931,* 41; CMS: G3/A3/0, Smith to Baylis, Mar. 16, 1909.

29. Several Igbo catechisms and other works were produced. The early examples included *Grammaire Ibo* (1904) by Father Ganot, *English-Ibo-French Dictionary* (1904); *Katekismi Ibo* (1901). This is in fact a summary of *Catéchisme de la foi catholique* (1898) by Monsignor LeRoy; *Katekisma Nk'Okwukwe Nzuko Katolik* (1904) by Father Volger and the catechists. This *Katekisma* was perhaps the most popular and successful. It was used in practically all Catholic schools in Eastern Nigeria up to the 1940s. The Efik language version for the Calabar mission was published in 1908. According to Father Leon Lejeune, "This work, edited with care by our catechists, is excellent from the point of view of the language. The religious truths are therein exposed in such a manner as to answer the principal objections broadcast in the country against our holy religion. As regards the print and format, the work is also most convenient. Everyone in the mission is very satisfied with it. It is for us missionaries an encouragement to continue the study of the Ibo language." Quoted in Ozigboh, "Christian Mission," 208. The *Katekisma,* of course, caricatured African religion and customs, African religion being described as idol worship and Catholics were thus encouraged to reject it ab initio.

QUESTION: Obu nkafie bu isekpulu alusi?

ANSWER: Eye, obu nkafie bu isekpulu alusi, makana madu melu fa. Ndu fa enwe, ike ikwu okwu fa enwe, nke fa na afu uzo, nke fa na'nu ife; ije fa eje, mmerube fa eme-rube, ife ma fa eli, we gabazia.

QUESTION: Is it folly to worship idols?

ANSWER: Yes, it is folly to worship idols, because they are made by man. They have no life, and they can neither speak, see, hear, walk, move, nor eat, etc., etc.

Katekism nke Okwukwe n'asusu Igbo (Onitsha: Roman Catholic Mission, 1920), question 258. English translation adapted from Okwu, "Holy Ghost Fathers," 268. Sadly, Catholic missionaries sought to stifle Igbo language by discouraging students from speaking Igbo on the college campus. At the Holy Ghost College, Umuahia in 1951–54, for example, students who spoke Igbo in class or on the college premises were made to wear a humiliating cardboard paper bearing the inscription Do SIGNUM (I bear a sign) which identified the wearer as an Igbo speaker!

30. CMS: G3/A3/0, Tugwell to Baylis, Aug. 3, 1912; ibid., Annual Letter, Oct. 4, 1910 by J. N. Cheetham; NNAE OWDIST 9/5/6, No. 42/19, "Half-Yearly Report on the Owerri Division, January 1st to June 30th, 1919." Cf. CMS: G3/A3/0, Smith to Baylis, June 22, 1900; ibid., Annual Letter, Dec. 7, 1912.

31. HGFA, B554/A/1, General Report to Superior General on the Visit to the District of Southern Nigeria (Nov. 1929), by Father Joseph Soul, quoted in Ozigboh, "Christian Mission," 341.

32. HGFA, 191/B/VI, Report on the School Question 1910; NNAE: OWDIST 9/5/6, No. 42/19, "Half-Yearly Report on the Owerri Division, January 1st to June 30th, 1919."

33. HGFA, 191/B/VI, "Notes recueillies par les Pères de Calabar et d'Anwa [Anua] sur les Ecoles au Niger," Apr. 26, 1914.

34. Quoted in Okwu, "Holy Ghost Fathers," 456, 475. Also see HGFA, *Bulletin de la Congregation* 25 (1911–12): 873–74.

35. HGFA, 553/B/111, "The Vicariate of Onitsha-Owerri, 1939–1946," Okwu, "Holy Ghost Fathers," 456, NNAE: OWDIST 10/1/3, "Annual Report 1938-Owerri Division," July 17, 1939.

36. CMS: G3/A3/0, S.R. Smith, Central District Report, in Minutes of Executive Committee Meeting, July-Dec. 1912. In the Owerri sector Reverend Payne acknowledged that the Catholic growth had rendered both the government and Anglican schools "insignificant." Ibid., Minutes of E.C. Meeting, Jan.-Dec. 1913.

37. CMS: G3/A3/0, Tugwell to Manley, Aug. 8, 1914; Dennis to Manley, Sept. 13, 1913. Cf. Anyabuike, "Missionary Enterprise," 326–28. Also see p. 344, where the reflective thinking of the Anglicans is clearly revealed: "No one who remembers the ascendancy which was ours . . . can now behold us playing [a subordinate] role without shedding substantial tears. The teachers in the almost insignificant field are alarmed, students in colleges know it, ignorant Christians in the villages bewail it that we are fast becoming a minority group, and it requires actual experience to appreciate the woes of a man who belongs to a minority group in any society."

38. CMS: G3/A3/0, Minutes of E.C. Meeting, Feb. 23, 1903; NNAE: OWDIST 10/1/2, No. 41, vol. IV, "Annual Report on the Owerri Division 1937," 17.

39. See J. F. A. Ajayi, *Christian Missions in Nigeria, 1841–1891. The Making of a New Elite* (Evanston, Ill.: Northwestern Univ. Press, 1969), chap. 8.

40. *Niger and Yoruba Notes* (1895), 12. It should be noted that CMS opposition to higher education was not limited to Nigeria. Rather it was widespread in Africa, especially East Africa. See Beidelman, *Colonial Evangelism,* 120.

41. CMS: G3/A3/0, Report of Financial Executive Meeting, Aug. 8–28, 1890, p. 3; Ben N. Azikiwe, "How Shall We Educate the African?" *Journal of African Society* 33 (April 1934): 143. See also Robert L. Koehl, "Transplanting British Universities to Africa and India," *Journal of Higher Education* 39 (Jan. 1968): 51. Koehl writes, "From the very beginnings of the mission schools Africans demanded nothing but the best. If the best was Greek and higher mathematics, then the students and the faculty too could not be put off with more 'practical education.' Education that fits men only to be inferiors, however well 'adapted' to the needs of the moment . . . , soon becomes debased into a mere tool of class tyranny."

42. CMS: G3/A3/0, Report on Schools by Blackett, Minutes of E.C. Meeting, July 1915. Cf. Jordan, *Bishop Shanahan,* 246–47 for the Catholic situation.

43. Howells quoted in Anyabuike, "Missionary Enterprise," 192; also see p. 209.

44. CMS: G3/A3/0, Dennis to Manley, Sept. 13, 1913; "Annual Letter," Nov. 1910, by G. T. Basden; Anyabuike, "Missionary Enterprise," 266–81; Ekechi, *Missionary Enterprise,* 198.

45. Anyabuike, "Missionary Enterprise," 270, 335.

46. Quoted in Okwu, "Holy Ghost Fathers," 456.

47. Jordan, "Catholic Education and Catholicism," 60–61.

48. "Owerri District Heavy Debt," in "Education (1950). Diocesan Education Board Documents." This document and others were salvaged at St. Paul's Church, Nkwerre in 1979. Over 99 percent of the documents in the box were eaten by ants. I am indebted to Archdeacon Chukwuezi for access to the documents. Hereafter cited as "Salvaged Documents (1950)."

49. "Salvaged Documents (1950)."

50. Ibid. Archdeacon Nkemena also added that overstaffing of schools was equally responsible for districts being in debt.

51. Ibid. See letter (No. OW 111/9/430. Umuahia-Ibeku) dated Oct. 24, 1950.

52. "Salvaged Documents (1950)."

53. "Owerri Field Notes," interviews with Nelson Opara, July 11, 1983; Winifred Emerenini, Nov. 25, 1983, and Reverend (now Bishop) Lambert O. Opara, Sept. 14, 1983. For a full discussion of the Zion mission see F. K. Ekechi, "The Ordeal of an African Independent Church: The Case of the Nigerian Zion Methodist Mission, 1942–70," *The International Journal of African Historical Studies* 20 (1987): 691–720.

54. Information based on data from Reverend Opara's private papers. I am indeed grateful to Bishop Lambert O. Opara for access to these papers, hereafter cited as M. D. Opara Papers.

55. Provincial Education Officer (PEO) to the Manager (Zion), Jan. 29, 1948, M. D. Opara Papers; "Owerri Field Notes," interview with Nelson Opara, July 11, 1983; "Memoirs on the Late Rev. M. D. Opara," by Law Obioma Emenyonu, M. D. Opara Papers.

56. "Owerri Field Notes," interviews with Nelson Opara, July 11, 1983; Winifred Emerenini, Nov. 25, 1983.

57. Opara to Hamilton (USA), July 3, 1952, and Opara to CMS Superintendent, Sept. 26, 1953, in M. D. Opara Papers.

58. Anyasodo to Opara, Jan. 28, 1952, ibid.

59. Amaefule to Opara, Aug. 3, 1948, ibid.

60. Opara to Anyasodo, Feb. 26, 1952; Opara to Amaefule (draft, n.d.), ibid.

61. Ajoku to Opara, Nov. 11, 1947, ibid. Attempts to interview Ajoku's relatives on this matter and others proved futile because of their reluctance to give out information.

62. Ajoku to Opara, June 14, 1946, ibid. For more details on the Ajoku-Opara controversy see Ekechi, "The Ordeal," 699–701.

63. Emerenini to Opara, July 14, 1961; J. N. Ndem to Proprietor (Opara), Mar. 23, 1961, M. D. Opara Papers.

64. Lloyd to Proprietor, Jan. 11, 1951, ibid.

65. "Owerri Field Notes," interview with Nelson Opara, July 11, 1983; P. C. Harmood to Deputy Director of Education, Jan. 24, 1950, M. D. Opara Papers.

66. Opara to PEO, Apr. 13, 1950, M. D. Opara Papers. By 1954 Reverend Opara had won election to the Eastern House of Assembly. Perhaps political influence played a vital role in the granting of approved status and financial assistance to Zion schools.

67. Harmood to Deputy Director, Jan. 24, 1950; Acting Inspector General to Proprietor, Dec. 14, 1951, M. D. Opara Papers.

68. See EMC's publication, *Evangelical Methodist Conference* (Altoona, Penn., 1952), 47 and 52–53. Special thanks are due to former and present officials of the Evangelical Methodist Church (USA) who kindly provided official and personal documents—particularly Dr. (Rev.) Mark Rhodes of the Manahath School of Theology.

69. See Ekechi, "The Ordeal," 705–17.

70. Handwritten biographical note for the Eastern House of Assembly; also Opara to Onyido, Sept. 14, 1948, M. D. Opara Papers.

71. "The Life of the Late Rev. M. D. Opara" (1971), by Rev. R. C. Onuekwusi, 2. See also "Memoirs on the Late Rev. M. D. Opara," by Law Obioma Emenyonu (Opara's brother-in-law), both in M. D. Opara Papers.

72. C. C. Nwa-chil, "The Spread of 'Western Education' in Nigeria," *Journal of East African Research and Development* 3 (1973): 145. For statistics see Nwabara, *Iboland*, 68–69.

73. See Ajayi, *Christian Missions*, 153–55. "The Secondary schools," he writes, "were in fact no more than senior primary schools, conducted in English, with a bit of Latin, mathematics and recitations of poetry." Also J. F. A. Ajayi, "The Development of Secondary

Grammar School Education in Nigeria," *Journal of the Historical Society of Nigeria* 2 (Dec. 1963): 517–35.

74. Otunti Nduka, "Background to the Foundation of Dennis Memorial Grammar School, Onitsha," *Journal of the Historical Society of Nigeria* 8 (Dec. 1976): 71.

75. CMS: G3/A3/0, Smith to Baylis, Aug. 16, 1905; ibid., Smith to Manley, May 26, 1913; Edward H. Berman, "American Influence on African Education: The Role of the Phelps-Stokes Fund's Education Commissions," *Comparative Education Review* 15 (June 1971): 132–45; HGFA, *Bulletin de la Congregation* 22 (1903–4): 789; CMS: G3/A3/0, "Annual Letter," Nov. 18, 1895, by Rev. Hardman.

76. Cf. Azikiwe, "How Shall We Educate the African?"; James Africanus Horton, *West African Countries and Peoples* (Edinburgh: Edinburgh Univ. Press, 1969); J. E. Casely Hayford, *Ethiopia Unbound* (London: Frank Cass, 1969); Hollis R. Lynch, ed., *Black Spokesman* (New York: Humanities Press, 1971), part 4.

77. Mbonu Ojike, *My Africa* (New York: John Day Co., 1946), 82.

78. CMS: G3/A3/0, Dennis to Baylis, Feb. 6, 1901; ibid., Baylis to Dennis, July 23, 1901. See Nduka, "Background," 78–81.

79. HGFA, 192/A/11, Shanahan to the Directors, Oct. 10, 1909; 191/B/VI, Training School for Nigeria, May 6, 1910.

80. Quoted in Nduka, "Background," 81.

81. CMS: G3/A3/0, Minutes of E.C. Meeting, July 14–26, 1915.

82. See Nduka, "Background," 69–72.

83. CMS: G3/A3/L7, Manley to Smith, Apr. 13, 1920. The CMS was suspicious of government interference, hence the rejection of any financial assistance from the government.

84. CMS Archives: *C.M.S. Annual Report, 1924–25*, 28. With the hostel for students, the total cost was £8,000. See Nduka, "Background," 89.

85. "Owerri Field Notes," interviews with John Egejuru, Oct. 2, 1975; Oparanozie Enyinna, Oct. 10, 1979.

86. HGFA, 554/B/111, Shanahan to Byrne, July 19, 1929; 554/B/IV, Grandin to Byrne, June 2, 1926, cited in Okwu, "Holy Ghost Fathers," 445. See also pp. 479–80.

87. NNAE: OWDIST 9/10/14, "Annual Report on the Owerri Division 1924," by F. Ferguson; James S. Coleman, *Nigeria: Background to Nationalism* (Los Angeles: Univ. of California Press, 1958), 340. Another leader said in 1933: " . . . education is the only real agent that will give rebirth to the dying embers of the Ibo national zeal. . . . It will be the means to free the Ibos from the throes of both mental and moral thraldom." Ibid.

88. Okwu, "Holy Ghost Fathers," 562; CMS: ACC4/F9, *Sowing and Reaping* (Nov. 1938), 7. Secondary schools for girls also occupied Anglican attention in the 1940s and 1950s. Item 161 of the Diocesan Education Board report on girls' schools for 1950 states: "A request was read for a Girls School in Umuduru District [Okigwe] and also from Nnewi District Women's meeting for the establishment of a Girls secondary school in each Archdeaconry. There was a general discussion on Girls Schools generally. It was agreed that the Education Secretary and the General Managers should go on considering the whole question of Girls education. Meanwhile efforts should be made to increase the number of lady teachers." In "Salvaged Documents (1950)."

89. See Jordan, "Catholic Education and Catholicism," 61–62.

90. Discussions on this matter are based on Okwu, "Holy Ghost Fathers," 530–41.

91. Okwu, "Holy Ghost Fathers," 439.

92. Cf. Ifeka-Moller, "White Power," 62, 67, for statistics. Bishop Heerey also conceded that "about two-thirds of our Christians and catechumens are in Owerri Province." Okwu, "Holy Ghost Fathers," 488.

93. See Ogike, *Centenary History*, 60 and 148; Okwu, "Holy Ghost Fathers," 485–93.

94. Okwu, "Holy Ghost Fathers," 488.

95. "Owerri Field Notes," interview with Chief Amadi Obi, Nov. 17, 1975. Chief Obi stated categorically that Bishop Heerey had a special dislike for Emekuku for reasons that are yet unknown.

96. Robert A. LeVine, *Dreams and Deeds: Achievement Motivation in Nigeria* (Chicago: Univ. of Chicago Press, 1966), 8; M. Goldway, "Report on the Investigation of Vocational Education in Eastern Nigeria," Official Document No. 13 of 1962, p. 2, Ministry of Education, Eastern Nigeria.

CHAPTER 6

1. Hastings, *History,* 46, 113–14.

2. Ibid., 113.

3. Cited in Okwu, "Holy Ghost Fathers," 521, 496.

4. Jordan, "Catholic Education and Catholicism," 61; Okwu, "Holy Ghost Fathers," 497, 498–99; SMA: 15550/14/8043, Father I. N. Cermanati to Monseigneur, May 12, 1911. "We are never fully staffed," complained Father Cermanati. "The work increases while the personnel to do it decreases." The earliest local priests were ordained in the 1930s. They were Father John Cross Anyogu (d. 1967), Father William Obelagu, Father Michael Iwene Tansi (d. 1964), Father Joseph Nwanegbo (d. 1965).

5. John Murray Todd, *African Mission: A Historical Study of the Society of African Missions* (London: Burns and Oales, 1962), 113.

6. Beidelman, *Colonial Evangelism,* 68; Hastings, *History,* 46; Okwu, "Holy Ghost Fathers," 496.

7. Cf. Okwu, "Holy Ghost Fathers," 496. "There is an old philosophical principle," Daniel Lifton of the Holy Ghost Fathers argued further, "that says a man has to exist before he can philosophise; or as Napoleon crudely translated it, an army fights on its stomach. The missionaries in Africa and elsewhere have never at any time found themselves in a position to make ends meet even for the barest necessities of life for themselves and their catechists—they have lived and worked in grinding poverty." *Annals* 10 (July-October 1928): 134–36.

8. Okwu, "Holy Ghost Fathers," 439–41. See also Jordan, *Bishop Shanahan,* 12, where the French pioneers were characterized as failures: "They came; they saw; they failed to conquer." Similarly the Irish were seen by the French missionaries (mostly Alsatians) as untrustworthy. Their doctrine, wrote Irish Bishop Heerey, is this: "An Irishman can't be straight even if he tries. Don't believe that Bishop, he can't be straight, he can't tell the truth. Frs. Groetz and Treich have said these words to lay people, and they say these words to the young Fathers." Quoted in Okwu, "Holy Ghost Fathers," 441.

9. Okwu, "Holy Ghost Fathers," 341, 434.

10. Ibid., 499–501; Ogike, *Centenary History,* 62; Njoku, *Advent of the Catholic Church,* 193–98.

11. Okwu, "Holy Ghost Fathers," 504, 505–6.

12. Ibid., 507.

13. "Owerri Field Notes," interview with Igbo Catholic priests at Owerri and Ihiala, Sept. 10, 1975.

14. Ekechi, "Portrait of a Colonizer," 33–40; Okwu, "Holy Ghost Fathers," 407–8.

15. Okwu, "Holy Ghost Fathers," 408, 409.

16. Ekechi, *Missionary Enterprise,* 218, 219.

17. "Owerri Field Notes," interviews at Egbu, Sept. 19, 1975. My informants asked to remain anonymous.

18. "Owerri Field Notes," information collected on Aug. 12, 1986.
19. "Owerri Field Notes," interview with Chief Obi, Nov. 17, 1975; Ogike, *Centenary History*, 48. See also Okwu, "Holy Ghost Fathers," 509–11.
20. See Colman M. Cooke, "The Roman Catholic Mission in Calabar 1903–1960,"(Ph.D. diss., University of London, 1977). I was not able to examine this thesis. Also Okwu "Holy Ghost Fathers," 338–48.
21. Quoted in Okwu, "Holy Ghost Fathers," 339.
22. Ibid., 485, 432.
23. Ibid., 488.
24. Ogike, *Centenary History*, 148–49.
25. Ibid, 176–77, 183.
26. See appendix B.
27. Hastings, *History*, 119.
28. Ogike, *Centenary History*, 198.
29. Okot p'Bitek, *Song of Lawino* (Nairobi, Kenya: East African Publishing House, 1966), 116.
30. Okwu, "Holy Ghost Fathers," 420.
31. Ibid., 547; Mobutu in Hastings, *History*, 191.
32. Beidelman, *Colonial Evangelism*, 165.
33. Samuel Wilson, ed., "Mission in the '80s," in *Mission Handbook: North American Protestant Ministries Overseas* (Monroe, Calif.: Missions Advanced Research and Communication Center, 1980), 12th ed., 10–12.
34. Hastings, *History*, 224.

CHAPTER 7

1. NNAE: OWDIST 10/1/3, "Annual Report 1938—Owerri Division," by A. E. Cook, 4.
2. Meek, *Law and Authority*, 105; Francis A. Arinze, *Sacrifice in Ibo Religion* (Ibadan: Ibadan Univ. Press, 1970), 19, 36, 52, and passim; Victor C. Uchendu, *The Igbo of Southeast Nigeria* (New York: Holt, Rinehart & Winston, 1965), chap. 4 and p. 98. For the role of the *ǫpara* see p. 41 and passim.
3. NNAE: CSO 26/29033/11, "Intelligence Report on the Ngwa Clan, Aba Division" (1934), by J. G. C. Allen, para. 95. Allen added that "the audience was swayed by the most eloquent man, no matter what his age or rank." Hereafter cited as Allen, "Intelligence Report."
4. Meek, *Law and Authority*, 115; Mazi E. N. Njaka, *Igbo Political Culture* (Evanston, Ill.: Northwestern Univ. Press, 1974); A. E. Afigbo, "The Indigenous Political Systems of the Igbo," *Tarik* 4 (1973): 13–22; Allen, "Intelligence Report," para. 93.
5. Meek, *Law and Authority*, 109.
6. Allen, "Intelligence Report," para. 98.
7. Ibid., paras. 84 and 86.
8. Ibid., paras. 85 and 88; Meek, *Law and Authority*, 113.
9. Allen, "Intelligence Report," para. 89.
10. CO 520/31, "Extract of report on the Owerri District for the quarter ending 30th June, 1905"; CO 583/34, Lugard to Bonar Law, July 3, 1915; CO 583/44, Lugard to Bonar Law, Feb. 18, 1916; NNAE: OWDIST 9/5/10, "Annual Report on the Owerri Division for the year ending 31st December, 1919."
11. CO 583/58, Report by E. Osborne (Mar.-May), enclosure in Lugard to CO (Conf.), July 21, 1917; NNAE: OW346/17 RIVPROF 8/5/353, "Report on the Owerri Division for

the year ending 30th June, 1917," 1; NNAE: OWDIST 9/5/ 10, "Annual Report on the Owerri Division for the year ending 31st December, 1919."

12. In retrospect, colonial officials found the supersession of traditional systems of law by the native courts ill-advised and harmful. Meek therefore recommended "the restoration of authority within the village-group to those classes of persons who were accustomed and best able to exercise it, namely, the heads of families, priests, holders of important titles, and rich or able men." In addition, "the Native Courts [should be] allowed to function as genuine native institutions and . . . not forced to conform to standards of English law, of which many of the sanctions are meaningless in terms of Ibo culture." *Law and Authority,* 336, 341.

13. PRO: *Southern Nigeria Annual Report* (1908), 36.

14. NNAE: 42/ 19 OWDIST 9/5/6, "Half-Yearly Report on the Owerri Division, January 1st to June 30th, 1919."

15. NNAE: CSE 1/85/3708, "Supplementary Intelligence Report No. 1 on the Ngwa Clan" (1933), by J. G. C. Allen, 69; CO 583/87, Minute by Harding on Clifford to Milner (Conf. A), May 19, 1920.

16. CO 520/31, "Overland Journey" (1905), 29; NNAE: 42/ 19 OWDIST 9/5/6, "Half-Yearly Report on the Owerri Division, January 1st to June 30th, 1919," 7; NNAE: OW 346/ 17 RIVPROF 8/5/353, "Report on the Owerri Division for the Half Year ending 30th June, 1917," 9; NNAE: OWDIST 9/5/ 10, "Annual Report on the Owerri Division for the Year ending 31st December, 1919."

17. NNAE: OW 346/ 17 RIVPROF 8/5/353, "Report on the Owerri Division, January 1st to June 30th, 1917," 8; OWDIST 9/5/ 10, "Annual Report on the Owerri Division for the year ending 31st December, 1919"; NNAE: 42/ 19 OWDIST 9/5/6, "Half-Yearly Report on the Owerri Division, January 1st to June 30th, 1919," 7.

18. CO 583/87, Minute by Harding on "Flogging in Nigeria," in Clifford to Milner, May 19, 1920; CO 538/80, Minutes, May 29, 1920. "I think we should tell Clifford politely but firmly that we did not send him to Nigeria to upset everything which his predecessor had done." CO 583/87, Minute, June 30, 1920.

19. NNAE: 42/29 OWDIST 9/5/6, "Half-Yearly Report on the Owerri Division, January 1st to June 30th, 1919," 3.

20. NNAE: OW 346/ 17 RIVPROF 8/5/353, "Report on the Owerri Division for the Half-Year ending 30th June, 1917," 5; NNAE: 70/ 1926 OWDIST 9/ 12/ 14, "Annual Report on the Owerri Division for the year ending 31st December, 1926"; NNAE OWDIST 9/5/ 10, "Annual Report on the Owerri Division for the year ending 31st December, 1919"; NNAE: 42/ 19 OWDIST 9/5/6, "Half-Yearly Report on the Owerri Division, January 1st to June 30th, 1919"; NNAE: 48/ 19 OWDIST 9/5/ 10, "Annual Report on the Owerri Division for the Year ending 31st December, 1919."

21. NNAE: 42/ 19 OWDIST 9/5/6, "Half-Yearly Report on the Owerri Division, January 1st to June 30th, 1919."

22. Ibid.

23. Ibid; NNAE: OW 346/ 17 RIVPROF 8/5/353, "Report on the Owerri Division for the Half Year ending 30th June, 1917."

24. NNAE: 42/ 19 OWDIST 9/5/6, "Half-Yearly Report on the Owerri Division, 1st January to 30th June, 1919"; NNAE: 70/ 1926 OWDIST 9/ 12/ 14, "Annual Report on the Owerri Division, 31st December, 1926."

25. NNAE: 42/ 19 OWDIST 9/5/6, "Half-Yearly Report on the Owerri Division, 1st January to 30th June, 1919"; NNAE: 45/ 1920 OWDIST 9/6/3, "Report on the Owerri Division for the half year—January-June 1920"; NNAE: OW 346/ 17 RIVPROF 8/5/353, Report on the Owerri Division for the Half Year ending 30th June, 1917; NNAE: 42/ 19 OWDIST 9/5/6, "Half-Yearly Report on the Owerri Division, 1st January to 30th June, 1919."

26. Afigbo, *The Warrant Chiefs,* 109–13; NNAE: OW 346/17 RIVPROF 8/5/353, "Report on the Owerri Division for the Half Year ending 30th June, 1917," 6.

27. HGFA, 191/A/111, Father Feral's journal; NNAE: OWDIST 9/8/1, "Nkwazema of Nekede—Petition from" (n.d.) Ibid., Resident to DO, Mar. 2, 1923.

28. NNAE: E/2146/10 OWDIST 4/3/1, "Cancellation of Warrants," DC to Provincial Secretary, June 20, 1910; OW 346/17 RIVPROF 8/5/353, "Report on the Owerri Division for the Half Year ending 30th June, 1917." Some of the chiefs were sentenced to various terms of imprisonment.

29. NNAE: OWDIST 10/1/2, "Annual Report, Owerri Province, 1937"; "Owerri Field Notes," interviews with Qha Owere Nchi lse, Sept. 28, 1979.

30. F. D. Lugard, *Political Memorandum No. 1* (1918), 11, cited in Afigbo, *The Warrant Chiefs,* 138; NNAE: 42/19 OWDIST 9/5/6, "Half-Yearly Report on the Owerri Division, 1st January to 30th June, 1919."

31. NNAE: 42/19 OWDIST 9/5/6, "Half-Yearly Report on the Owerri Division, 1st January to 30th June, 1919."

32. NNAE: OWDIST 7/1/7, "Annual Report 1945: Owerri Division"; NNAI: RG/G6, Report on the Eastern Provinces, Mar. 24, 1922, 6; NNAE: OWDIST 9/5/10, "Annual Report on the Owerri Division for the year ending 31st December 1919."

33. NNAE: OW 346/17 RIVPROF 8/5/353, "Report on the Owerri Division for the Half Year ending 30th June, 1917," 3–4.

34. Ibid., 6, 1–2.

35. NNAE: OWDIST 10/1/4, "Annual Report 1923," in "Annual Reports and Statistics, 1923," by A. F. M. White. Colonial officials were not, of course, oblivious to the regrettable cleavage between the young and the old, the result of European colonialism. Thus Allen ("Supplementary Intelligence Report") writes that "The attitude of both parties is easy to understand and is deserving of sympathy. On the one hand the elders, who in former times held authority in their hands, are asked late in life to change entirely their mode of existence and their outlook on the world, and thus very naturally they find themselves unwilling, in fact, unable to do. On the other hand the young men have for the first time tasted the sweet fruits of independence and comparative wealth, and in addition, have been taught to regard the religion of their fathers as a hollow pretence. While they eagerly desire to obtain the maximum share of the advantages imparted by civilisation their demands for progress are usually met with a firm refusal on the part of the elders to agree to anything which departs from the customs of their forefathers" (8–9).

36. NNAE: 6810 CSE 1/85/3637, "Intelligence Report on Native Administration, Awka Division," Feb. 4, 1930.

37. See note 35.

38. NNAE: OWDIST 10/1/4, "Annual Report 1923," in "Annual Reports and Statistics, 1923," by A. F. M. White; NNAE: 45/1920 OWDIST 9/6/3, "Report on Owerri Division for the Half Year—1st January to 30th June, 1920."

39. NNAE: 45/1920 OWDIST 9/6/3, "Report on Owerri Division for the Half Year—1st January to 30th June, 1920." The political climate in 1979 did not allow for local interviews in Ngor and Mbaise local government areas.

40. NNAI: CSO 26/29945, "Intelligence Report on the Obowo and Ihite Clans" (1933), by N. A. Mackenzie.

41. NNAE: OW 34/1925 OWDIST 6/8/1, "H. E. the Officer Administering the Government of Nigeria—Meeting with Chiefs of Owerri, 1925," hereafter cited as "H. E. and Owerri Chiefs, 1925."

42. NNAE: 117/28 OWDIST 9/14/106, "Handing Over Notes," 1928, by F. Ferguson; NNAE: 67/1927 OWDIST 9/13/47, "Memorandum," DO to Resident, Feb. 6, 1928.

43. NNAE: OW 5709 OWDIST 7/1/7, "Owerri Division. Annual Report, 1945," paras. 19 and 51.

44. "Owerri Field Notes," interview with J. K. Nzerem, Aug. 24, 1977; NNAE: OW 5709 OWDIST 7/1/7, "Owerri Division. Annual Report, 1945," para. 40. Unfortunately no copies of the *Bulletin* seem to have survived. Nzerem informed me his own copies were "burnt to ashes" when Nigerian soldiers set his house on fire at Naze during the Nigeria-Biafra war.

45. See Afigbo, *The Warrant Chiefs;* Harry A. Gailey, *The Road to Aba* (New York: New York Univ. Press, 1970); Nina Emma Mba, *Nigerian Women Mobilized: Women's Political Activity in Southern Nigeria, 1900–1965* (Berkeley: Univ. of California Press, 1982), chap. 3.

46. CO 583/17, Lugard to Harcourt (Conf.), Aug. 10, 1914; ibid., Minutes by D. L. H. Baynes (Aug. 11, 1914) and Harcourt; ibid., Minutes by Harcourt (Draft).

47. H. F. Matthews, "Direct and Indirect Administration with special reference to Taxation," paper read to Tropical Services cadets at Oxford, Oct. 29, 1926, RHL, Mss. Afr. s. 783 (Box 3/4).

48. NNAE: 67/1927 OWDIST 9/13/47, "Memorandum," DO to Resident (Port Harcourt), Feb. 6, 1928.

49. NNAE: 97/1928 OWDIST 9/14/88, DO to Resident, Sept. 30, 1929; NNAE: 67/1927 OWDIST 9/13/47, Resident to DO, May 13, 1929. See also Ruxton's Report, Oct. 29, 1928.

50. NNAE: 67/1927 OWDIST 9/13/47, "Memorandum," Falk to Divisional Officers, Apr. 17, 1928.

51. NNAE: 112/1930 OWDIST 9/16/27, Chief Nwansi to DO, May 29, 1931, and marginal note.

52. Mba, *Nigerian Women Mobilized,* 77; Afigbo, *The Warrant Chiefs,* 237–38.

53. NNAE: CSE 1/36/90, "Progress Report from Resident, Owerri Province," Dec. 27, 1929; ibid., Memo of Dec. 31, 1929; "Owerri Field Notes," interviews at Owerri in 1977 and 1979. For the commission report see *Sessional Paper No. 28. Report of a Commission of Enquiry appointed to Inquire into the Disturbances in the Calabar and Owerri Provinces, December 1929* (Lagos, Nigeria, 1930).

54. Sylvia Leith-Ross, *African Women: A Study of the Ibo of Nigeria* (London: Faber & Faber, 1939), 38.

55. NNAI: CSO 26/29945, "Intelligence Report on the Obowo and Ihite Clans" (1933); CSO 26/29033/11, "Intelligence Report on the Ngwa" (1934), 10; NNAI: CSO 26/3/27937, "Intelligence Report on the Ezinhitte Clan" (1932); CSO 26/31354, "Intelligence Report on the N & S Groups of the Isu Clan in Orlu Division" (1935), by G. I. Jones. "Every effort has been made," reported Jones, "to disabuse the elders of these erroneous impressions and with this end in view as few questions as possible were asked during the present inquiry about history or tradition."

56. NNAI: 6810 CSE 1/85/3637, "Intelligence Report on Native Administration—Awka Division" (1929), John Ross to Resident, Sept. 30, 1929.

57. NNAE: CSE 1/1/7 No. 30334, "Intelligence Report on the Oratta Clan, Owerri Province" (1935). The significance of extended-family rule was emphasized by Meek as one of the "practical administrative [lessons] learned" from a study of the indigenous political system. For "here we have the fundamental unit of law and authority, a grouping of consanguinous relatives which usually yields ready obedience to well-recognized head or heads, and is so closely knit together by common interests and common obligations that the conduct of one of its members is the close concern of all." *Law and Authority,* 333.

58. Allen, "Supplementary Intelligence Report," 63; NNAE: OWDIST 10/1/4, "Owerri Division. Annual Report 1939," by A. E. Cook.

59. NNAE: OWDIST 10/1/4, "Owerri Division. Annual Report 1939," by A. E. Cook.

60. Quoted in Afigbo, *The Warrant Chiefs,* 309.

61. NNAE: OWDIST 10/1/2, "Annual Report, Owerri Province 1937."

62. NNAE: OWDIST 10/1/4, "Owerri Division. Annual Report 1939," para. 13; NNAE OWDIST 10/1/3, "Annual Report 1938—Owerri Division," paras. 11 and 13.

63. NNAE: OWDIST 10/1/4, "Owerri Division. Annual Report 1939," para. 10.

64. See Meek, *Report on Social and Political Organization in the Owerri Division,* 3. But see NNAE: CSO 26/30334, "Intelligence Report on the Oratta Clan" (1935), where G. L. Stockley estimated the population of Oratta clan at 51,600 and the area at 185 square miles.

65. NNAE: 30334 CSE 1/1/7, "Intelligence Report on the Oratta Clan" (1935), by V. H. Moult.

66. Meek, *Report,* 2, para. 4.

67. Ibid., paras. 25, 3.

68. NNAE: CSO 26/30334, "Intelligence Report on the Oratta Clan." See also report by Moult.

69. NNAE: OWDIST 10/1/3, "Annual Report 1938—Owerri Division."

70. NNAE: 67/1927 OWDIST 9/13/47, Provincial Circular No. 38, Mar. 3, 1925; Meek, *Law and Authority,* 92; NNAE: OW5709 OWDIST 7/1/7, "Owerri Division. Annual Report 1945," para. 9.

71. NNAI: CSO 26/3/29835, "Report on Oguta Native Court Area" (1934) by V. H. Moult.

72. Ibid.

73. NNAE: OW5709 OWDIST 7/1/7, "Owerri Division. Annual Report 1945"; NNAE: OWDIST 10/1/3, "Annual Report 1938. Owerri Division"; DO to Resident, July 17, 1939, paras. 17, 18.

74. NNAE: OW5709 OWDIST 7/1/7, "Owerri Division. Annual Report 1945," paras. 14, 15, 18, 20.

75. Ibid., para. 26.

76. NNAE: OWDIST 10/1/3, "Annual Report 1938—Owerri Division," paras. 27, 22.

77. See D. C. Ohadike, "The Influenza Pandemic of 1918–19 and the Spread of Cassava Cultivation on the Lower Niger: A Study in Historical Linkages," *JAH* 22 (1981): 379–91. Dr. Ohadike argues forcefully that it was the influenza epidemic of 1918 that propelled Lower Niger Igbos to adopt cassava as a secondary crop. See also S. A. Agboola, "The Introduction and Spread of Cassava in Western Nigeria," *Nigerian Journal of Economic and Social Studies* 10 (1968): 369–85.

78. O. L. Oke, "Cassava as Food in Nigeria," *World Review of Nutrition and Dietetics* 9 (1968): 227–50; L. C. Okere, *The Anthropology of Food in Rural Igboland, Nigeria* (Lanham, Mass.: Univ. Press of America, 1983). For studies on women and the economy, see Susan Martin, "Gender and Innovation: Farming, Cooking and Palm Processing in the Ngwa Region, South-Eastern Nigeria, 1900–1930," *JAH* 25 (1984): 411–27; Bonnie Keller and Edna G. Bay, "African Women and Problems of Modernization," in Christopher C. Mojekwu, et al., eds., *African Society, Culture and Politics: An Introduction to African Studies* (Washington, D.C.: Univ. Press of America, 1978), 215–37; Phoebe V. Ottenberg, "The Changing Economic Position of Women among the Afikpo Ibo," in William R. Bascom and M. J. Herskovits, eds., *Continuity and Change in African Cultures* (Chicago: Univ. of Chicago Press, 1959) 205–23.

79. Ottenberg, "Changing Economic Position," 215.

80. NNAE: OWDIST 10/1/3, "Annual Report 1938—Owerri Division," para. 22. Cf. F. K. Ekechi, "The Cassava Palaver: The Gender Problem in African Economic Development," *Proceedings* (12th Annual Third World Conference, Chicago), 1 (1986): 130–42. For women's protest movements elsewhere see Mba, *Nigerian Women Mobilized,* chap. 4.

81. The officials' nervousness stemmed from the realization that if the 1938 women's pro-

test movement were not stopped, it might escalate to the 1929 revolt. When it later subsided, the officials breathed a sigh of relief, as reflected in the 1939 report: "There has been no revival of the women's movement reported in 1938 Report." NNAE: OWDIST 10/1/4, "Annual Report 1939," para. 2.

82. NNAE: OWDIST 10/1/3, "Annual Report 1938—Owerri Division," para. 22.

83. Though speculative and provisional, these inferences are by no means farfetched, as they are based on "impressions" derived from the reading of the annual reports. Perhaps when the official report submitted to the DO is located, these conclusions may be modified.

84. NNAE: OWDIST 10/1/4, "Owerri Division. Annual Report 1939," 21, para. 2. Cf. Ekechi, "The Cassava Palaver," 135–37. Also, F. K. Ekechi, "Aspects of Palm Oil Trade at Oguta (Eastern Nigeria), 1900–1950," *African Economic History* 10 (1981): 41–43.

85. Mba, *Nigerian Women Mobilized,* 67. She also writes, "Colonialism undermined the solidarity of the women by introducing new divisions based on education, wealth, and, in some areas, religious affiliation. . . . In the political area, colonialism not only deprived women of much of their precolonial authority in their own sphere, but by its exclusion of them from the colonial order, it served to reinforce their consciousness of being separate" (291).

86. NNAE: OWDIST 10/1/3, "Annual Report 1938—Owerri Division," paras. 22, 24, 62. The irony of it all was that while prices of palm produce were falling, farmers were at the same time encouraged to increase production and to plant more palm trees! But the Africans were not to be taken that easily, as the DO explained. "The progress made this year [1938] is disappointing, but this is hardly surprising in view of the effect of the fall in palm produce prices. Suspicion of the Government in encouraging palm cultivation is still very wide-spread, and is also an important factor in retarding planting" (para. 53).

87. NNAE: 41 vol. IV OWDIST 10/1/2, "Annual Report 1937. Report for the year ending the 31st December 1937"; NNAE: 41/V OWDIST 10/1/3, "Annual Report 1938," para. 61.

88. NNAE: OWDIST 10/1/4, "Annual Report 1939."

89. NNAE: OWDIST 10/1/3, "Annual Report 1938," DO to Resident, July 17, 1939. While the DO had high praises for the Oratta Clan Council, he seemed disappointed with the Oguta council which he characterized as "less satisfactory and at one period a few months ago I seriously considered recommending the closing of the Treasury, so apathetic was their attitude." But he admitted that "this suggestion provoked a storm of protest from the old Council members" and thus forced him to jettison the idea.

90. NNAE: 21/32 vol. III, OWDIST 9/18/16, "Handing Over Notes" of Mr. W. F. H. Newington, 1938, para. 5. Cf. G. I. Jones, "Councils Among the Central Ibo," in A. Richards and Adam Kuper, eds., *Councils in Action* (Cambridge: Cambridge Univ. Press, 1971), 63–79.

91. NNAE: EP 9419 MILGOV 5/1/9, P. N. Amadi and others to District Officer, June 15, 1936; Uchendu, *The Igbo of Southeast Nigeria,* 89. See also Uchendu, "Patterns of Igbo Social Structure," paper presented at the Workshop on Igbo Culture, University of Nigeria at Nsukka, April 5-9, 1977, 24; Donald C. Simmons, "Notes on the Aro," *Nigerian Field* 23 (1958: 28; F. K. Ekechi, "Education and Social Status in an African Society: The Igbo Example," *Umoja* (Journal of Black Studies), n.s., 4 (Fall 1980): 17–33.

92. NNAE: 21/32 vol. III, OWDIST 9/18/16, "Handing Over Notes"; Nnamdi Azikiwe, *Zik (A Selection from the Speeches of Nnamdi Azikiwe).* (Cambridge: Cambridge Univ. Press, 1961), 93–94; E. D. Jinehu, *The Osu Caste in Our Society* (Enugu: Tudor & Group Printers, 1981).

93. CO 520/31, "Overland Journey"; NNAE: OWDIST 10/1/4, "Annual Report. Owerri Division 1923"; "Owerri Field Notes," interviews with Osigwe Mere, Sept. 16, 1975; Owerri Council of Elders, Sept. 28, 1979; cf. K. David Patterson, *Health in Colonial Ghana: Disease, Medicine, and Socio-Economic Change, 1900–1955* (Waltham, Mass.: Crossroads Press, 1981), 20.

94. HGFA, B554/A/VIII, Bishop Heerey to Secretary of the Propaganda Fide, Rome, Nov. 5, 1932, cited in Ozigboh, "Christian Mission," 387. The bishop also expressed a great desire in 1938 to establish a Catholic leper settlement in the Onitsha-Owerri vicariate, again because "the Protestants have their leper colonies with hundreds of inmates. . . ." Okwu, "Holy Ghost Fathers," 395.

95. Ozigboh, "Christian Mission," 378. By 1932 the Protestants had several hospitals in Eastern Nigeria, which included the CMS Dobinson Memorial Hospital (1896) at Onitsha, transferred to Iyi-enu, Ogidi (1907); the United Free Church Society hospitals at Itu and Uburu; the Primitive Methodist Missionary Society at Ituk Mbang (Calabar) and Amachara, Umuahia; and the Qua Iboe Mission hospital at Etinam (Calabar).

96. Quoted in Ozigboh, "Christian Mission," 392; Sister Margaret Mary Nolan, *Medical Missionaries of Mary, 1937–1962* (Dublin: Three Candles, 1962), 36. In the words of Sister Nolan, "This decree is a landmark in the history of Catholic missions and was decisive in the history of MMM."

97. Njoku, *Advent of the Catholic Church,* 145.

98. NNAE: OWDIST 10/1/2 No. 41/IV, "Annual Report on the Owerri Division 1937," 17; NNAE: OWDIST 10/1/4, "Annual Report on the Owerri Division for the year ending 31st December 1939."

99. NNAE: OWDIST 10/1/3, "Annual Report—Owerri Division 1938," 15–16; NNAE: OW5709 OWDIST 7/1/7, "Owerri Division. Annual Report 1945," para. 49 (b); "Owerri Field Notes," interview with J. K. Nzerem, Aug. 24, 1977.

100. NNAE: EP747, vol. VI, CSE 12/1/227, "Chief Commissioner's Inspection Notes, Owerri Province."

101. NNAE: OWDIST 10/1/4, "Owerri Annual Medical and Sanitary Report for the year ending 31st December, 1939"; NNAE: EP747, vol. VI, CSE 12/1/227, "Chief Commissioner's Inspection Notes, Owerri Province"; "Owerri Field Notes," interview with J. K. Nzerem, Aug. 24, 1977.

102. NNAE: OWDIST 10/1/2, No. 41/IV, "Annual Report on the Owerri Division 1937"; NNAE: 41/III OWDIST 10/1/1, DO to Resident, Jan. 1937.

103. NNAE: OW5709 OWDIST 7/1/7, "Owerri Division. Annual Report 1945." Figures for each of the eight centers were as follows: Egbu (179), Mbieri (213), Atta (395), Obohia (236), Ihiagwa (175), Umuneke Ngor (145), Ife (178), Oguta (101).

104. NNAE: OWDIST 10/1/3, "Annual Report—Owerri Division 1938." For studies on ethnic unions see Austin M. Ahanotu, "The Role of Ethnic Unions in the Development of Southern Nigeria: 1916–1966," in Boniface I. Obichere, ed., *Studies in Southern Nigerian History* (London: Frank Cass, 1982), 155–74; E. P. Onyeaka Offodile, "Growth and Influence of Tribal Unions," *The West African Review* 18 (Aug. 1947); Audrey C. Smock, *Ibo Politics: The Role of Ethnic Unions in Eastern Nigeria* (Cambridge, Mass.: Harvard Univ. Press, 1971); Graham B. Kerr, "Voluntary Associations in West Africa: 'Hidden' Agents of Social Change," *The African Studies Review* 21 (Dec. 1978): 87–100.

105. NNAE: OWDIST 10/1/3, "Annual Report—Owerri Division 1938"; NNAE: OW5709 OWDIST 7/1/7, "Owerri Division. Annual Report 1945."

106. NNAE: OW5709 OWDIST 7/1/7, "Owerri Division. Annual Report 1945"; "Memorandum on the Future of Local Government in the Eastern Provinces of Nigeria," by R. A. Stevens, 1949, para. 13, RHL, Mss. Afr. s. 1068 (4), hereafter cited as "Memorandum."

CHAPTER 8

1. See Stevens, "Memorandum" para. 133.

2. Ibid., paras. 133. 3, 19.

3. Ibid., paras. 13, 20, 21. Quotations attributed to the Gibbons "Report," which was unavailable, are culled from Stevens's "Memorandum." Aspects of the Gibbons "Report" can be found in "Local Government Reorganisation in the Eastern Provinces of Nigeria and Kenya," *Journal of African Administration* 1 (Jan. 1949): 18–29 (hereafter, "Local Government").

4. Stevens, "Memorandum," quoted in paras. 20–22, 26. Also "Local Government," 19.

5. Ibid., paras. 1, 20, 23.

6. Ibid., paras. 23–24, 125.

7. Ibid., paras. 26, 28, 22, 21, 53, 54. Gibbons had recommended that "the Chief Commission, with the advice of the Local Government Board, should have powers of dissolving County and other Councils and to make arrangements for administration." In "Local Government," 21.

8. Ibid., paras. 56, 57. "I do not believe," Stevens insisted, "that any other course is really open to us now. . . . I personally have a complete confidence that the trust will not be misplaced" (para. 126).

9. Robert F. Ola, *Local Administration in Nigeria* (London: Kegan Paul International, 1984), 59; Philip J. Harris, *Local Government in Southern Nigeria* (Cambridge: Cambridge Univ. Press, 1957), 10, 21–24, 11. The Western Region Local Government Law was passed in 1953. According to Harris, in Northern Nigeria the term " 'local government' was not adopted . . . but in 1954 the Legislature . . . drew up the Northern Region Native Authority Law" (7).

10. Beidelman, *Colonial Evangelism,* 212.

11. Cf. Ekechi, *Missionary Enterprise;* Ilogu, *Christianity and Igbo Culture;* Isichei, *History;* Elizabeth Isichei, *The Ibo People and the Europeans: The Genesis of a Relationship, to 1906* (New York: St. Martin's Press, 1973); Chinua Achebe, *Things Fall Apart.*

12. Reaction from Professor D. I. Nwoga, April 7, 1977.

13. Discussion by Professor C. Ifemesia.

14. H. Kanu Offonry, "The Ibo People," *The West African Review,* 18 (Feb. 1947): 167; Dike Commission quoted in Nwabara, *Iboland,* 76.

15. Geofrey Z. Kapenzi, *The Clash of Cultures: Christian Missionaries and the Shona of Rhodesia* (Washington, D.C.: Univ. Press of America, 1979), 2. Cf. Toyin Falola, *Britain and Nigeria: Exploitation or Development?* (London: Zed Books Ltd., 1987), 2–3.

16. Whitaker, *Politics of Tradition,* 10–11, 458–59, 460, 463.

17. Swaisland to Nylen (USA), Apr. 7, 1961, RHL, MSS. Afr. s. 862, No. 13.

18. Eze Akanu Ibiam, Keynote Adddress at the Workshop on Igbo Culture, held at the University of Nigeria, Nsukka, Apr. 4–7, 1977.

19. Ibid.

20. Ibid.

21. A. E. Afigbo, "Towards Cultural Revival Among the Igbo-Speaking Peoples," *Añu Magazine* (Published by the Cultural Division of the Ministry of Education and Information, Oweri, Imo State, 1979), 12; "Owerri Field Notes," interviews at Emekuku, July 1977. Also see Frank A. Salamone, "Continuity of Igbo Values After Conversion: A Study in Purity and Prestige," *Missiology* 3 (Jan. 1975): 33–43.

SELECT BIBLIOGRAPHY

I. ARCHIVAL AND ORAL SOURCES

For the colonial records, the British archives (Public Record Office) and the Nigerian National Archives at Ibadan and Enugu contain the main sources.

The missionary archives included the Church Missionary Society (London); the Roman Catholic Holy Ghost Fathers (Paris) and Society of African Missions (Rome); and the Christ Methodist Zion Church (Mbieri, Owerri). The private papers of the late Reverend M. D. Opara (Mbieri, Owerri) were also consulted, thanks to the Reverend (now bishop) Lambert O. Opara. Reverend Opara's correspondences with the American Evangelical Methodist Church (Altoona, Pennsylvania) were provided by the EMC authorities, past and present.

Oral traditions were collected in Nigeria from 1973 to 1983. All the recorded traditions and interviews are still on tape and untranscribed.

II. BOOKS, PAPERS, AND ARTICLES

Afigbo, A. E. "The Indigenous Political Systems of the Igbo," *Tarik* 4 (1973): 13–22.

———. "The Missions, the State and Education in South-Eastern Nigeria, 1956–71." In *Christianity in Independent Africa,* edited by Edward Fashole-Luke et al., 176–92. Bloomington: Indiana Univ. Press, 1978.

———. "Oral Tradition and the History of Segmentary Societies." *History in Africa* 12 (1985): 1–10.

———. *The Warrant Chiefs: Indirect Rule in Southeastern Nigeria, 1891–1929.* New York: Humanities Press, 1972.

Agboola, S. A. "The Introduction and Spread of Cassava in Western Nigeria." *Nigerian Journal of Economic and Social Studies* 10 (1968): 369–85.

Ahanotu, Austin M. "The Role of Ethnic Unions in the Development of Southern

Nigeria: 1916–1966." In *Studies in Southern Nigerian History,* edited by Boniface I. Obichere, 155–74. London: Frank Cass, 1982.

Ajayi, J. F. A. *Christian Missions in Nigeria, 1841–1891.* Evanston, Ill.: Northwestern Univ. Press, 1969.

————. "The Development of Secondary Grammar School Education in Nigeria." *Journal of the Historical Society of Nigeria* 2 (Dec. 1963): 517–35.

Amissah, S. H. "The Present Position and Problems of the Church in Africa." In *Consultation Digest,* 45–51. Geneva: World Council of Churches, 1965.

Arinze, Francis A. *Sacrifice in Ibo Religon.* Ibadan: Ibadan Univ. Press, 1970.

Ayandele, E. A. *The Missionary Impact on Modern Nigeria, 1842–1914: A Political and Social Analysis.* London: Longman, 1966.

Azikiwe, Ben N. "How Shall We Educate the African?" *Journal of the African Society* 33 (Apr. 1934): 143–50.

Azikiwe, Nnamdi. *Zik (A Selection from the Speeches of Nnamdi Azikiwe).* Cambridge: Cambridge Univ. Press, 1961.

Basden, G. T. *Among the Ibos of Nigeria.* London: Frank Cass, 1966.

————. *Niger Ibos.* London: Frank Cass, 1966.

Baum, Robert M. "Rational Conversion and the Diola-Esulalu (Senagal) Religious Experience." Paper presented at the African Studies Association, Boston, November 3–6, 1976.

Beidelman, T. O. *Colonial Evangelism: A Socio-Historical Study of an East African Mission at the Grassroots.* Bloomington: Indiana Univ. Press, 1982.

Berman, Edward H. "American Influence on African Education: The Role of the Phelps-Stokes Fund's Education Commissions." *Comparative Education Review* 15 (June 1971): 132–45.

Brigid, Sister Mary, ed. *Bishop Shanahan and His Missionary Family.* (Killeshandra: Leinster Leader Ltd., 1967.

Burns, Sir Alan. *Colonial Civil Servant.* London: George Allen & Unwin, 1949.

Cary, Joyce. *Britain and West Africa.* London: Longmans, Green & Co., 1946.

Chinweizu et al. *Toward the Decolonization of African Literature.* Volume 1. Washington, D.C.: Howard Univ. Press, 1983.

Chuta, S. C. "The Ogbunorie and Ifanim Oracles: Encounters with the British in the Isuama Territory, 1910–1911." *Ikenga* 6, nos. 1, 2 (1984): 12–21.

Coleman, James S. *Nigeria: Background to Nationalism* Los Angeles: Univ. of California Press, 1958.

Cook, Arthur N. *British Enterprise in Nigeria.* London: Frank Cass, 1964.

Cooke, Colman M. "Church, State and Education: The Eastern Nigeria Experience, 1950–1967." In *Christianity in Independent Africa,* edited by Edward Fashole-Luke et al., 193–206. Bloomington: Indiana Univ. Press, 1978.

Edeh, Emmanual, M. P., C.S.Sp. *Towards an Igbo Metaphysics.* Chicago: Loyola Univ. Press, 1985.

Ekechi, F. K. "African Polygamy and Western Christian Ethnocentrism." *Journal of African Studies* 3 (Fall 1976): 329–49.

————. "Aspects of Palm Oil Trade At Oguta (Eastern Nigeria), 1900–1950." *African Economic History* (1981): 35–65.

————. "The Cassava Palaver: The Gender Problem in African Economic Development." *Proceedings* (12th Annual Third World Conference, Chicago), 1 (1986): 130–44.

———. "Colonialism and Christianity in West Africa: The Igbo Case, 1900–1915." *Journal of African History.* 12 (1971): 103–15.

———. "The Colonial Rebel: H. M. Douglas and the Nigerian Colonial Administration." *Nigeria Magazine,* forthcoming.

———. "Education and Social Status in an African Society: The Igbo Example." *Umoja* (Journal of Black Studies), n.s., 4 (Fall 1980): 17–33.

———. "The Igbo Response to British Imperialism: The Episode of Dr. Stewart and the Ahiara Expedition, 1905–1916." *Journal of African Studies* 1 (Summer 1974): 145–57.

———. *Missionary Enterprise and Rivalry in Igboland, 1857–1914.* London: Frank Cass, 1972.

———. "The Ordeal of an Independent African Church: The Case of the Nigerian Zion Methodist Mission, 1942–1970. *The International Journal of African Historical Studies,* 20 (1987): 691–720.

———. "Portrait of a Colonizer: H. M. Douglas in Colonial Nigeria, 1897–1920." *African Studies Review* 26 (Mar. 1983): 25–50.

———. "The War to End All Wars: Perspectives on the British Assault on a Nigerian Oracle." *Nigeria Magazine* 53 (Jan.-Mar. 1985): 59–68.

Emenako, Geoffrey E. *Oru Owerre and the Week of Weeks.* Owerri: Imo Newspapers Ltd., 1980.

Falola, Toyin, ed. *Britain and Nigeria: Exploitation or Development?* London: Zed Books Ltd., 1987.

Fashole-Luke, Edward, Richard Gray, Adrian Hastings, and Godwin Tasie, eds. *Christianity in Independent Africa* Bloomington: Indiana Univ. Press, 1978.

Flint, John. "Planned Decolonization and Its Failure in British West Africa." *African Affairs* 82 (July 1983): 389–411.

Gailey, Harry A. *The Road to Aba.* (New York: New York Univ. Press, 1970.

Gann. L. H., and Peter Duignan. *The Rulers of British Africa, 1870–1914.* Stanford: Stanford Univ. Press, 1978.

Goldway, M. *Report on the Investigation of Vocational Education in Eastern Nigeria: Official Document No. 13 of 1962.* Enugu: Government Printer, 1962.

Green, M. M. *Igbo Village Affairs.* New York: Frederick A. Praeger, 1964.

Harris, Philip J. *Local Government in Southern Nigeria.* Cambridge: Cambridge Univ. Press, 1957.

Hastings, Adrian. *A History of African Christianity, 1950–1975.* Cambridge: Cambridge Univ. Press, 1979.

Hayford, J. E. Casely. *Ethiopia Unbound.* London: Frank Cass, 1969.

Haywood, A. W. H., and F. A. S. Clarke. *The History of the Royal West African Frontier Force.* Aldershot: Gale & Polden, 1964.

Henige, David. *The Chronology of Oral Tradition: The Quest for a Chimera.* Oxford: Oxford Univ. Press, 1974.

Henry, M. D. "Confronting the Big Lie." *The Collegiate Review* 20 (Spring/ Summer 1984): 55–58.

Hensley, F. M. *Niger Dawn.* North Devon: Arthur H. Stockwell, n.d. [1948?].

Hives, Frank, and G. Lumley. *Juju and Justice in Nigeria.* London: John Lane, 1930.

Horton, James Africanus. *West African Countries and Peoples.* Edinburgh: Ediburgh Univ. Press, 1969.

Horton, Robin. "African Conversion." *Africa* 41 (1972): 85–108.

Horton, Robin, and J. D. Y. Peel. "Conversion and Confusion: A Rejoinder on Christianity in Eastern Nigeria." *Canadian Journal of African Studies* 10 (1976): 481–98.

Ifeka-Moller, Caroline. "White Power: Social-Structural Factors in Conversion to Christianity, Eastern Nigeria, 1921–1966." *Canadian Journal of African Studies* 8 (1974): 55–72.

Isichei, Elizabeth. *A History of the Igbo People.* New York: St. Martin's Press, 1976.

————. *The Ibo People and the Europeans: The Genesis of a Relationship, to 1906.* New York: St. Martin's Press, 1973.

————. *Igbo Worlds: An Anthology of Oral Histories and Historical Descriptions.* Philadelphia: Institute for the Study of Human Issues, 1978.

Jinehu, E.D. *The Osu Caste in Our Society.* Enugu: Tudor & Group Printers, 1981.

Johnston, G. D. "Ohaffia 1911–40: A Study in Church Developments in Eastern Nigeria." *Bulletin of the Society for African Church History* 2 (1966): 139–41.

Jones, G. I. *Report of an Inquiry into the position, status and influence of Chiefs and Natural Rulers in Eastern Nigeria.* Enugu: Government Printer, 1957.

————. "Time and Oral Tradition with Special Reference to Eastern Nigeria." *Journal of African History* 6 (1965): 153–60.

————. "Councils Among the Central Ibo." In *Councils in Action,* edited by A. Richards and Adam Kuper, 63–79. Cambridge: Cambridge Univ. Press, 1971.

Jordan, J. P. *Bishop Shanahan of Southern Nigeria.* Dublin: Clonmore & Reynolds, 1949.

————. "Catholic Education and Catholicism in Nigeria." *African Ecclesiastical Review* 1–2 (1959–60): 60–62.

Kalu, Eke. "An Ibo Autobiography." *Nigerian Field* 7 (1938): 158–70.

Keller, Bonnie, and Edna G. Bay. "African Women and Problems of Modernization." In *African Society, Culture and Politics: An Introduction to African Studies,* edited by C. C. Mojekwu et al., 215–37. Washington, D.C.: Univ. Press of America, 1978.

Kerr, Graham B. "Voluntary Associations in West Africa: 'Hidden' Agents of Social Change," *The African Studies Review* 21 (Dec. 1978): 87–100.

Kirk-Greene, A. H. M., ed. *The Principles of Native Administration: Selected Documents, 1900–1947.* London: Oxford Univ. Press, 1965.

Latin, David D. *Hegemony and Culture: Politics and Religious Change among the Yoruba.* Chicago: Univ. of Chicago Press, 1986.

Leith-Ross, Sylvia. *African Women: A Study of the Ibo of Nigeria.* London: Faber & Faber, 1939.

————. *Stepping-Stones: Memoirs of Colonial Nigeria, 1907–1960.* Edited by Michael Crowder. London: Peter Owen, 1983.

Linden, Ian. *Church and Revolution in Rwanda.* New York: Africana Publishing Company, 1977.

Lugard, F. D., "Political Memorandum No. 1, 1918," Nigerian National Archives, Enugu.

Lynch, Hollis R., ed. *Black Spokesman*. New York: Humanities Press, 1971.

Manley, G. T. "C.M.S. Policy in Pagan Africa." *Church Missionary Intelligencer* (1917).

Mba, Nina Emma. *Nigerian Women Mobilized: Women's Political Activity in Southern Nigeria, 1900–1965*. Berkeley: Univ. of California Press, 1982.

Meek, C. K. *Law and Authority in a Nigerian Tribe*. New York: Barnes & Noble, 1937.

———. *Social and Political Organization in Owerri Division*. Lagos, Nigeria: Government Printer, 1932.

Nduka, Otunti. "Background to the Foundation of Dennis Memorial Grammar School, Onitsha." *Journal of the Historical Society of Nigeria* 8 (Dec. 1976): 69–92.

Nolan, Sister M. M. *Medical Missionaries of Mary, 1937–1962*. Dublin: Three Candles, 1962.

Nwabara, S. N. *Iboland: A Century of Contact with Britain 1860–1960*. Atlantic Highlands, N.J.: Humanities Press, 1978.

Nwa-chil, C. C. "The Spread of 'Western Education' in Nigeria." *Journal of East African Research and Development* 3 (1973): 145–64.

Nwaguru, J. E. N. *Aba and British Rule: The Evolution and Administrative Development of the Old Aba Division of Igboland, 1896–*1960. Enugu: Santana Press, 1973.

Nwala, T. Uzodinma, ed. *Mbaise in Contemporary Nigeria*. New York: Gold & Maestro, 1978.

Obichere, Boniface I. "Oracles and Politics in West Africa: A Precolonial Legacy for Contemporary Nation States and Republics." Paper presented at the African Studies Association, Baltimore, November 1978.

———. ed. *Studies in Southern Nigerian History*. London: Frank Cass, 1982.

Offonry, H. Kanu. "The Ibo People." *The West African Review* 18 (Feb. 1947): 167–68.

Ogbu, Kalu. *Christianity in West Africa: The Nigerian Story* (Ibadan: Daystar Press, 1978).

Ojike, Mbonu. *My Africa*. New York: John Day Co., 1946.

Okonjo, Isaac M. *British Administration in Nigeria, 1900–1950: A Nigerian View*. New York: Nok Publishers, 1974.

Okoroh, Patrick D. *A Short History of Uratta*, 2d ed. Owerri: The Express Printing Press, 1963.

Ola, Robert F. *Local Administration in Nigeria*. London: Kegan Paul International, 1984.

Onyeche, G. C. "The Seed," unpublished manuscript, 1–7.

Oriji, J. N. "The Ngwa-Igbo Clan of Southeastern Nigeria: An Oral History Overview." *Oral History Review* 9 (1981): 65–84.

Ottenberg, Phoebe V. "The Changing Economic Position of Women among the Afikpo Ibo." In *Continuity and Change in African Cultures*, edited by William R. Bascom and M. J. Herskovits, 205–23. Chicago: Univ. of Chicago Press, 1959.

Patterson, K. David. *Health in Colonial Ghana: Disease, Medicine, and Socio-Economic Change, 1900–1955.* Waltham, Mass.: Crossroads Press, 1981.

Richards, A., and Adam Kuper, eds. *Councils in Action.* Cambridge: Cambridge Univ. Press, 1971.

Salamone, Frank A. "Continuity of Igbo Values After Conversion: A Study in Purity and Prestige." *Missiology* 3 (Jan. 1975): 33–43.

Simmons, Donald C. "Notes on the Aro." *Nigerian Field* 23 (1958): 27–33.

Smith, S. R. "The Progress of the Forward Movement in the Ibo Country." *Niger and Yoruba Notes* (Feb. 1902).

Smock, Audrey C. *Ibo Politics: The Role of Ethnic Unions in Eastern Nigeria.* Cambridge: Harvard Univ. Press, 1971.

Stevens, R. A. "Memorandum on the Future of Local Government in the Eastern Provinces of Nigeria." RHL: Mss. Afr. s. 1068(4), January 1949.

Talbot, P. A. *The Peoples of Southern Nigeria.* London: Frank Cass, 1969. Vol. 1, *Historical Notes.*

Taylor, John Vernon. *Christianity and Politics in Africa.* New York: Greenwood Press, 1979.

Taylor, W. H. "The Presbyterian Educational Impact in Eastern Nigeria, 1946–1974." *African Affairs* 83 (Apr. 1984) 189–205.

Tonkin, Elizabeth. "Investigating Oral Tradition." *Journal of African History* 27 (1986): 203–13.

Uchendu, Victor C. *The Igbo of Southeast Nigeria.* New York: Holt, Rinehard & Winston, 1965.

———. "Patterns of Igbo Social Structure." Paper presented at the Workshop on Igbo Culture, University of Nigeria, Nsukka, Apr. 4–7, 1977.

Vansina, Jan. "Once Upon a Time: Oral Tradition as History in Africa." *Daedalus* 100 (1971): 442–68.

———. *Oral Tradition.* Chicago: Aldine Publishing Co., 1965.

———. *Oral Tradition As History.* Madison: Univ. of Wisconsin Press, 1985.

Waddell, Rev. Hope Masterton. *Twenty-nine Years in the West Indies and Central Africa: A Review of Missionary Work and Adventure 1829–1858.* London: Frank Cass, 1970.

Whitaker, C. S. *The Politics of Tradition: Continuity and Change in Northern Nigeria, 1946–1966.* Princeton, N.J.: Princeton Univ Press, 1970.

Wilson, Samuel, ed. *Mission Handbook: North American Protestant Ministries Overseas,* 12th ed. Monroe, Calif.: Missions Advanced Research and Communication Center, 1980.

III. Theses

Anyabuike, Isaac D. E. "Christian Missionary Enterprise in Isu-Ama Igbo, 1900–1948: A Historical Survey." Ph.D. diss., Ibadan University, 1981.

Cooke, Colman M. "The Roman Catholic Mission in Calabar 1903–1960." Ph.D. diss., University of London, 1977.

Emezi, Cletus E. "British Administration in Owerri, 1900–1930." Ph.D. diss., University of Nigeria, Nsukka, 1978.

Okeke, D. C. "Policy and Practice of the C.M.S. in Igboland, 1857–1929." Ph.D. diss., Aberdeen University, 1977.

Okwu, Augustine S. O. "The Mission of the Irish Holy Ghost Fathers Among the Igbo of Southeastern Nigeria, 1905–1956." Ph.D. diss., Columbia University, 1977.

Oriji, John N. "History of Ngwa People: A Study of Social and Economic Developments in Igboland from the Precolonial Period to the 20th Century." Ph.D. diss., Rutgers University, 1981.

Ozigboh, R. A. "A Christian Mission in the Era of Colonialism: A Study of the Catholic Missionary Enterprise in South-Eastern Nigeria, 1885–1939." Ph.D. diss., Birmingham University, 1980.

Uzoechi, Innocent, F. A. "The Social and Political Impact of the Eastern Nigerian Railway on the Udi Division, 1913–1945." Ph.D. diss., Kent State University, 1985.

INDEX